Post-Mandarin

Post-Mandarin

MASCULINITY AND AESTHETIC MODERNITY
IN COLONIAL VIETNAM

Ben Tran

FORDHAM UNIVERSITY PRESS *New York* 2017

THIS BOOK IS MADE POSSIBLE BY A COLLABORATIVE GRANT
FROM THE ANDREW W. MELLON FOUNDATION.

Library of Congress Cataloging-in-Publication Data

Names: Tran, Ben, author.
Title: Post-Mandarin : masculinity and aesthetic modernity in colonial
    Vietnam / Ben Tran.
Description: New York : Fordham University Press, 2017. | Includes
    bibliographical references and index.
Identifiers: LCCN 2016014168 | ISBN 9780823273133 (hardback) | ISBN
    9780823273140 (paper)
Subjects: LCSH: Vietnamese literature—History and criticism. | Women in
    literature. | Masculinity in literature. | Postcolonialism in literature.
    | Gender identity in literature. | BISAC: SOCIAL SCIENCE / Gender Studies.
    | HISTORY / Asia / Southeast Asia.
Classification: LCC PL4378.05 .T64 2017 | DDC 895.9/2209—dc23
LC record available at https://lccn.loc.gov/2016014168

Printed in the United States of America

19 18 17   5 4 3 2 1

First edition

For Lev and Simone

CONTENTS

Post-Mandarin

Introduction

Established in 1070, Hanoi's Temple of Literature, or Văn Miếu, a complex of sacred courtyards and pavilions, stands as a monument to Confucian intellectual history in northern Vietnam.[1] The Temple of Literature was the setting where scholar-officials administered civil service examinations that identified mandarins who would constitute an "education-based government of talents."[2] Derived from the Chinese model, the Vietnamese mandarinate was an all-male political system premised on meritocracy.[3] The examination system aimed to appoint men of letters who had mastered a curriculum formed around the Five Books and Four Classics of the neo-Confucian tradition to government service. The mandarinal exam system conferred the title "superior men" (*quân tử*) on those who succeeded, authorizing them to apply their learning through governance. These mandarins were expected to exercise an "ethical power" informed both by their knowledge and morals.[4]

Stelae of etched stone memorialize the names of successful examination candidates, and each stela stands erect upon the back of a tortoise, a prominent symbol of memory and longevity. An exterior wall isolates the complex from today's bustling urban streets, overcrowded with cars and motorbikes relentlessly honking their horns. Now a tourist attraction, the remnants of the temple's intellectual tradition starkly contrast with contemporary Hanoi's brightly colorful signs and ads printed in the sans serif fonts of Vietnam's romanized alphabet, *quốc ngữ*.[5]

At a transitional moment between the mandarinal culture, with its classical Chinese language, and the print culture of *quốc ngữ*, Albert Sarraut, Indochina's governor-general at the time, stood at the Temple of Literature and delivered a speech that called for the cultivation of a new generation of native elites who, educated in a centralized Franco-Vietnamese school system, would work with the colonial government to guide the Vietnamese masses toward modernization. The year was 1919, and after serving an unprecedented two terms as Indochina's governor-general, Sarraut was preparing to return to Paris to take the position of minister of colonies. Explaining France's moral responsibilities to expand universal individual rights to Indochina, Sarraut advocated for French indirect rule under the "contrôle supérieur de la Métropole" and the implementation of a second-class indigenous citizenship for elite natives.[6] Without French guidance, he warned, Vietnam risked regressing to precolonial governance that, due to the arbitrary and corrupt rule of the royal court and its mandarins, stripped away individual rights. The governor-general did not want Vietnam to fall prey to the revolutionary ideas of "faux-savants" or "fausses élites," who derived their knowledge from Chinese-language works and, even worse, wanted to return Southeast Asia to Chinese influence.[7] Sarraut cast these warnings against the background of the Temple of Literature, linking these threatening intellectual impostors to the temple's Sino-centric history.[8] France's future minister of colonies contended that if he was to go forth and continue to work for the progress of Vietnam—because "you call me your father: a father does not abandon his children"[9]—then Vietnam must abandon its thousand-year old Confucian intellectual system and relegate the Temple of Literature to a past that had lost its viability in the present.[10] Sarraut assumes the role of a father to guide his Vietnamese subjects out of the supposed morass of Chinese education. His colonial paternalism operates at the symbolic and literal levels: as the figurehead of the Vietnamese family and the schoolmaster for the Vietnamese masses.[11]

Addressing an indigenous group collaborating with the colonial government, Sarraut outlined a plan to transform and streamline a loosely organized indigenous school system to impart France's "modern science of government" to the next generation of indigenous elite.[12] His educational policies intended to render Vietnam's mandarinal tradition obsolete, replacing the Sino-centric mandarinal exams with a French pedagogical model. Sarraut's educational reform was an intellectual disruption; it was equally a gendered shift away from the homosocial literary world of mandarins.[13] His educational agenda eroded the all-male preserve of the mandarinate, leaving a new generation of male intellectuals to grapple with the radically altered gender dynamics of Vietnam's intellectual and literary fields as women increasingly gained access to education and literacy.

The French government's attempts to modernize Vietnam, emblematized by Sarraut's speech at the Temple of Literature in Hanoi in 1919, did not lead to the unbridled development of Vietnam. Theoretically, Sarraut's expanded Franco-Vietnamese school system was supposed to provide universal education and opportunities on par with the elite schools that catered to French children. But in practice, Sarraut's educational agenda trained and produced laborers and bureaucrats for the colonial government and economy. The ambitious educational policies enacted after World War I reproduced the economic relations of exploitation that they were meant to ameliorate. For all the talk of development under the supervision of the colonial government, France never industrialized Vietnam for fear that indigenous commercial sectors would compete with French manufacturing and decrease French profits gained from Vietnam's resources and newly developed markets. This was the nature of colonial modernity in Vietnam. While my use of "colonial modernity" follows recent assertions about the inextricability of colonialism from modernity, I further understand it as a contradiction in terms rather than a mutualism of two constitutive parts.[14] Colonialism and modernity undoubtedly occurred simultaneously. However, as evidenced by Sarraut, the execution, rhetoric, and plans of modernizing the colonies often had the opposite effect: circumscribing the modernity that it vowed to implement. France's colonial agenda triggered the irreversible developments of modernity, but it also betrayed the modern era's promise of, to borrow Sarraut's words, the "most noble principles of rights and humanity."[15] The contradictions of colonial modernity serve as a guiding thread for my analyses of Vietnamese aesthetic modernity's emergence out of and against colonial modernity.

Sarraut's educational reform succeeded in producing the obedient, low-ranking cooperative civil servants and vocational workers that he envisioned. But his educational project also had unintended consequences. French educational policies created a new generation of anticolonial intellectuals who helped establish modern Vietnamese vernacular print culture.[16] The new Franco-Vietnamese school system replaced the character scripts of Examination Chinese and Vietnam's demotic script, Nôm, with French and *quốc ngữ*.[17] Although the French colonial government had appropriated *quốc ngữ*,[18] the Vietnamese romanized script proved to be more accessible than the character scripts and led to an increase in literacy among women, who had been excluded from the mandarinate.[19] After World War I, *quốc ngữ* became the primary language of print culture, a print culture that now consisted of women literate in the same language as that of the new class of male intellectuals. As the vernacular press increasingly addressed women as readers and subjects of contemporary social issues,[20] it also emerged as the foundation of a modern literature that critiqued French imperialism and fostered anticolonial nationalism. Cultivating national culture and consciousness, this burgeoning vernacular print culture harkened back to the etymological roots of *quốc ngữ*: "national script." This intersection between the rise of Vietnam's modern, national literature and women readers' entrance into the literary world is this book's focus.

Gaining momentum in the 1920s, Vietnamese print capitalism flowered by the 1930s alongside many other cultural transformations of modernity, including urbanization, increased capacities of printing presses, and the emergence of working and middle classes that had leisure time to read.[21] Moreover, a cohort of intellectuals educated in the Franco-Vietnamese system began publishing, editing, and contributing to print newspapers and journals at an incredible and unprecedented pace of production. During this period several important Hanoi journals debuted, playing a significant role in the production of modern Vietnamese literature and serving as a vital forum for intellectual debates.[22] By the 1930s Hanoi's intellectuals earned their social and intellectual capital not from the hallowed spaces of the Temple of Literature but rather from the newly established newspapers and publishing houses of the period. Native intellectuals who penned Vietnamese literature no longer fostered their careers and intellectual lives as civil servants. Instead, the majority of them earned a living from print.[23] I employ the term "post-mandarin" to describe the Vietnamese aesthetic modernity and cultural field that emerged from the ruins of the Chinese-influenced mandarinal system. The dissolution of the previously all-male preserve gave rise to a post-mandarin literature that differed from Vietnam's earlier literary traditions in its orthography, its stylistic norms, its subject matter, its material conditions, its educational infrastructure, and, most significantly, its shifting gender dynamics.[24] I analyze how this new print cultural world gave rise to Vietnamese aesthetic modernity by looking at the intellectual and literary seismic shifts that displaced the all-male mandarinate and gave women greater access to the world of letters. *Post-Mandarin* illuminates the complex gender dynamics—between alienated native intellectuals and modern native women—of anticolonial nationalism and aesthetic modernity in the colonies.

It is clear that Vietnamese aesthetic modernity stems from the influence of French colonial policies, particularly education reform. But rather than understand post-mandarin intellectuals merely as receptacles of the French Enlightenment, I argue that Vietnam's colonial modernity fostered the conditions of possibility for a national public that engaged, transformed, and refuted European ideas. In the chapters that follow, I examine the cultural and aesthetic amalgamations particular to Vietnamese aesthetic modernity:

reportage intermixed with autoethnography, pornography as aesthetic modernity, sociological prose with romanticist novels, and queer politics and socialist realism. Vietnam's aesthetic modernity does not derive from or rehearse European literary history. Instead, during Vietnam's rapid colonial modernization, which occurred in mere decades, the aesthetic movements and intellectual discourses that developed over centuries in Europe were received in intermixed, reconfigured, and even inverted forms. Post-mandarin writers extracted from and reconstituted European aesthetics to create literary works, particularly in fiction and nonfiction prose, that addressed the sociocultural contexts of their time.

The post-mandarin authors I examine are Nhất Linh, Khái Hưng, Thạch Lam, Tam Lang, Vũ Trọng Phụng, and Nguyễn Công Hoan. In conventional accounts of modern Vietnamese literature, the first three are read as romanticists who advocated for individualism and Westernization through their participation in the Tự Lực văn đoàn (Self-Strengthening Literary Group), the latter three as critical realists who mimetically depicted the shortcomings of colonial society. According to this literary history, these writers represent oppositional literary movements that significantly contributed to modern Vietnamese literature.[25] However, I read them collectively to identify historically and intellectually significant but neglected contiguities—contiguities that I am qualifying as post-mandarin.

These Hanoi-based writers depicted everyday reality under French colonial rule through techniques and styles appropriated from European literature for their purported objectivity, including investigative journalism, ethnographic writing, and sociological analysis.[26] Yet the elaboration of post-mandarin in the chapters below aims to demonstrate that these presumably objective forms of representation were complicated, and indeed compromised, by the disruption of Vietnam's indigenous intellectual history as well as the dispersion of the mandarinate's all-male preserve. Post-mandarin intellectuals confronted historical vicissitudes that not only eroded Vietnam's intellectual institutions but also dissolved the gendered boundaries that gave shape and order to the male homosocial world of letters.[27] Shifting away from the male-to-male literary address, post-mandarin authors began to write for and about women. They simultaneously intermingled in a literary world orienting itself to women while maintaining the social and moral authority of their mandarinal predecessors.[28]

Gender—understood as the perceived differences between the sexes produced and maintained by social relationships, knowledge, and power—was a central modality in the development of Vietnam's modern national literature. Post-mandarin male authors grappled with the possibilities and limitations of modernity through their representations of women's sexuality and desires. They examined women's roles as colonial subjects in order to imagine themselves anew as modern national authors.

Vietnam's aesthetic modernity emerges from the post-mandarin intellectual's representation of women. Post-mandarin literature had a vicarious nature because male authors represented and spoke for Vietnamese women—disproportionately, compared to women speaking for or representing themselves. This asymmetrical relationship between male subjects and female objects of representation was complicated by the predicament of the post-mandarin intellectual. French-educated intellectuals' attempt to represent and integrate the masses was not premised solely on authoritarianism or elitism, but also on masculine anxiety about women's modern subjectivities. Educated in the Franco-Vietnamese school system, yet excluded from intellectual professions and positions of command and organization, post-mandarin authors at times viewed themselves as more vulnerable, inadequate subjects of modernization than Vietnamese women, who were no longer perceived as being bound to domesticity and tradition.[29] Although the discourse of nationalism was mapped onto women's bodies and desires, it also signals a masculine vulnerability that stemmed from women's modern subjectivities. Therefore, I argue, post-mandarin literature must be read through the vexed masculinity of the native intellectual in relation to his representation of the modern indigenous woman. Post-mandarin authors identified with and represented women in order to forge a modern subjectivity and a national identity.

Post-mandarin male intellectuals exchanged the tunic, winged hat, and horned shoes of the mandarin for the three-piece suit, fedora hat, and heeled leather shoes of the modern European man.[30] This sartorial transformation signaled a shift toward European tastes and sensibilities. The critics Hoài Thanh and Hoài Chân have remarked that modern Vietnamese literature resulted from the Europeanization of Vietnamese epistemology that accompanied the material changes of modernity.[31] Members of the Self-Strengthening Literary Group, for example, equated the potentialities of modernity strictly with Westernization, tirelessly attacking Confucianism as a vertical social order—structured by a bureaucrat's duty to the emperor, a son's obedience to his father, and a wife's submission to her husband—at the expense of individual will and desire.

Post-mandarin intellectuals constituted a deracinated cohort, unable to access the mandarinal intellectual history because a diminishing number of intellectuals knew the languages of that textual world. John McAlister and Paul Mus have characterized native intellectuals' inability to read character

scripts as an incomprehension of past worldviews and even their own society: "In Europeanizing the Vietnamese intellectuals and accepting them into
their ranks the French both shattered their mental apparatus—their traditional conception of the world—and put their behavior outside the sociological context in which they were raised."[32] Although McAlister and Mus were
wrong to view twentieth-century Vietnamese society as timeless, untouched
by the profound transformations of modernity, they captured the alienation of
European-educated colonial subjects. With the imposition of European colonial education, native intellectuals' mental bearings and coordinates no longer
mapped onto indigenous society or its intellectual history, which had been
rendered illegible.[33] Yet this cultural amnesia was only part of the native intellectuals' predicament. I read modern Vietnamese literature's claims, rhetoric,
and commitments to nationalism and modernity through the colonized intellectual's double bind: post-mandarin intellectuals had been deracinated by the
mandarinate's demise, yet were armed with new, modern knowledge. They
embraced the critical rationality of the European Enlightenment to assail the
instrumental rationality of French colonialism, working toward an organic
cultural nationalism, to borrow Pheng Cheah's formulation.[34]

Frantz Fanon has argued that the native intellectual's role is to "substantiate [national culture's] existence in the fight which the people wage against
the forces of occupation."[35] As a "mimic man," the colonized intellectual had
to resist the allure of the colonizer's culture and progress with a "retrograde
consciousness" that led to his integration with the anticolonial movement.[36]
Fanon limns the contours of a national literature, contending that national
literature engages and compels the reading masses to join in the struggle for
liberation. For Fanon, national culture culminates not only with a revolutionary and national literature but also with a "new history of man," a culture
of new humanism.[37] The post-mandarin intellectual is kin to Fanon's mimic
man, the native intellectual educated by the colonizers.

Feminist scholars, however, have observed that studies of liberation movements, Fanon's included, have construed women as mere symbols of nationalism.[38] In her influential essay "Can the Subaltern Speak?," Gayatri Spivak
writes, "Between patriarchy and imperialism, subject-constitution and object-
formation, the figure of the woman disappears, not into a pristine nothingness,
but into a violent shuttling, which is the displaced figuration of the 'third-world
woman' caught between tradition and modernization."[39] Such male-centric narratives of anticolonialism recount the struggles for liberation, but too often in
these accounts women are silenced and reduced to instrumental or symbolic
mediators in the struggle between the hypermasculine colonial male and the

native revolutionary.[40] In this account the third world woman has little or no agency. For Spivak, the subaltern woman's dubious position results in a muted voice that does not represent itself authentically and cannot be recovered.

Focusing more on modernity, Lisa Rofel has suggested that gender is a central modality through which "modernity is desired and imagined."[41]

> Gender differentiation—the knowledges, relations, meanings, and identities of masculinity and femininity—operates at the heart of modernity's power. Discourses on women's place in colonized societies among both colonizers and elite colonized men; the use of women to represent by turns "tradition," the essence of culture, the constitutional "lack" in third world countries' ability to modernize, or resistance to the West; the "feminization" of non-western cultures, the construction of hypermasculinity through which the West imagines its power, and, more recently, the focus of development aid on women, the sexualization of local/global interactions—these multiple processes demonstrate ways in which gender is invoked to naturalize power.[42]

Taking up Rofel's argument about the centrality of gender, this book underscores how post-mandarin intellectuals mediated their intellectual authority and their critique of colonial modernity through representations of women. But at the same time, I am deviating from Rofel's figurative readings of women as symbols of tradition, the nation, the third world, or the non-West, arguing that Vietnam's masculine discourse on national literature hinged on women's different subject positions within the historical context of colonial modernity: sexual partners, patients in the colonial dispensary, transgressive romantic lovers, speakers negotiating sociolinguistic structures, and readers of novels. Post-mandarin writing challenges an understanding of modernity's gender norms that views men as primary mobile agents capable of transformation and women as static or symbolic figures responsible for upholding tradition in the domestic sphere.[43]

Scholars of Southeast Asia have questioned the subaltern woman's lack of agency and voice, offering important counterexamples of women as active participants of social change in different historical periods. In *The Flaming Womb* Barbara Watson Andaya has argued that women in Southeast Asia, compared with China and India, had relatively high position; she goes on to suggest that despite the changes of the early modern period (1400–1800)—the spread of world religions, modernization of state governments, and the region's increased participation in the world economy—women's status did not necessarily decline.[44] More specific to the context of Vietnamese modernity, Nhung Tuyet Tran has argued for two primary models for Vietnamese womanhood: as the embodiment of Vietnamese tradition and as the liberated figure of a non-Western modernity.[45] In *The Passage of*

Literature Chris GoGwilt focuses on the Indonesian *nyai*, or concubine, particularly as portrayed in Pramoedya Ananta Toer's *Buru Quartet*, as the central figure for the awakening of Indonesian nationalism. Pramoedya's *nyai* proves to be the most significant mentor for Minke, the novel's male protagonist coming of age as a national hero and author.[46] Although not recognized by Dutch colonial law, this female character from Pramoedya's novel prefigures Indonesian nationalism while also serving as the ideal against which to measure the dystopia of the postcolonial Indonesian state. As GoGwilt contends, the *nyai* character is a prominent figure not only in Indonesian nationalism and the formation of its male national heroes but also in English, Creole, and Indonesian modernisms, forming the "shared literary and linguistic points of reference for a matrix of transnational modernisms."[47] Through his study of the *nyai*'s literary and historical legacy, Gogwilt reorients our understanding of transnational modernism. Following the lead of GoGwilt and others, I explore the agency of women in the formation of national consciousness—specifically, how women affected colonized intellectuals' masculinities, literary ambitions, and national identity. *Post-Mandarin* argues that the inseparable relationship between masculinity and femininity underlies the overlapping discourses of nationalism and modernity—and the aesthetic modernity that derived from and contributed to these discourses.

Post-mandarin intellectuals educated in the Franco-Vietnamese system grappled with the dissolution of the mandarinate's all-male preserve and the subsequent reconfiguration of the intellectual field's gender relations. With the development of print capitalism, women emerged as a targeted reading demographic and as consumers of advertised goods. The burgeoning *quốc ngữ* press fueled ongoing debates about modernity and nationalism that centered on women. Pamphlets, books, tracts, and newspapers discussed new political concepts in direct relationship to women's rights.[48]

The prominent critic Hoàng Ngọc Hiến goes so far as to gender *quốc ngữ* literature as women's literature.

> Before the Revolution [of 1945] . . . I studied in French language schools. In my family there were two bookcases. The French-language bookcase belonged to my father, a primary school teacher. My father—who believed that only French was the key to knowledge and culture—only allowed us to read books in French. Many friends, in reading my literary criticism, have praised its clarity. Perhaps I acquired "French clarity" from my father's bookcase. The Vietnamese language [*quốc ngữ*] bookcase belonged to my mother and sister. But when my father was gone, I went to the Vietnamese bookcase and snatched the opportunity to devour all that I could read: *Ngày nay* [Today], *Tao Đàn* [Literary coterie], *Tiểu thuyết thứ bảy* [Saturday novel],

the prose of the Self-Strengthening Literary Group, the novels of Vũ Trọng
Phụng, the stories of Nguyễn Tuân, Nam Cao. . . . My mother's and sister's
bookcase imparted to me a love of the Vietnamese language and of Vietnamese literature.[49]

By no means was *quốc ngữ* writing addressed exclusively to women, but the
strong association between femininity and the modern Vietnamese vernacular (and, analogously, masculinity with the French language) is apparent
in this passage. Hoàng Ngọc Hiến's identification with *quốc ngữ*'s implied
female reader reveals the complex gender relations of this national literature. The development of Vietnam's national literature stemmed from a literary corpus composed by male writers increasingly addressing a female
readership, in sharp contrast to the homosocial literary world of the mandarins, where male authors wrote primarily for male readers. Not only did
post-mandarin intellectuals write for women readers and, at times surrep-
titiously, take the place of women readers, but they also established their
cultural and intellectual capital through their representations of women.
The post-mandarin address to and representation of modern Vietnamese
women significantly contributed to a new national literature.

Post-mandarin intellectuals focused their attention on women who were
sex workers, female patients treated for sexually transmitted diseases in colonial dispensaries, and nonconformist lovers who questioned social norms.
They depicted modernity through women's sexuality, and in doing so these
authors assumed the unassimilated first-person voice of investigative journalism, the "objective" lens of sociological analysis, and the third-person
omniscient narrator. As if they were employing a disembodied third eye giving authoritative accounts, the post-mandarin intellectual viewed himself as
the arbiter of social values. However, as post-mandarin writers appropriated
European methods of representation and critique, they experienced acute
anxiety about their masculine identity as modern, yet deracinated, figures of
intellectual authority. Chapter 1 analyzes the journalistic genre reportage as a
form of bodily knowledge, indicative of the post-mandarin's uncertain masculinity. It focuses on Tam Lang and Thạch Lam's writings on prostitution,
a recurring theme in Vietnamese reportage. The male chroniclers' persistent gaze at commercial sex workers exposes the narrators' sexual anxieties
as they observe the erotic relationships between European men and native
women. Despite their European knowledge, native intellectuals viewed Vietnamese women as more intimately tied to modernity because of this sexual
involvement. These literary narratives portray Europeans sexually initiating
Vietnamese women into modernity, while the male post-mandarin intellectuals remain mere observers of these encounters. Excluded from these

relationships, the male narrators and protagonists of these works come to see themselves as racially and sexually inadequate—and thus inadequate modern subjects.

The relationship between post-mandarin intellectuals and indigenous women's subjectivities in Vietnam complicates previous articulations of colonial masculinity as a struggle between European and indigenous masculinities or as a "politics of substitution" in which "the fantasy of the native is precisely to occupy the master's place" by possession of the white woman.[50] As the mimic men strived to establish national identity and culture, there was an unequal power dynamic over native women but also masculine anxiety from their gaze at native women. Post-mandarin authors questioned the repressive power of the colonial regime, as well as the emancipatory potential of modernity. It was through their representations of native women that they examined how the contradictions of colonial modernity translated into everyday reality with the hope of overcoming those paradoxes.

Post-mandarin authors employed reportage to document and interpret women's sexual experiences. In Vietnam, reportage transformed the aesthetic norms of literature. It rekeyed prose writing with renewed cultural and political significance, making way for the modern Vietnamese novel. This is, of course, not to say that prose forms were new or invented in Vietnam after World War I. Instead, post-mandarin authors reconfigured the methods and values of prose, which in Vietnam's Confucian literary hierarchy was subsumed under poetry and historiography.[51] This alteration of prose occurred, in large part, because of the masculine gaze at women in order to depict colonial society. Post-mandarin authors focused on women's various identities—as prostitutes, medical patients, lovers, and readers of romance. Vietnamese aesthetic modernity shifted toward cultural representations increasingly structured around the interrelationship between the erotic and aesthetics.

I use the terms "prose" or "prosaic" to refer to narrative sequences with no metrical structure that in fiction primarily took the form of novelistic realism and in nonfiction the form of investigative journalism. Post-mandarin aesthetic modernity was contingent on the everyday. Employing the techniques of ethnography and sociological analysis to observe the practices of everyday life, post-mandarin writers indiscriminately aestheticized everything so as to break down the distinctions between the everyday and the literary, bringing pedestrian acts and ordinary objects, particularly the taboo subject of sexual desire, into the world of aesthetic representation. Their inclusive analysis of prosaic realities instantiated what previously had been unrepresented or deemed inappropriate for aesthetic representation. This prosaic turn, for me, is the pivotal point for Vietnamese aesthetic modernity.

Since the late 1990s proponents of a "new modernist studies" have convincingly argued for a more inclusionary definition of modernism that would move beyond the geographic and temporal parameters of Western Europe and North America.[52] It calls for a different understanding of modernism's formal stylistic qualities and a blurring of the distinction between forms of high and popular art. Scholars have shed light on alternative and late modernisms in the far reaches of the globe and have demonstrated how modernist aesthetics has been deployed as an effective instrument of anticolonial resistance. New modernist studies offers a possible paradigm to examine Vietnamese literature that emerged out of and against modernization under French colonialism. Yet, for multiple reasons in addition to the reasons outlined above, I am reluctant to view interwar Vietnamese literature as merely a variation of modernism. On the one hand, interwar Vietnamese writers were the contemporaries of French and European modernists; on the other hand, there seems to have been a missed connection because post-mandarin authors had a greater affinity to nineteenth-century authors, such as Balzac, Hugo, and Flaubert.

In *Modernist Commitments* Jessica Berman insightfully redefines modernism in terms of its ethical and political demands in various situations, echoing the work of Susan Stanford Friedman.

> [Modernism] escapes nominal definition, even as a plurality, and exceeds our efforts to describe it through its differences from what came before and after. Even where modernism seems to exhibit certain formal preoccupations, such as textual defamiliarization, refusal of strict verisimilitude, or play with the vagaries of space and time, it is clear that these are neither necessary nor ubiquitous conditions but rather signs or symptoms of a particular attitude toward a specific literary horizon of expectations. Nor can we pretend that such a list of preoccupations stands in for the practices, relationships, or problematics that motivate the great variety of modernisms as they emerge worldwide.[53]

In her reconsideration of modernism, Berman questions the distinction between self-conscious, experimental modernism and politically engaged literature. She challenges the reductive valuation of twentieth-century third world literatures as either liberal modernism or socialist realism—a binary categorization that emerged during the Cold War. This is a distinction that, particularly when understood as the difference between Europe's metropolitan avant-gardism and the colonies' peripheral aesthetics, privileges high modernism at the risk of neglecting the pluralism of modernism.[54]

In the spirit of Berman's suggestion to think of modernism beyond a checklist of formal preoccupations, I want to examine Vietnam's pivotal turn toward aesthetic modernity through the documentation of everyday life—or the prosaic. Aesthetic modernity in the colonies, as made evident by the case of Vietnam, challenges the assumed antimony of realism/modernism, an antimony premised on the chronological development of Western European literary history. The defining aspect of modern aesthetics is not necessarily the crisis of representation or art's intransitive focus on its own materiality—what Rey Chow has recently called "medial reflexivity"[55]— but rather the democracy of prose in printed form. For post-mandarin literature, prosaic representation is a crucial inaugural moment of aesthetic modernity, as opposed to high modernism or avant-garde movements.

Jacques Rancière has suggested that aesthetic modernity is the dissolution of art into life and life into art, so that the functions of art merged with the social forms of resemblance. According to Rancière, aesthetic modernity's inclusive analysis of prosaic realities destabilized the hierarchies of representation, both aesthetically and politically. The resulting literary realism functioned transitively, as it incarnated literary locutions in the external world through its renegotiation of what is sayable and who is able to speak—what he calls the "the distribution of the sensible."[56] Therefore, Rancière identifies the crucial turn to modern aesthetic not with medial reflexivity but rather with literary realism. He specifically chooses the term "aesthetic modernity," rather than "modernism," to underscore this point. And in order to extend his claims to the Vietnamese context, I too opt for "aesthetic modernity" and not "modernism."

Insofar as thinkers such as Benedict Anderson and Amilcar Cabral attribute the incarnation of anticolonialism to culture,[57] they presuppose prose's aesthetic and political significance. In contrast, Rancière's emphasis on the representation of prosaic realities explains why anticolonial, as well as postcolonial, literature often resembles nineteenth-century European realism (as in the works of Jose Rizal and Pramoedya Ananta Toer or more recent peripheral realisms like Roberto Bolaño's and V. S. Naipaul's works) more than the high modernism or the avant-garde movements of interwar Europe. It is not that colonial and postcolonial literatures, modern Vietnamese literature among them, were belated or backward but rather that we should redefine their political and cultural significance in terms of the prosaic.

While Rancière situates aesthetic modernity in the European context, I view the elements of aesthetic modernity crucial for Rancière—the realist novel and the prosaic—as the points of intersection between European and indigenous cultures during colonial modernity. For Rancière, the regime of aesthetic modernity begins with novelistic realism because its unconditional representation of all subjects was the "material realization of a common humanity still only existing as an idea."[58] The aesthetic regime's political efficacy was located in its reconfiguration of the sociopolitical order so that the *sans-part*, those who had no share in the common world, can be seen and heard as political subjects. Realism's depiction and analysis of prosaic realities collapsed the hierarchical differences of subject matter, genres, and art forms. This was, to borrow a line from the novelist César Aira, a "destructive realism, strong enough to dissolve all preconceived ideas."[59] In addition to its indiscriminate representation, this literature democratically addresses all.

> Literature is the reign of writing, of speech circulating outside any determined relationship of address. . . . The same goes for this new literature that no longer addresses itself to a specific audience, one sharing the same position within the social order and drawing ordered rules of interpretation and modes of sensibility from that ethos. . . . That is what the democracy of writing consists in: its garrulous mutism cancels the distinction between men of speech-in-action and men of noisy suffering voice, between those who act and those who merely live. The democracy of literature is the regime of the word-at-large that anyone can grab hold of, either to appropriate the life led by heroes or heroines of the novels for themselves, or to turn themselves into writers, or to insert themselves into the discussion of common affairs.[60]

In Vietnam's post-mandarin contexts, the democracy of literature's circulation beyond "any determined relationship of address" occurred with print's circulation beyond the field of immediate experience and face-to-face contact. This material development is not only important for the imagined communities of nationalism as Benedict Anderson has suggested but also, I argue, causally related to the dissipation of the mandarinate's gendered boundaries. Indeed, in many of the post-mandarin works discussed here, male native intellectuals are often reading and at times intercepting texts initially intended for women readers, including personal diaries, intimate correspondences, public health poems concerning women's hygiene, and women's newspaper columns, collectively referred to as *nữ văn giới* (the world of women's letters).

Vietnam's post-mandarin case suggests that the democratization of literature—the indiscriminate representation of subjects, along with a more accessible world of letters—meant a reorganization of gender boundaries. While women were integral subjects of print culture, men addressed the possibilities and limitations of modernity by encroaching on the world of women's letters, or *nữ văn giới*. Chapter 2 illuminates the revolutionary project of post-mandarin prose, focusing on Vũ Trọng Phụng's depiction of women's everyday reality in Hanoi's sex industry. Phụng's literary project merged reportage writing with the realist novel, developing a unique modern prose style that was labeled pornographic. I argue that Phụng's so-called pornographic content signals Vietnam's radical literary turn toward the prosaic. This chapter reads nonfictional reportage as a genre entwined with fictional realism. Phụng's works pervert Vietnamese literature through their representations of characters, particularly commercial sex workers, that had been considered too vulgar for representation. He includes such profane characters in his works to confront the realities of colonial modernity's most pressing issues. For Phụng, reportage becomes a vehicle to address modernization and also a stepping-stone toward the modern novel.

When viewed through Vietnam's post-mandarin literature, modernity is not merely an absolute description of the "new" that opposes or disavows tradition, a rational world premised on science and empiricism, the penetration of capitalism's development, or the continuation of the European Enlightenment project. Post-mandarin writers responded to modernity as the juxtaposition of the everyday of the present and the remnants of the past (whose presence remains in a historic site like the Temple of Literature or surviving character-based inscriptions, present today throughout Hanoi like unearthed fossils). Post-mandarin modernity was a merger of different signs. Print culture was a microcosm of this confluence, as most, if not all, post-mandarin literature was published serially in newspapers or journals next to designed graphics, cartoons, news stories, advertisements, headlines, word games, and so on. As Harry Harootunian has suggested, idiosyncratic modernities outside of Europe should not be construed as alternative or subaltern derivatives but rather as manifested through the everyday, where the revenant of the past overlaps with modernity's developments.[61]

Post-mandarin intellectuals were caught between the jarring coexistence of Vietnam's Confucian past and colonial modernity. Although the French educational system rendered illegible the character-based scripts associated with Vietnam's mandarinal intellectual history, Confucianism's aesthetic legacies and social effects still lingered: it was the system of reference against which post-mandarin literature responded. When Vũ Trọng Phụng, for example, made his prose sexually explicit, he was reacting to a hierarchy of content that prevented the pressing issue of colonial sex from being aesthetically represented and thus politically addressed.

The various social effects of Confucianism's modes of authority—in social mores, familial hierarchies, social collectivism, and language—were singled out and criticized by other post-mandarin authors. The post-mandarin writers who most acerbically opposed Confucianism were the members of the Self-Strengthening Literary Group. They organized their campaign to modernize

Vietnam around the objective of vanquishing Confucianism as a social order that determined an individual's social position and negated personal desire. Despite the group's hyperbolic denunciation of Confucianism in the name of unbridled modernization, their attempt to exorcise Confucianism was an acknowledgment of its hold on Vietnamese society. The group understood modernity as the coexistence between incompatible systems of values that pitted social collectivism against individualism, and they examined this tension by writing about women who violated the Confucian social norms through their romantic relationships. For the Self-Strengthening group, Confucianism was a presupposed and accepted social force that constrained individuals, who, in turn, behaved accordingly, unaware of the imposed rules and norms. The group saw the Confucian social world as a kind of chessboard whose parameters and regulations dictated and limited individual movement and will.

Self-Strengthening authors employed the genre of the novel to observe and critique Confucianism's accepted social practices and rules. Chapter 3 examines how Nhất Linh, the leader of the Self-Strengthening group, sociologically observed romantic relationships in his novels to assail Confucianism's conscription of women into specific social expectations. Nhất Linh's *Đoạn tuyệt* (Breaking away) reveals the social norms and rituals that continued to determine women's social roles during the 1930s. The novel attempts to expose the social facts—what the text calls "invisible strings" (*những dây vô hình*)—that imposed restrictive gender roles. My reading recasts this "romanticist" novel as a sociological analysis of gendered roles and expectations that had the illusion of being natural and self-evident.

One of the defining attributes of this modern Vietnamese literature is its incorporation of the first-person pronoun *tôi* (*je* in French or *I* in English). Associated with European influence, the first-person grammatical category was antithetical to Vietnam's Confucian sociolinguistic system. The complex system of pronouns in the Vietnamese language is based on familial relations. One's relationship to a family member through age, gender, or marriage extends into the social realm. Each pronoun in the complex system specifies one's age, seniority, and gender in relation to the person being addressed, as if he or she were within one's family. It is the organization of kinship relations that determines social and even political relations.

For the Self-Strengthening group, Confucianism penetrated all aspects of social life, from ritualized events to personal inclinations and behavior. The group's authors viewed it as an institution of doctrines and principles enforced and regulated by the familial collective, particularly through the reinforcement of gender differences and sociolinguistic structures. Chapter 4 looks at the sociolinguistic element of the Self-Strengthening project. Focusing on Khái Hưng's

Nửa chừng xuân (In the midst of spring), the chapter examines how the author addressed the cultural translation of the first-person grammatical category into Vietnam's Confucian sociolinguistic order, revealing the gendered implications of the changes taking place during the post-mandarin period. I argue that although male Vietnamese writers adapted the European first-person pronoun to express individual autonomy, modern female authors and protagonists remained circumscribed by sociolinguistic structures and thus were unable to assume the first-person voice. Khái Hưng's novel illuminates this disparity by examining how the female protagonist must relate herself discursively with and against existing sociolinguistic structures. The heroine's subjectivity is formed not through an adaptation of European individualism but rather through the chasm between the imported first-person grammatical category and the sociolinguistic structures particular to Vietnam. For the Self-Strengthening group, individualism was not, as many critics have noted, a Western concept or ideology to be grafted onto Vietnamese society. Rather, the emergence of the first-person grammatical category reveals how linguistic differences are premised on gender differences. Modern Vietnamese literature, then, is not the emergence of an autonomous first-person voice and the subsequent abandonment of Vietnam's complex system of person references (which is still in use today), but rather it is the tense juxtaposition of the two systems that is most evident in the gender differentiation of the post-mandarin context.

My elaboration here of post-mandarin literature through an analysis of gender and sexuality is an attempt to revise Vietnam's Communist historiography as it was codified and implemented institutionally beginning in the 1940s.[62] This dominant narrative, inflected by Stalinist and Maoist orthodoxy, explains the emergence of modern Vietnamese literature as the fulfillment of Vietnamese socialism, the teleological end of anticolonial revolution, legitimating the Communist insurgency and its rise to state power. I challenge this historiography by examining the post-mandarin gender and sexual dynamics that shaped the literary and intellectual fields from which Vietnamese Marxism emerged. Chapter 5 illuminates this cultural history by looking at how and why post-mandarin intellectuals engaged with André Gide's call for national and individual particularity, a particularity that was mediated through sexuality. The chapter argues that Gide's influence in Vietnam—specifically as "queer internationalism"—during the 1930s underlies the emergence of critical and socialist realism. These claims question the historiography of the Vietnamese anticolonial revolution and its privileging of class determinism.

In the 1940s state-sanctioned narrative, critics characterized romanticist literature as individualistic, apolitical, amoral, and escapist, while realist literature was seen as socially conscious, political, and grounded in reality. Vietnam's

Communist literary history has situated romanticism in a bipolar system as the reactionary other to the venerated literary category of realism. Romanticism has been charged with being a passive and negative movement that worked against the struggles of anticolonialism and nationalism.

Such a reading of modern Vietnamese literature is exemplified by the literary criticism of Trường Chinh. As one of the primary architects of the Vietnamese Communist Party's cultural policies, Trường Chinh begins his *Marxism and Vietnamese Culture* (*Chủ nghĩa Mác và văn hóa Việt Nam*) by defining culture with Marx's conceptions of base (*cơ sở hạ tầng*) and superstructure (*kiến trúc thượng tầng*). The economic relations of production determine the superstructure, which includes politics, law, and culture.[63] Trường Chinh goes on to claim that culture "influences economics and politics, at times with extraordinary force."[64] Therefore, the August Revolution of 1945 had altered the relations of production, and it was a conflict that was (and would continue to be) waged in ideological forms that led the masses to become conscious of their economic and material conditions. Of these ideological forms, Trường Chinh focused exclusively on literary culture.[65]

Trường Chinh associates the development of modern Vietnamese literature with the capitalist system under French colonialism and the rise of the Vietnamese bourgeois class after World War I. During World War I, the French colonial government exploited the Vietnamese population through taxation and recruitment into the armed forces. After the war, the laboring class (*giai cấp công nhân*) struggled against the repression of French imperialism, preexisting feudalism, and an emerging Vietnamese bourgeoisie—three elements that capitalized on the postwar economic boom. According to Trường Chinh, the indigenous bourgeois class may have had the intention of opposing the French, but such political intention would conflict with its economic interests, since it had to maintain business relationships with the colonial power. It was not until the founding of the Indochinese Communist Party in 1930 that a new proletariat movement displaced the stagnant, futile bourgeois revolution. The proletariat movement gained momentum, and its efforts culminated in the 1945 revolution.

Consistent with his distinction between the bourgeois and proletarian movements, Trường Chinh conceptualizes Vietnam's national culture (*văn hóa dân tộc*) as a bifurcation. There was "the culture, which betrayed our nation, of the French colonialists and of the traitors, representative of the many feudalistic landowners and the comprador bourgeoisie (this culture gained prominence in French-controlled areas); meanwhile, there was the culture of patriotism and resistance, a culture for the nation and the people, the culture of a new democracy (this culture established itself in the realm of liberation)."[66] Any artist who was deemed unpatriotic was viewed as reveling in the French colonial legacy.

Trường Chinh claims that Vietnam's demand for bourgeois, romanticist litera-ture signaled the French's success in lulling the younger generation into debauch-ery and political ignorance.[67] Conversely, as Trường Chinh would explain it, realism documents and exposes the causes and effects of contemporary society's gritty reality, while the culture that betrays the revolution distorts reality.

Although Trường Chinh is right to suspect the transmission of French lit-erature as an arm of the colonial project, he is wrong to assume that Vietnam-ese colonial writers were all seduced by the French colonialists' instrumental use of culture. Rather, as discussed in the following chapters, post-mandarin authors translated, adapted, and challenged European ideas of modernity, ratio-nality, universalism, and nationalism to critique Vietnam's sociopolitical situa-tion. Moreover, influential French writers and thinkers, ranging from Rousseau to a romanticist like Victor Hugo to André Gide, were also engaged political theorists—working on ideas ranging from constitutionalism to republicanism.[68] While there are, of course, differences among Vietnam's cultural Marxists, the dominant framework of realism versus romanticism can be traced back to the 1930s and up to the 1980s.[69]

Although this binary of realism and romanticism is intended to organize texts into a comprehensive narrative of revolutionary communism, ultimately it obscures the transformative literary projects forwarded by writers of this period. This literary historical narrative is based on certain misconceptions. The political impetus for the binary system of realism and romanticism places more emphasis on an author's political associations than his or her works. There is a presupposition here that a writer's political leanings and membership can accu-rately explain his aesthetic practice. As a result, critical readings of purportedly romanticist literature as a failed literary movement are less an accurate concep-tualization of modern Vietnamese literature than an exercise of political parti-sanship. Vietnam's orthodox literary history has, as other critics have observed, skewed and overlooked the plurality of discourses and questions addressed by modern Vietnamese literature.[70]

My book posits post-mandarin disruptions as the crucial factor in the devel-opment of Vietnam's intellectual and literary fields during colonial modernity, looking at the prosaic turn in works that do not conform to the political tenets of state-approved realism. I examine this literature not along ideological lines and alliances but rather through the imperative to represent so as to transform colonial society. Post-mandarin realism and its more democratic representation emerged from the altered gender relations after the abandonment of the man-darinate's all-male preserve. The elaboration here of the post-mandarin not only rethinks modern Vietnamese literature's most significant prose forms—realism, romanticism, and investigative reportage—but also sees them as interrelated.

These genres do not represent opposing political ideologies articulated in different literary forms and styles; rather their political significance and aesthetic innovation are underwritten by the fraught and shifting gender dynamics of colonial modernity. It is the entwined predicament of post-mandarin male writers and modern Vietnamese women that I examine in this book.

CHAPTER 1

Autoethnography and Post-Mandarin Masculinity

Mình cứ việc điều tra ngay ở chính mình!

(We should just investigate ourselves!)

—Nguyễn Công Hoan

In the epigraph above,[1] Nguyễn Công Hoan, an important figure in Vietnamese realism during the 1930s, addresses his fellow Vietnamese writers and declares that they must look inward, within their own society, to find the materials for a new modern literature. The author Vũ Trọng Phụng cites Nguyễn to legitimate his own investigative journalism on domestic servants' labor conditions and defend himself against his editor's charges of vulgarity. The controversies that surrounded Phụng's work raised larger literary questions regarding the new genre, *phóng sự* (reportage). To what extent, the men were debating, should bare moments of *sự thực* (truth) be published? Did the sexual and physical exploitation of household workers constitute a suitable subject of journalistic writing—or was it a form of voyeurism, inappropriate for public consumption? Nguyễn Công Hoan's call for self-investigation served as a credo for a new Vietnamese prose that represented everyday life, including those elements that seemed too raw and perverse to merit aesthetic representation.

Reportage stands as a foundational pillar in Vietnamese aesthetic modernity; it was entwined with the development of the modern Vietnamese novel. Vietnam's post-mandarin authors merged the techniques of investigative journalism with the principles of French naturalism, an offshoot of and correction to literary realism. Echoing the aims of naturalism to treat the deterministic forces of heredity and the environment scientifically, reportage emphasized the objective representation of material objects and subject matter. In the case of Vietnam, as this chapter explores, the empirically based research and the observation of reportage were based on the writer's subjective point of view—a presupposition that was complicated by the predicament of the post-mandarin male intellectual.

As a foundation of Vietnamese aesthetic modernity, reportage briefly dovetails with, yet quickly diverges from, impressionism's influential role in European modernism. Both reportage and impressionism begin with the observer's subjective sensual perception. But whereas impressionism provides a perceptual totality in which a sensuous moment is mediated by another memory or perceptual moment, the subjective perceptions of the reportage investigator do not retreat into the recesses of personal memory[2] but rather transpose, as if to verify, the observed external reality. The centrality of reportage in modern Vietnamese culture illustrates the imperative of scientific and social scientific methods for French-educated intellectuals. However, post-mandarin writers rarely addressed another crucial aspect of the genre: its reliance on the subjective experience of the first-person participant observer. A careful reading of the post-mandarin's subjective experiences illuminates how their masculine anxiety steered the development of reportage to focus on the lives of women, particularly sex workers. It was precisely the subjective nature of reportage writing, dressed in the guise of objectivity, that played a central role in Vietnamese aesthetic modernity. Therefore, Vietnamese reportage merits consideration, more than typically attributed to the genre elsewhere.

Vietnamese writers of the 1930s employed *phóng sự* to portray the prosaic, in both senses of the word—that is, as a prose genre and as the everyday. But as the controversy surrounding Phụng illuminates, they did so with attention to the lurid details of colonial sex. Post-mandarin writers embraced the immersive experiences of reportage investigation that enabled them to observe and document the everyday. Unlike the preceding generations of intellectuals legitimized by civil service exams, *phóng sự* authors worked in a post-mandarin literary field structured by print capitalism, employing the market-driven newspaper as their primary medium. The drive for collective, self-reflexive analysis—"We should just investigate ourselves"—signaled their intellectual and literary turn away from the literati's authority based on the mastery of poetics toward the firsthand observations of investigative journalism.[3] Moreover, I argue here that the inward turn toward "ourselves" hinged on the conceptualization of a new Vietnamese collectivity that included and seriously considered the place of women. The new collective identity, which breached previous gender divisions, meant that the situation and, indeed, the fate of sex workers were inextricably tied in with that of post-mandarin intellectuals. It was with this consternation that Vietnam's colonized intellectuals set out to write reportage.

As a literary term, *phóng sự* refers to nonfiction prose writing based on objective observations of events or milieus. Breaking down the term's constitutive parts, *phóng* has several meanings: (1) to enlarge, (2) to imitate (in terms of writing or art), and (3) to project. *Sự* denotes event or occurence. Read literally, then, the term *phóng sự* means to project something by mimesis and enlargement. The visual connotations of *phóng sự*—"to enlarge," "to give a close-up"—refer to one of the genre's defining attributes: the eyewitness who documents what he experiences.[4] *Phóng sự* narrators directly observe the immediate present, attempting to depict or gather information about a social scene, social situation, or current affair with a focus on the working classes and urban underclass. Examples are works that document the laborious life of rickshaw pullers or the social crisis of prostitution. The genre depends on narrators who employ a language of objectivity and mimetic transparency to describe their subjects.

Phóng sự's development during the 1930s dovetailed with the rise of reportage in locales beyond Indochina. Like reportage in other national contexts, *phóng sự* works focus on social spaces and the immediate present, presuppose the accurate and authentic depiction of the real, and appear in newspapers.[5] Moreover, Vietnamese scholars often translate the term as "reportage." In the French, Soviet, Chinese, and central European contexts, reportage has been closely associated with cultural leftism, particularly the Communist Party during the interwar period.[6] Practitioners and scholars of reportage consider the genre antithetical to and distinct from bourgeois writing, such as the nineteenth-century realist novel from Europe.

Leftist readings of reportage adequately characterize some of Vietnam's *phóng sự* or reportage texts—particularly those that are viewed as exemplifying critical and socialist realism. Nevertheless, there remains a large number of *phóng sự* texts that are more concerned with Vietnam's *dân tộc* or *ethnos* than communism, more concerned with sexual relations than class relations. *Phóng sự* writing had multiple purposes: to critique the mandarin class, to assert an identity against Indochina's "other" ethnic groups, to address peasant life, to chastise the new bourgeois and petty bourgeois classes, to question colonial policies, and to ponder modernity's possibilities and uncertainties. Of course, these works responded to imperialism's exploitation of the working classes. However, they were also concerned with the formation of anticolonial consciousness through the self-awareness that comes from the writing of one's own culture. In addition, Vietnamese literary historians agree that *phóng sự* is an important foundation of modern Vietnamese literature.[7] This has not been the case elsewhere, such as in Anglo-American and European literature, where reportage is a peripheral genre.[8]

During the 1930s, when the genre flourished in post-mandarin circles, Vietnamese writers composed *phóng sự* works to critique and reform colonial society. Exploiting the genre's realistic depictions and straightforward prose, *phóng sự* authors claimed that the genre was authentic, objective, and thus suitable as an expression of moral authority. They employed the first-person voice while assuming a neutral perspective so as to shed light on social issues. It is precisely this first-person voice that signaled both the innovation of the genre and its central contradiction: its inherent objectivity stems from a writer's subjective point of view. These authors presumably operated with transparency and accuracy in their recordings of the real, like the workings of a camera. Nevertheless, *phóng sự* writing required a subjective witness to do the recording. To borrow George Orwell's definition, the point of straightforward reportage prose is to "report contemporary events truthfully, or as truthfully as is consistent with the ignorance, bias, and self-deception from which every observer necessarily suffers."[9]

I argue that *phóng sự*, with its blend of documentation and personal testimony, is a form of autoethnography, a mode of ethnographic writing in which the author, a male Vietnamese participant observer,[10] documented and wrote his own culture in order to define himself through an other. A significant other for these male writers, as I discuss momentarily, was the indigenous female sex worker. Colonial Vietnam's *phóng sự* writing focuses, to a large extent, on local culture and the everyday—a web of significances that is, nowadays, typically relegated to the purview of urban sociology or social anthropology. Much like the field-worker, the reportage narrator immerses himself in a given culture for the purposes of investigative fieldwork. This reportage writing, like ethnography, is "the attempt to understand another life world using the self—as much of it as possible—as the instrument of knowing. . . . The ethnographic stance (as we may call it) is as much an intellectual (and moral) positionality, a constructive and interpretative mode, as it is a bodily process in space and time."[11] Moreover, like the participant observer in the field, the reportage narrator's presence in a given cultural context signals his interest and investment in the "experiential density of 'being there'"—to borrow a description of ethnography.[12]

Autoethnography is a genre of writing in which the author or narrative voice speaks about his or her community for that community's own consumption. However, I am not claiming that autoethnography represents some kind of authentic self-expression, cultural authenticity, or unproblematic "insidedness." It is not a given that the reportage author is privy to the supposed intimate and subconscious knowledge that everyone *within* a particular culture possesses. Rather, I am interested in how these works illuminate the ways that culture forms through asymmetry and difference, in this case through the native, male autoethnographic voice. I question the access and privilege of the indigenous heterosexual male's ethnographic voice. If the privileged voice belongs to a colonial subject, then, following James Buzard, I want to "look at the rhetoric by means of which autoethnographers indicate their fitness for their task, and even at the degree to which *they* take for granted their right to perform that task."[13]

Through *phóng sự*, Vietnamese writers counteracted exogenous colonial discourses, working toward a self-determined articulation of a totalized ethnic and national culture.[14] The insistence on a collective cultural identity runs consistently throughout *phóng sự* texts. In *Tôi kéo xe* (I pull a rickshaw), considered one of the earliest and most significant *phóng sự* works,[15] Tam Lang expresses solidarity with urban coolies by defining *xã hội* (society) as all "people who come from the same origin and who all live together under the same system, and that includes you and me."[16] The genre's nationalist aspirations are evidenced in its depiction of a collectivity based on a singular, autochthonous origin and common ethnicity. Thus critics have characterized Tam Lang's writing style and contributions as "bearing [the Vietnamese] national character" (*mang tính cách dân tộc*).[17]

The term *dân tộc* shares the multiple meanings of the Greek word *ethnos* (ethnic group, people, nation). In the Vietnamese language, the phrase is used to translate the French term *ethnologie* (ethnology) into the Vietnamese term *dân tộc học*. While French ethnographic observations about colonial Vietnam circulated among Vietnamese readers and intellectuals, there was, interestingly, no equivalent Vietnamese term for *ethnographie*. This void is surprising given the multitude of neologisms in late nineteenth-century and early twentieth-century Vietnamese language that accounted for ideas and concepts imported from Europe. Nevertheless, the absence of a term equivalent to *ethnographie* does not mean a corollary lack of writing about the *ethnos*, or nation. Instead, it points to French ethnography's institutionalization—becoming more and more professionalized as a practice within the colonial enterprise and later within academia while the colonized subject's practice of ethnography was less confined and more ubiquitous. We can locate Vietnamese ethnographic writing in various guises, such as popular travel writing or, most pertinent here, reportage.[18]

This autoethnographic writing was not only a tool of anticolonial nationalism; it also negotiated the new post-mandarin gender relations between Vietnamese men and women. In multiple *phóng sự* works, the narrator acts as a participant observer writing his own culture, defining the self through his engagement with a female other. I examine *phóng sự* chroniclers' investigative journalism as an embodied interaction in which the narrator's subjective viewpoint starkly contradicts his claims to objectivity, revealing the instability of *phóng sự* writers as post-mandarin intellectuals grappling with their own masculinity and sexuality. As I demonstrate below, the claims to objectivity actually point to a larger anxiety among *phóng sự* authors about their masculinity as they struggled to overturn the twin authorities of the mandarin intellectual and the European colonizer. *Phóng sự* authors exercised their intellectual authority while displacing their masculine anxieties, turning to the indigenous female sex worker as a figure for their own abjection and thus the other of this embodied, ethnographic relationship.

Phóng sự authors saw the indigenous female sex worker as symptomatic of the cultural and material transformations triggered by colonial modernity. Yet their engagement with the lives of these women led them to question their own indigenous, male sexuality, a concern that explains the splintered subjectivity at the core of this genre.

Tam Lang's *Tôi kéo xe* (I pull a rickshaw), published serially in 1932 and in book form in 1935, depicts the shadowy, unknown world of Hanoi's *cu li xe kéo* (rickshaw coolies). Physical violence and deplorable conditions, human exploitation, opium addiction, and prostitution riddle this underworld. In order to chronicle the rickshaw world, the narrator assumes the identity of a rickshaw puller both to observe and to participate in the trade. Pushing the limits of investigative writing, the narrator sets out to endure a rickshaw coolie's physical toil, psychological humiliation, and economic hardships. The participant observer experiences firsthand the trade's everyday tedium and the dark underside of opium addiction and prostitution rings. He then distills his empirically derived social knowledge into a work of prose to influence social practice and political policy: ultimately, to fade out the practice of human rickshaws.[19]

Near the end of *Tôi kéo xe*, the narrator makes explicit his intentions by addressing the city officials responsible for initiating social changes.[20] He offers pragmatic solutions: abandon the most abject practices of rickshaw pulling while still retaining jobs for these laborers. Tam Lang, therefore, proposes switching to the technologically advanced and more humane pedicab. The abolishment of the rickshaw would effectively alter Vietnamese society's inhumane treatment of rickshaw coolies as "human horses" (*người ngựa*). Tam Lang's reportage contributed to the critical discourse of social progress and universal rights that ultimately reshaped policy regarding the rickshaw trade.[21] Tam Lang's *phóng sự* writing represented an important example of effective social and political advocacy while also capturing the difficult reality of the post-mandarin figure.[22]

Born Vũ Đình Chí in 1900, Tam Lang came from a reputable family of Confucian scholars. Vũ Đình Chất, Tam Lang's father, opposed French colonialism and joined the Đông Kinh Nghĩa Thục (Tonkin Free School), a short-lived anticolonial movement that sought to modernize Vietnam by importing ideas from Europe and Japan. However, with few career options, his father reluctantly worked as a civil servant for the French colonial government. Unlike his father, Tam Lang was educated in the Franco-indigenous system (after an initial foray into Chinese-language education). He continued with his studies and trained as a schoolteacher. Tam Lang eventually quit his training to pursue a career as a newspaper journalist. *Tôi kéo xe* marks Tam Lang's break from his family's lineage of scholars and educators and his venture into the post-mandarin field of print capitalism. The reportage not only documents the life of the rickshaw worker but also captures the social and historical pressures that shaped the emergence of the post-mandarin intellectual.

In *Tôi kéo xe*, Tam Lang fails to meet the physical demands of participant observation required by reportage journalism.[23] As the son of a Confucian intellectual, he had no experience with manual labor. Throughout the reportage, the narrator notes the physical toll on a body and mind unaccustomed to such work. In one scene, he writes, "I felt like a naked person in the street pulling an ox-cart with a board mounted on it which bore my full name and, also, the names of the close members of my family."[24] By publicly taking on the role of the rickshaw coolie as a participant observer, the author exposes the declining status of the public intellectual from elite mandarin to everyday laborer in the print-cultural field.

Capturing the generational fall from Confucian scholar to "human horse," Tam Lang finds as his primary interview subject *anh* Tư, who is also the son of a fallen Confucian scholar. Tam Lang's consistent use of "*anh*" (older brother) suggests that they are from the same generation. Although this interview is supposed to provide a counterpoint to the narrator's own outsider position, *anh* Tư's social position is analogous to the narrator's own familial situation. The *phóng sự* text captures the men's unexpected positions as participant observer of and laborer within the rickshaw underworld. Their abrupt generational decline is thrown into greater relief by their surroundings, a dilapidated opium den located in an area untouched by *văn minh* (civilization) or *tiến hóa* (progress).[25] As the two men smoke and commiserate with each other, Tam Lang comes to identify with Tư. In the chapters focused on Tư (ten of the text's twenty chapters), the encounters between the two men are represented as a dialogue; however, the narrator often fades into the background, merely transcribing Tư's observations with occasional commentary. The text takes on Tư's voice for chapters at a time and blurs the distinction between observer and subject. Even though the story is clearly not Tam Lang's own, its presentation in the text—the long, uninterrupted passages; the preservation of Tư's deictic *tôi*'s (I's); the occasional quotation mark—camouflages the interviewee. In effect, Tư's words become the narrator's own.

> Those elementary lessons Tư taught me became paragraphs and chapters.
>
> Each pipe was an end stop! Each piece of candy was a semicolon!
>
> But how indifferent they were! In fifty or sixty sentences there was not a question mark or an exclamation mark.[26]

Void of interrogative or exclamatory sentences, Tư's narrative of declarative sentences is clearly informative and valuable to Tam Lang. The matter-of-fact voices may suggest a disinterested or impartial observer, but in fact they indicate torpor and despondency from the consumption of opium. The opium-induced narrative cuts through the reportage's intended objectivity, pointing the reader to the colonial transformations of the intellectual and literary fields that led both the interviewer and the interviewee to the decrepit den as, respectively, journalist and coolie—the primary subjects of this groundbreaking reportage.

As the reportage's primary informant, Tư represents a new brand of *thầy*, or teacher, not one who is vaulted by scholarly erudition and cultural capital, but rather one who has experienced, with humiliation, the travails of working in a society where his family's intellectual lineage no longer has relevance. Tư's father was a scholar and teacher of classical Chinese texts, but, marginalized in the French colonial system, he forged a government seal and consequently was sentenced to a colonial prison in Sơn La, where he died. Wholly dependent on the patriarch's income, Tư, an only child, and his mother could no longer support themselves, and the family's finances became precarious as they sought medical treatment for an unspecified blinding illness that affected his mother. There was no social support system since all of his father's students had dispersed. Tư claimed that as an intellectual heir he had no marketable skills or knowledge capable of generating an income. Therefore, he turned to the rickshaw trade, and eventually became Tam Lang's *thầy*.

Tam Lang describes Tư as a *thầy* who has gone through two phases.

> My teacher, an unfortunate Confucian scholar whose mouth has been blackened by a pen-brush for half his life, was more than poetic and literary.

—And yet, he continued, in those wretched conditions were many pitiful stories. If one can filter out the layers of muck, one can find a few tears.[27]

The pedagogical content—and consequently, the content of the reportage—is no longer textual and academic but rather full of everyday experiences and instructive work techniques, such as correctly balancing a rickshaw or efficiently shifting one's body weight. Tam Lang's "teacher" does not speak from a position shored up by Confucianism's political legitimacy or hierarchical order but rather, more precisely, from the demise of that system. The teacher was no longer the master of Chinese classical texts but instead the informant who had experienced the realities of the urban world. Tam Lang identifies with this fallen Confucian scholar's disillusionment, cynicism, and resignation because the situation mirrored the post-mandarin transformation that affected the author. Soon enough, Tư loses the only material object that symbolized his family's past history, áo thâm nhà nho (the Confucian scholar's tunic),[28] and it is at this point that he displaces, quite maliciously, his wretchedness onto the vulnerable women whom he coerces into prostitution.

Tư explains that after being stripped and ruthlessly beaten he lost all moral sensibility and social decorum. He began to pursue the callous work of a pimp, a line of work facilitated and masked by rickshaw pulling. Tư's first story concerning prostitution involves forgery, much like the crime behind his father's demise. Both father and son, as marginalized figures, felt compelled to falsify and assume another's identity. But specifically in the latter's case, he employs this fraudulent persona to exploit a woman made defenseless by an illicit love affair. Tư's scheme perpetuates a chain of marginality, making contiguous his loss of social standing as a mandarin's son and a young woman's fear of social condemnation for her love affair and entrance into prostitution.

Tư hatched the plot when he gave a ride to a young woman secretly heading for a rendezvous with her lover. He then began to shadow the couple. The rickshaw puller notes the lovers' personal profiles and addresses, their families, and their meeting patterns. He studies their coded correspondence in order to produce a forged letter, imitating the male lover's "feminine" handwriting, their secret seal, and their use of couriers. One evening, as the woman is leaving for her illicit excursion, a young boy, coached by Tư, delivers the fake letter to her, and after some reluctance, the woman agrees to go to a predetermined hotel room. At the hotel a room had been staged for an intimate escapade. But rather than her lover, the Vietnamese hotel proprietor enters. The woman tries to escape, but the door is already locked. As if to make the trapped woman feel at ease, the hotel owner feigns intimacy with her family relations, information that had been relayed by

Tử. Continuing to play his role of innocent rickshaw puller, Tử leaves the room and hears the double bolted door lock, an ominous sign for the young woman. The next morning the men reconvene to further their collaboration: to defile and scandalize the name of the young woman and her family with an account of all her sexual exploits should she not comply with the hotel owner's demands of servicing other men. Consistent with the other situations of prostitution detailed by Tử, the men's exploits depend on their ability to blackmail women suspected of sexual activities that violate extant social structures and value systems. These women were young lovers, nightclub patrons, runaways, and sex workers.[29]

Reportage writers depicted the social conditions and government policies that lead to the problems of prostitution in order to reflect on the crisis of colonial Vietnamese society writ large. But they were also imbricated in the genre's complex, unequal, and even exploitative gender dynamics. Tử displaces his marginalized position onto the woman. Likewise, through the lens of female prostitutes, these male authors grappled with their own uncertain subject position during colonial modernity. Their ability to examine the lives of these women depended on their circumscribed mobility in the colonial setting; in contrast, the observed female prostitutes were held at the legally sanctioned brothel houses and the colonial dispensary.

Reportage writing was contingent on this limited mobility, or, to borrow James Buzard's phrasing, "metaphor of knowledge as travel."[30] The initial moments of *Tôi kéo xe* emphasize travel as knowledge: Tam Lang's editor attempts to inspire him to look beyond his local conditions with tales of other investigative journalists who worked abroad, including Albert Londres, Maurice Dekobra, Jack London, and Louis Charles Royer. However, the author rebuts this argument, claiming that the colonial government had not granted permission for a family relative to travel to Cambodia, a neighboring French colonial territory, no less to distant places like Shanghai and New York. Citing the work of Maryse Choisy, who famously went into disguise to investigate Paris's brothels, Tam Lang decides to work in his native environs, traveling to an unfamiliar urban area and immersing himself as a participant observer for the purposes of his investigative reportage.

Although he remains in Indochina, Tam Lang, like many of his fellow reportage writers, voluntarily enters and, eventually, exits the cultural world he investigates. For example, when the "king of reportage," Vũ Trọng Phụng, reemerges from the petty world of household servants, he declares, "I am I again."[31] Unlike Rimbaud's well-known dictum, "Je est un autre" (I is another), the reportage writer's declaration connotes a grammatically correct identity—in control and empowered—between self and other, between writer and subject, between participant observer and subject. The male writer's flexible position starkly opposes that of the indigenous female prostitute trapped in the sex industry.

The confinement of the local woman here resembles the immobility of the native subject in the ethnographic encounter, while the mobility of the reportage narrator is analogous to the travels of the anthropologist. Identifying the difference in mobility as the problematic conception of place in ethnographic fieldwork, Arjun Appadurai suggests that this is a kind of metonymic freezing.

> [It] is the problem of the culturally defined locations to which ethnographies refer. Such named locations, which often come to be identified with the groups that inhabit them, constitute the landscape of anthropology, in which the privileged locus is the often unnamed location of the ethnographer. Ethnography thus reflects the circumstantial encounter of the voluntarily displaced anthropologist and the involuntarily localized "other."[32]

Not only are ethnographic subjects limited to a particular place, but they are presumed to speak "from" and to speak "of" a certain locale without "distortion or residue."[33] Metonymic freezing occurs when ethnographers assume the boundedness of a given culture and the informant's representative voice and essentialize a culture with hegemonic ideas and images taken as the cultural whole.[34]

Rather than assume that the ethnographic voice represents a uniformity that overrides any internal differences of a given cultural space, I approach autoethnography through the intersection of voice and space in Vietnamese reportage to question the access and privilege of the participant observer's voice, which consistently belongs to the indigenous heterosexual male. The internal hierarchies of the cultural space expose the differences between the mobile male voice and the immobile female subject—between native man and native woman—a relationship of unequal power and gender dynamics. As I elaborate below, the male reportage writer's flexible position starkly opposes that of the involuntarily localized other—the indigenous prostitute confined to the state-sanctioned brothel and colonial dispensary—even as the male narrator identifies her plight with his own.

To illustrate this power relationship and its importance in Vietnamese literature of the time, I turn to Việt Sinh's 1933 reportage, *Hà Nội ban đêm* (Hanoi at night), whose subject is prostitution. Việt Sinh was the pen name of Thạch Lam, the youngest of three brothers who spearheaded the Self-Strengthening Literary Group. Founded in 1932, the group quickly emerged as pioneering authors, editors, and publishers of modern Vietnamese literature. The

Self-Strengthening group espoused and promoted the reportage genre as a means to expose and modernize Vietnam's Confucian social structures and illuminate how they were buttressed by French colonialism.

In *Hà Nội ban đêm*, the narrator of *phóng sự* is a participant observer entangled in the gender relations of Vietnamese society during the French colonial period, relations characterized by two situations of unequal differences. First, there is the difference between European and Vietnamese men. When the narrator takes on a heterosexual male identity as a participant observer of prostitution, he is trying to establish his own position against that of the European male. Second, it examines how colonial modernity alters the relationship between native men and native women, a disparate set of relations.

Published serially in the Self-Strengthening Literary Group's weekly journal *Phong hóa* (Customs), *Hà Nội ban đêm* depicts Việt Sinh's experiences as he went out at night to explore Hanoi's various brothels (see figure 1). Việt Sinh's editor introduces *Hà Nội ban đêm* in the following manner.

> As the ill effects of prostitution in Hanoi worsen each day, we believe that it is necessary to know about its harmful effects.
>
> This reportage . . . gives an account of the truth, what was heard and seen, what occurred in Hanoi—none of which is fictional. To the best of our abilities, *Phong hóa* will expose the reader to the secrets of the profession, while also presenting to the reader the tribulations and sufferings of a social group that we should empathize with, rather help than scorn.[35]

Hà Nội ban đêm then pursues this straightforward purpose of exposing the social epidemic of prostitution.[36] Throughout the text, Việt Sinh collects information and data so that he can examine colonial sex and the ineffective French mission to civilize and to modernize.

Hà Nội ban đêm is thick with ethnographic description. The narrator depicts the dark, narrow streets and the sly, incognito guides who show him the way to the brothels. Minute details are recorded with each step: the different surfaces the foot feels with each stride; the changing smells, as if they were microclimates, from the night's damp sky to the alleys' stench to the women's chemical smell of arsenic, mercury, and bismuth (from prophylactic medicines). The observer's eye notes the naked lightbulbs, the different kinds of beds (European, Hong Kong, or Vietnamese), the yellow, stained mattresses, and the mosquito nets.

In the opening moments of the reportage, the narrator and his friend Tràng Khanh walk to a neighborhood that is foreign to them. They approach the last house on the street and knock on the door. A young woman's voice asks, "Who is it? Is it you, *me*?"[37] The doorkeeper is expecting a *me*, which

Figure 1. Original serialization of "Hà Nội ban đêm" (Hanoi at night). Published in *Phong hóa*, March 10, 1933.

is a term for a Vietnamese woman married to a European. Tràng Khanh, the narrator's friend, declares that they are "*me*," demanding entry and startling the doorkeeper, who hurries away and leaves the door cracked. Tràng Khanh opens the door wide to enter uninvited. Once inside, the narrator is overwhelmed by feelings of uncertainty and fear in the strange setting. He writes, "I was shuddering: the room's atmosphere was eerily silent and cold. Wafting about was a peculiar smell, a mixture of incense, rot, perfume, and human odor."[38] Moments later, they are greeted by the brothel's rotund manager, who has a distinct air about her like a woman of "*số đỏ*" (a term I address below). Unlike the rattled doorkeeper and the petrified narrator, the hostess maintains equanimity, barking out orders to her staff while inviting the narrator and Tràng Khanh to make themselves at home. For two men who have ventured into Hanoi's streets at midnight to give authoritative accounts of prostitution, the tables seemed to have turned on them from the beginning: had either man been the expected Vietnamese woman married to a European, they would have been more welcome. Whereas the female owner is assured of her position and power, the narrator is vexed by his feelings of estrangement and uncertainty. Throughout *Hà Nội ban đêm*, the narrator comments on prostitution's effects on women, but as we have already witnessed from this opening scene, the reportage also concerns the male narrator's dubious position.

The first installment of *Hà Nội ban đêm* was published on March 10, 1933, in *Phong Hóa*, and the main illustration on this issue's cover questions male sexual identity amid the changes offset by colonial modernity (Figure 2). The illustration's caption reads, "Nam Việt Kỳ Quan." "Nam Việt" refers to Vietnam, and "Kỳ Quan" denotes a "wonder" and, if taken separately, suggests an awkward (*kỳ*) mandarin (*quan*). The punch line plays on the image of the Vietnamese mandarin as an odd, antiquated wonder of the world. The cartoon derides the author Tản Đà (born Nguyễn Khắc Hiếu), identifying him by his name as well as the titles of his major works on the jars and heart-shaped placards. Tản Đà never succeeded in passing the imperial exams. Nevertheless, he was targeted for his background in Confucian letters. Working in various genres and styles, his work merged Vietnamese literary tradition with French influence. Tản Đà was a transitional figure between Vietnam's precolonial poetic tradition and the French-influenced New Poetry (*Thơ mới*) movement that was inaugurated in 1932. Although he anticipated some of the central motifs of the New Poetry movement, including individualism and romance, he was not modern enough for the publishers of *Phong hóa*. They consistently derided his inebriation and saccharine poetics, and here they depict his works as repugnant. In the image, he displays his works as if they are goods available for trade or exchange, but they seem to be fermenting or rotting, giving off a smell that offends the irreverent woman and servant behind him. The *kỳ quan* figure is immune to the smell because his nose is desensitized and reddened from excessive drinking. A nametag labels him a "banished immortal," aligning him with a lineage of Chinese poets, including Li Bai from the Tang dynasty. A literary figure like Li Bai may be celebrated for his drunken eloquence, but in the cartoon's modern context inebriation signals lack of hygiene and self-awareness that contributes to Tản Đà's doomed affection and desire.

The *kỳ quan* is courting a group of women identified as *xian*, immortals or transcendents from the heavens, figures from a value system that is considered, in the context of *Phong hóa*, cosmological and unworldly. The women wear the Han Chinese clothing. Moreover, in the same way that the poet, already out of touch with modern times, addresses anachronistic female figures, the character script that identifies both the mandarin and his audience has been eradicated by French colonial policies—unlike the romanized alphabet used to address *Phong hóa*'s readers.

The illustration of the uncouth mandarin starkly contrasts with the introductory image of *Hà Nội ban đêm*'s narrator (Figure 3). While the mandarin is seated, holding court in an unidentifiable space, unable to comprehend his environs, the reportage figure is on his feet, walking the cramped, urban streets of Hanoi. Courtesans do not come to him; rather, he approaches a woman, slightly leaning in to engage her. Unlike the oblivious and drunk mandarin, this character will depend on his senses to observe and document Hanoi's world of prostitution. The narrator's masculinity and male sexual identity are not anachronistic like the mandarin's. Instead, they are as ambiguous and uncertain as his blacked-out body in the drawing. Nevertheless, in both cases the man's sexual identity is determined in relation to women. In this initial drawing, he sports a fedora, a cross-cultural signifier of hard-boiled masculinity, and as suggested by many of the illustrations that accompany the serialized reportage, he never seems to take it off.[39] Christopher Breu has argued that this hard-boiled masculinity presents a fantasy of moral detachment and affective displacement.[40] My point here is to dispel such illusory veneers of manhood, and by extension the presumed objectivity of reportage, by questioning the authority and voice of the participant observer.

As the narrator sets out to enter the brothel world, he is overcome with uncertainty. This anxiety, particularly as it pertains to the narrator's masculinity and sexual identity, manifests itself in the text, undercutting his

Figure 2. Caricature of Vietnamese mandarin. Published in *Phong hóa*, March 10, 1933.

attempts at objective reporting and documentation. Therein lies the irony of Việt Sinh's reportage on prostitution.

The narrator's gaze through the scope of *phóng sự* is a decidedly male heterosexual perspective that refrains from expressing erotic desire. When the narrator of *Hà Nội ban đêm* makes his entrée into the world of prostitution, he takes on an identity that is consistently male and heterosexual. Việt Sinh makes no mention of witnessing sex, let alone taking part in a sexual act. He only ventures to brothels where men visit women, never an establishment with male prostitutes. The narrator's lack of interest in male-to-male sexual relations contradicts the concerns of the period's French doctors and social engineers, who concluded that venereal diseases, particularly syphilis, were interrelated with the "social diseases" of pederasty and opiomania.[41]

The author's male, heterosexual abstinence contrasts with the sexuality present in *Un mois chez les filles* (A month among the girls), the 1928 work by Maryce Choisy, whom Tam Lang specifically cites as one of the strongest influences on his work. Claiming to have invented the *reportage vécu* (lived reportage), Choisy penned a work detailing her experiences in Parisian brothels. She argues that as a woman she has a privileged position from which to observe prostitution, claiming that men like Goncourt and Zola have written about prostitution but never from the perspective of a female journalist. In her preface to the American translation (which was a best seller), she writes that *A Month among the Girls* was the "first time a decent

Figure 3. Illustration of reportage participant observer.
Published in *Phong hóa*, March 10, 1933.

woman dared to tell her sisters what their husbands and sons did in those
places not mentioned in polite society."[42] But whereas both Tam Lang and
Việt Sinh maintained their appearance and identity as heterosexual men,
taking interest only in male-female sexual transactions, Choisy dressed as a
man to enter establishments with male prostitutes for male customers. She
delighted in having a convincing male appearance. And from the keyhole
perspective, Choisy reports the graphic details of sexual interactions. In further contrast to Việt Sinh, Choisy repeatedly expresses physical attraction to
this or that woman.

Although he insists on a heterosexual identity, Việt Sinh constantly preempts any possibility of his own sexual knowledge, desires, or engagement.
This explains the two names in the byline of *Hà Nội ban đêm*: Tràng Khanh

and Việt Sinh. Members of Việt Sinh's own literary group, Tự Lực văn đoàn, coauthored and cosigned a number of fiction and nonfiction works. In these collaborative efforts (such as novels or short story collections), both authors contributed to the creative process. However, in *Hà Nội ban đêm*, Tràng Khanh's voice is absent throughout. Every utterance of "I" clearly belongs to Việt Sinh, and Tràng Khanh is only referred to in the third person or by his proper name. There is no indication that Tràng Khanh picks up a pen to write about his experiences and observations. As a matter of fact, Tràng Khanh merely accompanies and acts as a foil for Việt Sinh. Whenever Việt Sinh gains access to an exclusive establishment, whenever the narrator is on friendly terms with a brothel owner, such knowledge and access are credited to the sexual experiences and knowledge of this friend Tràng Khanh.

When Việt Sinh cannot effectively use his friend as a stand-in for intimate or compromising moments, he abruptly switches from the first-person pronoun to the person-reference *anh* (older brother). These are odd scenarios in which the narrator, at great lengths, refers to himself in the third person. In one case, the narrator portrays a scene in which a woman, visible from the street, plays coy to lure and swindle a man inside her home. The woman's name is Nam, and her family background is given. However, the man enters the scene merely referred to as "*anh*" or "he." We never learn his name.

> Probably because he noticed her flirting he became more courageous each day. Then one night he walked by the house and saw her standing by the door. He was determined to get close and talk to her. . . . He kept standing there to talk with her, and after a while she will earnestly look at him while retreating further into the house. He kept following her inside . . . and there will be that moment when, the door shuts, he sits next to her to converse intimately.
>
> She has a long story to tell but at the beginning most likely she will look at him and say: "Strangely, you look like Khang."[43]

Standing outside the house, the narrator projects a scenario that is inconsistent on a number of levels. He mixes the present and imperfect timeframes with the future timeframe. When the anonymous "he" moves inside and the door shuts, another odd grammatical inconsistency occurs. An independent clause is wedged into the middle of a complete sentence: "there will be that moment when, the door shuts, he sits next to her to converse intimately." The narrator's modality vacillates, and his use of terms like *chắc* (probably) and *thế nào* (most likely) underscores the probability of events. Like the fluctuation between timeframes, the tentative narration undercuts the straightforward observations that a reportage narrator is supposed to make.

Even more peculiar, when the door closes, the narrator, who is purportedly standing outside, speculates that the woman inside will say, "You look just like Khang." This name is suspiciously similar to the narrator's friend, Khanh. In the same way that the speculative narrator on the outside is like but is *not* the anonymous "he" on the inside, the narrator is like but is *not* Khang. Similarly, even though the narrator wears a fedora and a suit, like a European man, he is *not* a European man. The native male's physical location outside the room corresponds with his ethnographic position as an outside observer. The narrator's likeness to a European man and to the woman's past lover, along with his identity as neither, situates him at a threshold. His narrative perspective drifts between insider and outsider, consistent with his vacillating modality and use of tense. His undetermined identity differentiates him from both the outsider and the insider, despite any resemblances.

The male autoethnographer's displaced bodily presence reveals a compromised position: he is the subject of agency and authoritative voice—observing and writing—yet he is also subject to colonial sexual norms. The narrator's unsure footing affects the text's modality. Whenever the narrator senses the limitations of his body—when it is limited in its ability to see, hear, or comprehend a given situation—the narrative defaults into uncertain epistemic modality and is realized nongrammatically through terms like "*chắc*" (perhaps) and "*thế nào*" (most likely). This modality cuts against the authoritative position the narrator is trying to assume. Unlike an omniscient narrator, he is limited to his body, and whenever he cannot orient his body within a particular space, behind a closed door, window, or a curtain, he can only speculate.

One of the narrator's implicit concerns is to insert himself between the European colonizer and the desired Vietnamese woman. This fraught colonial romance between European male and Vietnamese woman not only provokes the narrator's anxiety but also explains, for Việt Sinh, Vietnam's modernization. Women who married Europeans during this period were called "*me*"—a transliteration of the French term *mère* (mother). Often the term was further qualified as "*me tây*," which idiomatically came to mean "Westerner's wife." In *Hà Nội ban đêm*, the narrator writes entire installments about these *me* women. He was taken aback that female sex workers during this period were fluent in the French language, French leisure (such as shooting billiards), and French culture (singing and playing French songs with stringed instruments).[44] These bicultural, cosmopolitan women were catering to a French or European clientele. He views these prostitutes as similar to native women who marry foreigners. The narrator assumes that they marry foreigners not for love but rather for material gain. For the narrator, to be a European's kept woman, even if sanctioned by marriage, is to take part in a form of prostitution. This labeling accepted and repeated the categorization already set by the French colonial legal system.[45] The narrator's concerns about these women's fidelity to Vietnamese men actually conceal a much stronger anxiety that Vietnamese men, unlike these female prostitutes, are not modern enough or are somehow unable to gain entrance into the modern world. Recall the opening scene when the narrator and Tràng Khanh are at the door, and a *me* figure was expected, not the men. These women's French cosmopolitanism belies the narrator's seeming mobility. He cannot cross over into the European circles to which these women have access by way of their sexual relationships.

Indeed, the narrator views these women, both the prostitutes and the wives of European men, as the initiators of Vietnam's modernization process—or, to play off the transliteration of *mère*, the figurative mothers of Vietnamese modernity.[46] Việt Sinh explains how Vietnamese women who were sexually intimate with Westerners became Europeanized.

> New exterior transformation always precedes and incites new interiority. When a woman has cut her hair short, has worn heels—she is no longer abiding by traditional philosophies, a woman's three obediences to her father, her husband, and her son, or a woman's four virtues of domesticity, tolerance, behavior, and geniality.[47]

He continues:

> These women are the first Vietnamese women to encounter Western civilization. . . . But eventually, no matter what the customs and manners of the West, these women come to understand and accept these customs and manners as their own. These women are a particular social type because they bridge two different civilizations. These women have boldly adopted all that was new about speech, fashion, and even spirit.[48]

The narrator claims that Vietnam's modernization (which he conflates with Europeanization) began with the commodified, sexual relationship between European men and indigenous women; it then spread, by way of unconscious imitation, to the different women within the demimonde and then to those beyond the demimonde. Việt Sinh's understanding of modernity differs from that of French officials, who often viewed such women as urban degenerates. French writings from the 1930s explained marginal, urban figures like the *me* as indigenes who had been "deracinated" and "decultured"—no longer of the Vietnamese race and culture but "never to become French."[49]

Việt Sinh, however, sees these sexual relationships as modernization's starting point—a starting point from which the indigenous male narrator is excluded. Moreover, he draws a direct connection between prostitution and other institutions of French colonialism. In *Hà Nội ban đêm*, he devotes much of his attention to a French establishment known colloquially as *số đỏ*. Literally, *số đỏ* means "red number." *Số* is "number" with the secondary meaning "fortune" or "fate," and *đỏ* is "red." The term refers to the red-numbered addresses of licensed brothels in Hanoi (all other address numbers were painted white on a blue background in accordance with the Napoleonic Code and are still seen in Paris and Hanoi, with some modifications, today). Figuratively, Việt Sinh employs the term to refer to one who is ill-fated—whose fortune and luck are ultimately doomed. The term's progression from its literal to its figurative meaning proves Việt Sinh's thesis that Hanoi's crisis of prostitution runs parallel with France's failed mission to civilize and modernize Vietnam. (As discussed in chapter 2, the modern woman's misfortunes run parallel to but differ drastically from that of indigenous men who emerge as national heroes.)

The French colonial government established officially licensed brothel houses in Hanoi city proper, which was directly governed as a municipality (unlike the city's outskirts, which were indirectly ruled). The decision to manage and regulate prostitution, rather than outlaw it, stemmed from government and health policies in France. The French colonial government also sought to monitor the spread of sexually transmitted diseases among commercial sex workers by establishing dispensaries to house and educate infected prostitutes about venereal diseases and sexual hygiene. If a woman showed symptoms of sexually transmitted diseases, she was admitted and detained at the dispensary.[50] These facilities implemented standard procedures that were both invasive and ineffective, from mandatory gynecological exams to useless and even harmful treatments for sexually transmitted disease. Often detaining patients indefinitely,[51] the dispensaries operated much like prisons, with thick walls, iron gates, barred windows, and wretched living conditions.[52] The French government had built and utilized such dispensaries immediately after establishing colonial rule in Hanoi. Despite the French colonial government's efforts to control and eliminate sexually transmitted diseases, this problem, as Việt Sinh bitterly observes, grew at an alarming rate.

Given the framework set up by French colonial law and public health measures, Hanoi's prostitutes were destined for two scenarios: indefinite incarceration at the dispensaries due to lingering symptoms of venereal disease; and remanding to the red-numbered brothel houses, which served as the only viable means for shelter and work for former sex workers.[53] To go back to an early scene from *Hà Nội ban đêm*, the woman who greets the narrator and Tràng Khanh has a distinct way about her—one that he likens to that of a số đỏ woman. It is precisely this type of ill-fated woman who introduces the men to Hanoi's underground world of prostitution.[54] Taken together, these two colonial institutions explicate Việt Sinh's idiomatic use of số đỏ to mean "ill-fated." This doomed fate is how Việt Sinh understands Vietnamese modernization under French colonialism.

While well aware that prostitution existed before the French reached the shores of Vietnam, Việt Sinh argues that for all of French colonialism's pretenses about civilized culture, science, hygiene, and public health institutions (evident by the dispensaries), the problems of prostitution—the social and moral corruption, as well as the alarming rate and effects of venereal diseases—worsened during French colonialism. In Việt Sinh's eyes, French claims to modernity and civilized society were as artificial as the disenfranchised women who dressed in trendy, modern clothes to work in the brothels.

Việt Sinh goes on to argue that prostitution is a contagion that will infect the entire Vietnamese race. He writes, "The diseases of prostitution are always lurking in a woman's deteriorating body until her death. Not only does this pathology affect women, but it also infects all of society. It spreads out and infects the entire race."[55] With this diagnosis, Việt Sinh addresses, on the one hand, the problems that stemmed from France's ineffective policing of prostitution, which was harming an entire population—from the spread of venereal disease to rampant sexual exploitation. But, on the other hand, he also outlines how the widespread disease of prostitution points to larger social symptoms: moral bankruptcy, radically changing sexual relations, and the misleading enterprise of modern progress.

Việt Sinh employed his pen like a scalpel to objectively diagnose this crisis of prostitution as historically contingent on French colonialism. But there is a looming dilemma here: if this contagion of prostitution will affect the entire race, then the narrator himself, the participant observer, is vulnerable to this self-diagnosed, contagious, and therefore unavoidable misfortune. As much as he was invested in writing about the culture of Hanoi's prostitution, Việt Sinh had to grapple with his own social position, particularly his sexuality and masculinity—that liminal position between the European man and the modern Vietnamese woman. Việt Sinh's unsure footing destabilizes his analysis of the condition of số đỏ women. While he sees these women as a distinct social type conscripted to colonial modernity's failures and hypocrisies, he also viewed them as cosmopolitan types liberated from the confines of Vietnamese tradition and culture. While he presumed to hold them in an objective view, he also identified with them, taking them to be harbingers of modernity.

Việt Sinh understood prostitution as a social epidemic that foreshadowed the process of colonial modernization already under way. His focus and understanding of *số đỏ* women necessitate a revision of prostitution as a rhetorical trope during the colonial period and of the relationship between modernity and tradition. First, Việt Sinh does not discuss prostitution as a symbol of Vietnam's compromised position under French colonialism. For him, prostitution during the period was symptomatic of larger social problems, including the spread of sexually transmitted diseases, ineffective medical treatment, the regulation of colonial subjects and their bodies, failing colonial institutions, a legislature plagued with loopholes, inconsistent and corrupt legal enforcement, impoverished living and working conditions, and the formation of an exploited social group. His view of modernization grounds any abstract or symbolic rhetoric—prostitution figured as colonialism—in material reality.

Second, Việt Sinh's insistence on sex workers' ineluctable ill fate also suggests that modernization was a process under way and irrevocable. By writing *Hà Nội ban đêm*, he makes the case that prostitution and its related issues demand modern solutions, such as modern medicines, rather than the arrested modernization imposed by the French. To talk about modernization as irreversible preempts the possibility of returning to any native or traditional past. Thus Việt Sinh was not a colonial subject attempting to restore the native self or precolonial tradition.

Rather, Việt Sinh addressed the colonial situation—Vietnam's irrevocable, yet thwarted, modernization under French control—through the investigative genre of reportage. But as I have demonstrated above, this "objective" subjectivity of the reportage writer derived from colonial modernity's reorganized power and authority. While the male participant observer assumes an authoritative voice over the ill-fated female sex worker, the presence of the European male and the emergence of the modern Vietnamese woman cast doubts and anxiety on his masculinity. And as the next chapter shows, the presumed objectivity of reportage's documentation carried over and translated into fictional realism. The first-person voice may be evacuated from realist novels, but, as I argue, the authoritative voice is still male and preoccupied with modern women. It is this dual concern about the prosaic and the modern woman that gives reason to define aesthetic modernity as realism.

CHAPTER 2

Pornography as Realism, Realism as Aesthetic Modernity

Hold the penis from below,
From the base to the hole at its end.
If you see even a little pus there, watch out!
That's where the danger comes from;
You must pay attention; don't play with it!
Then look at his penis,
See if there are any strange marks.

—Vũ Trọng Phụng, *Lục xì*

Medical experts circulated the bawdy ode quoted in the epigraph[1] to teach female sex workers how to identify symptoms of venereal disease in their male clients. As part of a larger public health campaign to cure Vietnamese women of sexually transmitted diseases and to educate them about hygiene and sex, officials shoehorned safe sex and antivenereal content into poetic forms that were easy to recite and memorize. The women, at once prisoners and patients in Hanoi's colonial dispensary, were required to rehearse such songs as an entire class and, if they wanted to be released, to recall them from memory. Vũ Trọng Phụng cites these lines in his investigative reportage *Lục xì*, excoriating the treatment of sex workers at the hands of the colonial regime. For Phụng, these poetic warnings about sexually transmitted diseases were at best campy and at worst ineffective. The singsongy public health measures not only failed to protect women from disease, but they also failed to diagnose the colonial roots of the problem that led to such troubling conditions for female sex workers.

Published in 1937 when Phụng gained access to Hanoi's Municipal Dispensary, *Lục xì* details the institution's political context and history and goes on to report various aspects of the sex workers' experiences. The narrative describes the dispensary's gruesome conditions and invasive gynecological exams and details the administrators' essentializing and racist view of the Vietnamese as unhygienic and uneducated. Phụng's reportage further demonstrates how French colonial authorities' policing of women's bodies reflected their broader view of Vietnamese culture as unsanitary and primitive. He reproached public officials who, aiming for realistic representations, tried to fit graphic and vulgar content into lighthearted poems—a critique that he also leveled against his contemporaries.

In his own work, Phụng employed the genre of reportage to avoid campy and playful representations of colonial sex that were far removed from the grim reality that sex workers faced. His persistent use of the genre to close the gap between literature and reality led not only to groundbreaking techniques and content in reportage but also to an overhaul of the Vietnamese novel. For his contribution to and mastery of the genre Phụng earned the title "King of Reportage" (*Ông vua phóng sự*). But extending the significance of Phụng's literary accomplishment to fiction, I contend here that Phụng's tireless focus on the lurid details of colonial sex, coupled with his genre-bending work with reportage, makes the Vietnamese novel into a more democratic forum of aesthetic and political representation. The unorthodox themes, content, characters, and plot of Phụng's "pornographic realism" cracks the veneer of Vietnamese fiction's isolation from external reality, fusing the world of the novel with everyday colonial reality.[2] The novel's analogue structure (which I discuss further below) with the exterior world is a key aspect of Benedict Anderson's conceptualization of the nation as an imagined community. But rather than follow Anderson's explanation that the novel was an analogue for the real world due to empty homogenous time, the present chapter considers how the reconfiguration of the novel's structure was premised on the prosaic turn toward colonial sex.

Phụng was born in 1920 to working-class parents. His father died from tuberculosis when he was a seven-month-old infant. The same disease would, twenty-seven years later, claim the author's own life, prematurely ending a prolific literary career in both fiction and nonfiction. Phụng's educational and intellectual background was a direct result of French educational policies, although he only had six years of primary schooling. He published in the romanized alphabet of *quốc ngữ* and knew no Chinese. Phụng was an avid reader of French literature, immersing himself in a range of works, from pulp fiction to canonical literature. He also engaged with the popular Freudian ideas and Marxist-Leninist thought that reached Indochina. Within the post-mandarin literary field, Phụng was in many ways an outsider: he did not come from a family of intellectuals; he did not complete his primary education; he was mired in constant poverty, struggling to support his widowed mother; sartorially, he did not follow trendy European styles but rather preferred to wear a turban and gown; and his political vision of left-leaning colonial republicanism differentiated him from neoconservative and bourgeois as well as Marxist thinkers.

The reception of Phụng's work has evolved from skepticism about its perverse nature—and outright censorship in Communist Vietnam (1960–85)—to the reevaluation and rehabilitation of his oeuvre in the early 1970s, mid-1980s, and late 2000s.[3] Two primary issues provoked the controversy surrounding Phụng's legacy: his prurient depiction of colonial sex and his denunciation of communism in the late 1930s. Vietnamese communism, the author feared, would be an ineffective imitation of the Soviet model that would lead to totalitarianism.[4] Peter Zinoman has described Phụng's politics as "late colonial republicanism"—"a moderately progressive political tradition with strong French roots." "Despite the protean nature of 'Republicanism' as a concept," Zinoman continues, "late colonial republicanism denotes a fairly stable cluster of political concerns and commitments and, as importantly, provides a useful alternative to the communist/anticommunist frame of analysis."[5] Zinoman goes on to read Phụng's career and literary works through the lens of this political paradigm, perceptively going into detail about the historical and intellectual milieus surrounding the somewhat schizophrenic appraisal of Phụng's literary legacy. By contrast, this chapter focuses on Phụng's aesthetic vision as a "realist"—a self-description he employed more readily than any political moniker.

Writing against the divorce of social reality from poetic form, Phụng employs the prosaic genres of reportage and the novel to diagnose accurately and realistically the social epidemics of Vietnam's colonial modernity, particularly the crisis of colonial sex. Phụng's entwined employment of these two genres, I argue, marks the modern turn of Vietnamese literature toward the prosaic. Phụng's work exemplifies this turn at multiple levels: at the formal level, where the prosaic description of the everyday trumped verse's constricting rhyme and meter; at the level of content, where all subjects and contents constitute a new aesthetics; and at the level of the newspaper, where the aestheticization of the prosaic is delivered and contiguous with daily news and advertisements for everyday goods. Here, I focus on two of Phụng's novels: *Làm đĩ* (To be a prostitute) and *Số đỏ* (Dumb luck)—to show how and why he incorporates the prosaic into his reportage and novels. Both works illuminate how the prosaic turn of Vietnam's aesthetic modernity and national literature occurs when post-mandarin intellectuals mediate their investigation of colonial society through women's sexual lives and pasts—though never giving voice to women. Phụng's innovations with literary realism—or more accurately put, Phụng's perversion of literary realism—were attempts to update a system of representation that could no longer effectively depict and address the crisis of colonial sex.

In a special issue of the journal *Tao Đàn* commemorating Phụng's life, the critic Trương Tửu explains Phụng's commitment to realism: "He was a child born straight from life. His artistic talent was not established through mimesis. It comes from individual experience and individual effort. Therefore, in the capital of modern Vietnamese literature, he holds a flag that he wove himself. He staked out a position—at the very left—as the vanguard and standard of realism."[6] Trương Tửu goes on to explicate Phụng's work by interpreting his literature through his hardscrabble life. Rather than read Phung's realism sociologically, however, I argue that it is a further development of the post-mandarin condition discussed in chapter 1, whereby the emergence of the native male intellectual investigating female sex workers and the demimonde became aestheticized in fiction. Phụng incorporated reportage's documentation of the prosaic into Vietnamese fiction, reconstituting literary aesthetics so that they could effectively represent and address the crisis of colonial sex.

Phụng's fusion of reportage and the novel overturned the separation of poetics and common reality that characterized Vietnamese literature up to this point. In the penultimate chapter of his reportage *Cơm thầy cơm cô* (Household servants), Vũ Trọng Phụng describes his contempt for the lack of realism, of "life," in Vietnamese literature:

> Facing truth that is not normally considered worth writing down on paper, we find ourselves frightened and astounded by humanity.
> Novels tell us things that people say is fiction.
> In life, on the other hand, there are things that a novel wouldn't want to report.
> And so I started despising humanity, because I came to believe that not one of us is able to see clearly the reality of life.
> There are really so many books about human beings that aim to teach us about each other, and, yet, they fail. All the things people learn from books. . . . They are vague, mistaken, literary. Literature is one thing, life is another.[7]

In this passage Phụng critiques Vietnamese literature, as practiced by both his predecessors and his contemporaries, finding fault in a criterion of representation that safeguarded the aesthetic realm from gritty, prosaic subject matters. Phụng's frustration explains and justifies his penchant for bizarre (*lạ lùng*), implausible (*không . . . có thật được*), lewd (*nhơ bẩn*), and distasteful (*chướng tai*) stories. According to Phụng, Vietnamese literature did not reference its immediate surroundings or conditions; it failed to represent marginalized characters and the wretched conditions of their lives.[8] His strategic attacks against the literary field point to the restrictions of Vietnamese aesthetics: a system of art forms anachronistically and conservatively premised on a hierarchy of content that deemed prosaic subjects too vulgar for aesthetic representation. To disrupt literature's isolation from everyday reality, Phụng claimed, an author must represent human subjects and material conditions viewed as unworthy of aesthetic representation. He employed the *phóng sự* and novelistic genres for their amoeba-like ability to absorb all things prosaic, seeking to contaminate the purely fictional world of the novel. In his literary oeuvre these genres bleed into each other, erasing the division between the aesthetic realm and the everyday world, between fiction and nonfiction. Phụng upends Vietnamese literature through the representation of pedestrian characters, characters such as sex workers and perverted street hawkers that his critics deemed too vulgar for aesthetic representation. Yet for Phụng, the inclusion of marginalized characters and prosaic issues in aesthetic representation was the only means to effectively address colonialism's pressing issues.

Aesthetic representation here is an act of political and social representation. Modern Vietnamese literature's efficacy derives from the melding of art into life and life into art, as it indifferently and democratically represented all subjects, renegotiating who and what are represented and visible in the common world. In my efforts to understand realism as aesthetic modernity in the colonial setting, I turn to Jacques Rancière's articulation of aesthetic modernity. Rancière understands the politics of aesthetic modernity as a reordering of the hierarchy of representation, a reconfiguration of what is perceived, what determines the common world.

> The way in which the world is visible for us, and in which what is visible can
> be put into words, and the capacities and incapacities that reveal themselves
> accordingly. It is on this basis that it is possible to theorize about the politics
> of literature 'as such,' its mode of intervention in the carving up of objects
> that form a common world, the subjects that people that world and the powers they have to see it, name it and act upon it.[9]

Political representation and aesthetic representation are contiguous and undifferentiated, and this is precisely the political work of aesthetic modernity. Moreover, aesthetic modernity here is not the incommunicable modernism that pivots on antimimetic revolution or art's concentration on its own materiality. Instead, Rancière traces literary modernity back to nineteenth-century realism's "law of universal equivalence"—the equality of represented subjects that undermines the hierarchies and divisions of art. He takes as his examples Victor Hugo, Balzac, and, most significantly,

Flaubert for his absolute indifference in the representation and stylization of all pedestrian objects and subjects. Notably, these writers also appealed to Vietnamese authors during the period of colonial modernity, more than their modernist contemporaries. Moreover, Rancière points out that in the French context the term "literature" did not refer to the arts of speech and writing until after the nineteenth century. Prior to this, "literature" designated the "knowledge held by men of letters."[10] I argue that the European shift from the man of letters to the novelist resembles the transition from the Confucian scholar to the post-mandarin writer in Vietnam. Anticipating Rancière, Đặng Thai Mai begins his *Outline of Literature* by pointing out the difference between the Confucian and European-inflected notion of *văn học* (literature).

> In the teachings of Confucius, literature only meant general knowledge and thorough understanding of ethics, general letters.
>
> These days, in China—as well as in our country—that term has a different meaning. This old term is an imported item. . . . Under the influence of Europe and America, the term "*văn học*" now encompasses a meaning entirely different from its previous "connotations." Like the French term "*littérature*," the term "*văn học*" has two meanings. Literature is a subject of culture and includes all creative works in poetry or prose. Literature also means the study of those works.[11]

It is obvious that Rancière's timetable for aesthetic modernity is quite different from the condensed and accelerated modernization that took place in Vietnam. However, the crucible of Vietnamese colonial modernity allows us to see more vividly Rancière's claims about aesthetic modernity vis-à-vis realism, particularly through the entwined relationship between the prosaic genres of reportage and the novel. But whereas realism precedes reportage in France, in colonial Vietnam this order is inverted.

The compressed temporality of colonial modernity in Vietnam amplifies the role of the prosaic as the starting point of aesthetic modernity. Most Vietnamese reportage and fiction were first published in journals or newspapers, giving shape to both the form and the content of print capitalism. Anderson has argued that the newspaper medium and the novel provide the necessary conditions for nationalism's equal and horizontal comradeship. He emphasizes how the formal structures of the novel and newspaper—rather than their representation of nationalist themes, characters, plot, or content—are necessary for imagining the nation. These forms of print capitalism foster the temporal mode of simultaneity that allows readers to imagine themselves as members of a community beyond face-to-face interactions. From this vantage point, he convincingly argues that print capitalism's newspapers

and novels are contemporaneous analogues for the imagined nation. However, Anderson presupposes that their causal and formative powers are
contingent on the turn toward the prosaic. It is no accident then that Anderson's primary novelistic examples are of realism—from the works of Balzac to Pramoedya Ananta Toer's *Buru Quartet* (not to mention that both
authors have prominent characters who chronicle everyday life as journalists). Anderson's emphasis on the nation's temporal simultaneity overshad-
ows *how* a social space, which the imagination renders as analogous to the
nation, is represented in both the newspaper and the novel.[12]

Both the newspaper and literary realism are contingent on, as Rancière
has put it, a "logic of descriptive and narrative arrangements [that] becomes
fundamentally indistinct from the arrangements used in the description
and interpretation of the phenomena of the social and historical world."[13]
Although Rancière identifies this writing logic primarily with fictional realism, his articulation of a writing mode that assigns meaning to the "empiri-
cal," prosaic world also applies to post-mandarin forms of prosaic writing:
ethnography, reportage, sociological writing, and literary realism. The dismantling of subject matter and mode of representation gave modern Vietnamese aesthetics its political and social bearings in the everyday—and thus
revolutionized literature. The imagination of the nation is not technologically determined but rather is prosaically determined. This reverses Anderson's view that the advancement of technological conditions makes possible
the imagining of the nation: for Anderson, the coherent imagination of the
nation is facilitated by the technologies that allow for perceived simultaneity.
But in the Vietnamese case, the imagined community is founded primarily
on prosaic representation, which, in part, makes print culture more pertinent. Only when an author like Vũ Trọng Phụng insists on the representation of prosaic subjects does the revolution of aesthetics and the imagining
of the nation occur. This substantiation of the prosaic into aesthetic form
redefined *văn học*, or literature, in Vietnam.

In concert with the serial publication of *Làm đĩ*, Phụng's editors and
colleagues published essays to argue for the literary merits of the novel—a
genre that previously did not merit consideration as proper literature. In a
1936 essay titled "Văn học tiểu thuyết là cái quái gì?" (What is this literary
novel?), the capacious intellectual and editor Phan Khôi (who serially published Phụng's *Làm đĩ* in the journal *Sông Hương* (Perfume River)) took issue
with the term "literary novel" (*văn học tiểu thuyết*).[14] The qualifier "literary,"
he chided, implied the genre's negligible status. Phan went on to critique the
marginalization of the novel as anachronistic and nostalgic because it narrowly limns the Vietnamese novel (*tiểu thuyết*) according to its peripheral

position in Chinese literature and etymological roots in *xiaoshuo*—trivial discourse or gossip—while failing to account for the Europeanization of the Vietnamese novel and its rising aesthetic prominence.

> The East, including the Chinese as well as us Vietnamese, has long understood the novel as chatter from street corners and markets—chatter that is not considered literary. The West takes an oppositional approach: in literature, the novel is not marginalized; it is given a prominent position. . . . Recently the revitalized and popularized novel has come to a crossroads with the West and our tradition. This means that the Eastern paradigm has yielded to that of the West.[15]

The novel has transformed and gained significance as it gives aesthetic form to the real through literary mimesis, through recording the "chatter" of the street. And by doing so, realism reessentializes the referential world. David Wang's observations of Mao Dun's realism apply here: "As far as the call for reflecting an arguable reality is concerned, realism is not so much a promise as a pact, pointing to aesthetic, cultural, and ideological terms of writing and reading the real."[16] What was once street chatter now merited literary valuation as a source for knowledge and aesthetics.

Phụng's novelistic innovations dovetailed with a larger campaign in Vietnamese *belle lettres* to get at the "truth." A series of articles penned by prominent thinkers published in *Sông Hương*'s first issues argued that Vietnamese history should be grounded in the "truth" of quotidian reality. In the inaugural issue's lead article, "Vấn đề học thuật nước ta" (On the education of our nation), Hoài Thanh encouraged thinkers to move away from the superficial motivations—status and fame—of Vietnamese intellectualism and work toward "researching the truth, even the truths that we consider ordinary and trivial, not worthy of attention."[17] Hoài Thanh argued that pedagogical methods had been dictated by entrenched traditions and moral conservatism more than the intellectual pursuit of knowledge and truth. In the lead story of the second issue, Phan Khôi argued for a more pragmatic educational curriculum, claiming that the Chinese and Vietnamese pedagogical traditions were rooted in a poetics isolated from ordinary life.[18] Vũ Ngọc Phan "insist[ed] on the due attention to the truth" so as to stem the obviation of historical accuracy, primarily through historical novels.[19] On the same page, an ad for Phụng's *Làm đĩ* declares the novel a realist work that depicts the neglected reality of sexual desire. The editor of *Sông Hương* delayed the serial debut of Phụng's novel to build anticipation among its potential readers for its sexual realism. However, the juxtaposition of Phan's article to Phụng's novel illuminates the journal's vision to ground Vietnamese poetics—both fiction and nonfiction—in prosaic reality.

Phụng used the term *tiểu thuyết* (novel) indiscriminately to characterize both his reportage and his novelistic writing—as if there were no differences between the nonfictional and fictional genres. I argue that the
deliberate elision of these categories effaced the boundary separating the
realm of art from nonart. In other words, Phụng's promiscuous use of the
term *tiểu thuyết* signals his attempts to unravel the novelistic genre's connection with fiction and to couple it with the *phóng sự* genre. For example, in his
phóng sự work *Household Servants*, he titles one of his chapters "Tiểu thuyết
của con sen Đũi" (Servant Đũi's novel). The chapter gives the nonfictional
narrative of an impoverished young servant caught in her mistress's web of
sexual exploitation. Phụng counterpoises this graphic depiction against the
idyllic scenery populated by two romantic couples from well-known novels, *Tố Tâm* and *Ngọc Lê Hồn*, in which the promises and ideals of unfulfilled love prove tragic for the heroines. Elsewhere in his *phóng sự* writing, he
uses *tiểu thuyết* to refer to the narratives of peasants and prostitutes, apply-
ing the term to nonfictional narratives of characters and scenarios previously excluded from novelistic representation.[20] The interconnections that
Phụng forged between the two genres negate claims that reportage was a
writing genre distinct and demarcated by its formal features and delimited
aesthetics.[21]

In *Làm đĩ* Phụng interweaves fiction and nonfiction so that they inform
and buttress each other.[22] And he does so to realistically depict colonial sex:
young Vietnamese men and women were becoming sexually active while
oblivious to the consequences because society as a whole had failed to educate them about the issue. Phụng composed a novelistic work that featured
the fictional diary of a sex worker named Huyền. The female protagonist
narrates her descent from the daughter of a mandarinal family to her life as a
prostitute. She openly details the sexual exploitation, experiences, and urges
that led her to work in a brothel. Phụng validates this marginalized woman's
voice by framing it as reportage, rather than as a novel, about two men who
set out to investigate colonial sexuality.

Làm đĩ is a first-person, fictional account of a sex worker's travails—
structured as a fact-finding mission of autoethnography. In order to counter
the unrealistic representations of youthful love in Vietnamese and European
novels alike, Phụng plays out the end game of colonial sex for young women:
prostitution. He was well aware that his attempts to portray the "truth" about
the colonial crisis of sex made him vulnerable to attacks. Yet he held his
ground.

Phụng's contemporaries and critics viewed works like *Làm đĩ* as unneces-
sarily and dangerously pushing a personal obsession toward pornography.

SÔNG HƯƠNG

LÀM ĐĨ

CHUYỆN DÀI của SÔNG HƯƠNG — Số 1   VŨ-TRỌNG-PHỤNG

Khi bậc làm cha mẹ sẽ cứ mãi mãi không đủ tư-cách truyền lại cho con cái phần gia tài cao-thượng ấy theo một quan-niệm hoàn toàn đạo-đức và bằng sự thấu triệt đã cả mọi lẽ sinh lý học, tùy theo niên bạn và trí thông minh của chúng, thì sự làm lẫn đáng ghê tởm sẽ cứ mãi mãi làm uế-tạp mất cái của báu ấy mà tạo hóa đã phú cho ta, và số ngăn trở cho bọn bận sinh sẽ không còn biết lần đường vào dễ đi đến chỗ tận thiện tận mỹ.

Giáo sư W. Liepmann

sau khi bị độ hai ba cái tát. Ghét, yêu, yêu, ghét, chúng tôi đã vô tâm theo một môn triết học cao xa thăm thủy mà người ta dạy cho trai gái phải theo để giữ cho được bền chắt

cách lếu láo vô tội, mà nó cần đến thơ chim gái thì nó có tội, tôi thiếu tiền đi xem chiếu bóng thì tôi có nó.

Ít lâu sau đó, tôi được tin rằng ông

Figure 4. Original header of *Làm đĩ* (To be a prostitute). Published in *Sông Hương*, August 8, 1936.

While adversaries characterized Phụng as a "pervert," a "decadent," and a "vulgar naturalist" infatuated with "sexual theories" and "female sexuality,"[23] Phụng bitterly realized that these attacks pigeonholed his work as "pornographic writing" (*văn khiêu dâm*),[24] condemning it for titillating readers and ignoring its larger social, political, and aesthetic provocation. I argue, however, that the supposedly gratuitous perversion of Phụng's literary oeuvre sought to puncture an aesthetic and political system of representation that failed to capture the realities and consequences of sex during colonial modernity.

In his preface to *Làm đĩ*, Vũ Trọng Phụng describes the work as a *realist novel* (*tả chân tiểu thuyết*), with the expressed intention to spur moralists and parents to confront more directly the moral turpitude of lust.[25] As the headline for *Làm đĩ*'s serial installments suggests (figure 4), the novel promised to be graphic and revealing if not tantalizing. By the 1930s the taboo subject of sex had manifested as pervasive, alarming problems of prostitution, incest, rape, sexual exploitation, and sexually transmitted diseases. Moreover, the discursive and poetic circumvention of sex willfully ignored the sexualized nature of French colonialism. If, as Ann Stoler has noted, "no subject is discussed more than sex in colonial literature [and] sexual prescriptions by class, race and gender became increasingly central to the politics of rule and subject to new forms of scrutiny by the colonial state,"[26] then, for Phụng, such prescriptions and their effects needed to be exposed and counteracted. Of the Vietnamese intellectuals during this time, Phụng most persistently addressed the crisis of colonial sexuality, and his overt inclusion of sexual content was part of his political and aesthetic practice of realism.

Vũ Trọng Phụng criticized novels with amorous plotlines because their representations of youthful love, despite their celebration of individual liberation and a modern ethos, failed to account for carnal desire. For Phụng, moralists and contemporary novelists alike turned a blind eye to the libidinal and bodily desires that derailed love from its ideals and thus exacerbated a series of pressing social issues. In the preface Phụng writes, "To speak of love, yet to not address lust, is merely the work of impractical idealists."[27] He went on to claim that his novelistic writing runs counter to sterile representations of love, rendering love more accurately as lust in all its vulgarity and lewdness. In this sense, his adamant assaults against romantic love resembled Lu Xun's objections to the May Fourth proponents of free love and its potential for individual liberation and sovereignty. But whereas Lu Xun sought to disabuse the delusions of love with a "concomitant transformation of the socioeconomic system,"[28] Phụng focused his attention on colonial sex. He based his aesthetic paradigm on the conviction that sex could not be divorced from romantic desire; otherwise, any aesthetic representation and intellectual debate about love would fail to reflect and address modern social realities.

Moreover, Phụng drew a direct connection between colonial Vietnam's sexual crisis and Westernization.

> The encounter between East and West has brought sweeping changes to our material life. What can be more irrational than acknowledging that modern living, including music halls, movie theaters, modern fashion, dance halls, perfume, and cosmetics, intensifies sexual desire, yet refusing to acknowledge the need to inform young people about sexual desire so that they act responsibly and morally?[29]

In Phụng's view, any uncritical embrace of Westernization and modernity's veneer, from its trendy fashions to its proselytizing rhetoric, that does not address its possible corruption of the social body is as empty and unrealistic as an idealized love story.[30] Instead, he pleaded for public dissemination of information that in a straightforward manner instructs about sex and its consequences. He criticized parents, intellectuals, and moralists for their willful silence on carnal desire. In practice, he turned to the *phóng sự* and novelistic genres to destigmatize the literary discourse of sex.

Phụng structures *Làm đĩ* with a reportage frame around the novelistic content. As in Việt Sinh's *Hà Nội ban đêm*, the narrator sets out with a male sidekick. The two men were childhood friends who parted ways when they pursued post-mandarin careers: the narrator as a published writer and Quý as a schoolteacher of the French language. In an effort to rekindle their friendship, the men visit a brothel. Although they did not initially set out to do investigative reporting, their interaction with the sex workers quickly defaults into an interview. They ask the young women, "Why have you been corrupted at such an early age?"[31] The men's investigative pretense displaces their own pleasures as they set out to learn why young women have become sex workers. Thus the format of investigative interviewing generates the novel's form and content.[32]

But before the two visitors assert their authority as participant observers, one of the sex workers challenges their male perceptions of prostitution. Duyên, the first prostitute they encounter, exposes her male visitors' pretense of naïveté, as well as their marginal position within the sexual relations and economy of the time. At first, she offers a sharp feminist critique that exposes the men's lack of knowledge and experience with the demimonde, pointing out that men are unaware of their complicit and hypocritical roles in commercial sex.

> You men are the root cause of prostitution, but it is women who become depraved from it, while being condemned by men's scrutiny and judgment. As for us women, how can we be as unconscionable as you men? We were living with our parents, enjoying familial bliss, when, suddenly, a young, good-looking lover comes and seduces us. . . . We follow his lead, become deceived and depraved, and then other unconscionable men taunt us, further depraving us! You men are as promiscuous as demons, but no one says anything. But for us women, anything suggestive ruins our lives! For heaven's sake, why do you men have to be so classless, so savage?[33]

According to Duyên, men venture out to fulfill their desires and curiosities, oblivious to the repercussions for women who, conversely, experience firsthand the crisis of colonial sexuality and the ensuing social condemnation. In addition to the compounding damage it incurs for women, this male naïveté fosters men's ignorance about the shifting social norms of sexual modernity.

Though Duyên's words do not register with her clients, they prove to be self-fulfilling, as the men persist in their unreflective ways. They continue to fix their gaze on Duyên, promptly asking if she finds her predicament saddening or regretful. In response, she vilifies their inability to adapt to the sexual relations of colonial modernity. Duyên claims that as long as Vietnamese men insist on traditional marriage and its associated gender roles, they remain out of touch with modernity. The men may pay a visit to the modern, legalized brothel, but it is the Vietnamese woman who experiences and understands the changing sexual and marital relationships of the time.

> You men are shocked to see me like this, but if you were I, there would be nothing strange or disconcerting. It is even a greater misperception to say that I won't be able to get married like normal women. Why wouldn't I be able get married? According to traditional morals, to be a prostitute is to have no future. But is that true in life? More accurately, a greater number of women who are principled and talented cannot find husbands, or they marry worthless, adulterous men who beat and abandon their wives. But a corrupted prostitute is more likely to marry a perfectly good man and become a Madame![34]

While Vietnamese men, like the narrator and his companion, deem "corrupted" women undesirable for marriage, Duyên had encountered more accepting foreign men who passed through Hanoi during the colonial period. These included "Western executives from this and that company, soldiers, lawyers, law clerks, Indian moneylenders, Chinese restaurateurs, casino owners, politicians, businessmen."[35] Given the number of foreign suitors, her eligibility for marriage no longer depends on the narrator and Quý's outdated value system and gender norms. Duyên's account aims to disabuse the men's presumptions that any promise of a future is contingent on marriage to a Vietnamese man. The definition of marriage, Duyên suggests, is no longer premised on Vietnamese gender expectations and ethics but on more cosmopolitan standards. Vietnamese women, particularly sex workers, are no longer confined to the norms of Vietnamese marital arrangements.

Unlike his sidekick, Quý, the narrator seems cognizant of these gendered differences in experience and knowledge pertaining to colonial sex. He attempts to resolve these discrepancies by including the perspective of a female sex worker and by retaining the framework of *phóng sự* to push the genre beyond the male narrator's limitations. If *phóng sự* investigators intended to document colonial prostitution but were limited in their efforts at objective, accurate representation due to their marginalized masculinities, then *Làm đĩ* corrects this shortsightedness by deferring to a woman's experiences and narrative.

And if, as in *Hà Nội ban đêm*, the male chroniclers had epistemological and ontological angst, then, Phụng seemed to realize, embedding a woman's firsthand account, albeit a fictional one, in the literary work would circumvent their uncertainty. Therefore, while at the brothel the male narrator acquires a memoir written by Huyền, the second prostitute whom the men meet. Huyền does not make pointedly bold and accusatory claims like Duyên; however, she is keenly aware of the factors that led her to prostitution, developing and recording her views by composing her personal narrative.

Huyền's manuscript details the various pitfalls that caused her to alienate her respectable family and resort to prostitution. She documents her experiences and travails, earnestly revealing that she was curious about sex at an early age and that without adequate knowledge about sex she was seduced by men. Huyền's intention to expose her story unveils the silencing of women's sexual desires and experiences. Initially, she thought that the manuscript was unfinished, but the narrator convinced her that it had already achieved its most important purpose: "it depicts all that is true, all that is objectionable,"[36] or, as Quý reluctantly puts its, "all of that frightening truth."[37] This "truth" that is both objectionable and frightening derives from the heroine's frank confession of her sexual past. The overall structure, then, of *Làm đĩ* comprises the frame story of the men's investigation at the brothel and Huyền's personal memoir. Together the two constitute what Phụng called a "reportage novel."[38]

It is precisely the inclusion of this narrative that, for Vũ Trọng Phụng, constitutes a novel or *tiểu thuyết* that effectively addresses and represents the "truth" (*sự thực*) of colonial sexuality. When the narrator presents Huyền's memoir, he states, "We 'researched' Huyền's downfall. . . . Here is her novel [*tiểu thuyết*]."[39] The original ellipsis, which is further accentuated with a line break, denotes an omission or void on the part of the men's investigative pursuits, which are, nevertheless, contiguous with and supplemented by Huyền's manuscript.

By situating the personal narrative in the reportage framework, Phụng dissolved the boundaries of social reality and literature, of fiction and nonfiction, of the plausible and implausible. In his *phóng sự tiểu thuyết*, or reportage novel, Phụng mixed the seemingly disparate fictional and nonfictional realms. While the male narrator resembles the author Vũ Trọng Phụng, Huyền does not refer to any particular person. Instead, she is a fictional composite of various news stories about women caught in one scandal or another. The collusion of the nonfiction reportage with the fictional memoir blurs the author's identity, calling into question the autobiographical aspects of the frame narrative[40] while at the same time making more plausible the fictional character of Huyền and her stories. *Làm đĩ*'s structure shifts the spotlight away from the male visitors at the brothel to Huyền's narrative.

The novel's dissolution of the boundaries between fiction and nonfiction carries over to the work's portrayal of the crisis of colonial sexuality. Huyền comes from a well-off mandarin family no longer in touch with the realities of colonial society; her upstanding parents and caretakers never truthfully answered her childhood questions about sex and reproduction. As adults refused to address the child's precociousness, her curiosity about sex continued in the schoolyard, where other children made wild speculations about the reproductive process. The children argued over the supporting evidence for their various theories, whether the evidence was fictionalized (*bịa*) or witnessed (*được mắt thấy*).[41] The playground debate mirrors the social dilemma that, for Vũ Trọng Phụng, catalyzes the crisis of sexuality: uninformed, fictionalized accounts that mask and stray from the realities of sex. And in literature this translates into lofty love stories devoid of romance's ulterior motive: erotic desire. Rather than continue with the childish banter based on uninformed speculation, the inclusion of Huyền's narrative dispels the purely imaginative, unrealistic aspects of literature with an experiential account. Otherwise, Huyền explains, the status quo continues to have detrimental effects.

> I know that all pre-nubile boys and girls have a harmful obsession: they are overcome with bodily urges, yet they are all groping in the dark . . . but the more curious they are, the more constricted they become. And for this reason, they acquire misinformation that undercuts any higher meaning, any legitimacy of love. They're a herd of horses chaotically running in search of science, but before they come to any discovery, they've become entangled, they've tripped each other, fallen over each other, broken.[42]

As her sexual curiosity persists, yet goes unaddressed, Huyền starts to consult with neighborhood boys. Collectively, they begin to test out their theories about sex through physical experimentation, games, and masturbation. Episodes of "playing husband and wife"[43] stir up new sexual, bodily feelings. At the age of thirteen, her sexual urges and thoughts increasingly consume her. When she begins to menstruate, she again asks her mother about sex. But her mother says to wait until marriage, and she will learn all that she wants to know. The protagonist's carnal desire becomes an uncontrollable entity alienated from her "soul" (*linh hồn*).

Huyền grapples with her conflicting selves. For a brief period, she tries to live according to prescribed moral standards of a woman willing to dedicate herself to one husband. Her critical reflections lead her to believe that a "pure social cosmos that revered the soul had been upended by materialism."[44] However, Lưu, a family relative, moves into her home, and they come to have intimate feelings for each other. The two cousins try to avoid the taboo of incest, but they cannot resist over time, and Huyền loses her virginity. Afterward, she makes an observation that is somewhat peculiar but consistent with the novel's themes and ambitions of getting at the truth, or *sự thực*, of sex: "Life has come to me as something that is real."[45] For her, sex breaks through the protective walls of her family and allows her to engage with real life. This development undermines Quý's hypothetical justification, in the frame narrative, for his conservative stance: if men were to imagine their sisters or daughters falling into sexual pitfalls, then they would not condone women's sexual liberation. Circumventing social norms and familial boundaries, the cousins' sexual relationship disproves Quý's naive assumptions about the asexual nature of intrafamilial bonds—the assumptions that daughters and sisters are to be sexually inactive and that there is no sexual tension between relatives.

Huyền's narrative deviates from the standard novel of adultery in both European and Vietnamese canons by reversing the gendered fates of the novel's lovers. She does not succumb to suicide or an inexplicable illness, as in *Madame Bovary, Anna Karenina*, or *Tố Tâm*. Phụng relishes Huyền's story precisely because the heroine's life does not prematurely end amid the portentous bliss of love. But it is as if Phụng takes part in authorial biopolitics, keeping Huyền alive and healthy so as to play out the inevitable outcome of colonial sex: prostitution. The author even goes so far as to render her infertile so as not to have a pregnancy detour Huyền from her path to commercial sex. Phụng's drive to play out this scenario explains why he had to base the text on fiction and not documentary nonfictional work, such as reportage. The writer's intent brings us to a recurring irony of post-mandarin writing: Phụng wants to constitute and reflect on the realities of colonial society but can only do so by mediating them through the private lives of women.

Huyền and Lưu never reveal their consummated relationship to their family. During this time, Huyền's parents arrange a marriage proposal, which the heroine obligingly accepts. Unable to propose a viable solution to preserve the couple's past love, Lưu commits suicide by overdosing on opium. There is a black secretion at the mouth, reminiscent of Emma Bovary's suicide. Huyền, however, continues with her arranged marriage, determined to preserve her secret relationship and to enact revenge for Lưu. Her memoir reveals a fierce, yet rational, woman, challenging the sanctimonious and fetishistic expectation that a bride should be a virgin. Citing a "Western doctor," the heroine points out that the hymen is a thin fold of tissue susceptible to tearing not only during sex but also in an incidental fall or slip.

Subsequently, Huyền prepares herself to challenge her husband and his family's expectations that she be a virginal bride. However, her husband, unexpectedly, does not seek to consummate the wedding for the entire first week of their marriage—an unforeseen occurrence that continues the reversal of the adulterous heroines' novelistic fate: the groom reveals that he has syphilis and is waiting for it to subside. Here, the one who has contracted the venereal disease and practices self-monitoring is not a woman subject to the colonial dispensary but rather a man. Whereas the transmission and modern surveillance of sexually transmitted diseases had previously implicated a woman's sexual past and regulated her sexual activity, in this novel venereal disease implicates the husband and conceals Huyền's sexual past.

The husband's confession reveals his vulnerability as a carrier and transmitter of sexually transmitted diseases, even though the colonial dispensaries did not test men. The narrative further makes plain that men may embrace more liberated relations with women—but not without consequences. Unwittingly cuckolding himself, Huyền's husband pushes her to develop a friendship with Tân, a self-proclaimed bachelor for life. Their relationship quickly turns sexual, and Huyền asks, "Isn't this my husband's fault? Yes, my husband, with his civilized mind, indulges his wife as if a Westerner."[46] The heroine accuses her husband of an uninformed embrace of Western individual liberties, particularly in the form of sexual freedom.

When Huyền proposes to divorce her husband, so as to maintain her relationship with Tân, the bachelor rejects the prospects of a long-term commitment because the mundane expectations of married life occupy and overwhelm a wife, who is then only capable of offering true love to a man other than her husband.[47] Neither man comes to terms with Huyền's sexual desires and past, failing to offer her a viable future: the husband refuses to legally divorce her, yet disavows their life together, and Tân refuses any form of relationship other than a sexual one.

Tân's idealization of extramarital sex parallels the very ideologies of love that Phụng finds reprehensible in his literary adversaries. As the novel comes to its conclusion, this more "civilized" sexual relationship proves to be an inconsequential affair for the male lover while leading the female lover into prostitution. Citing the savagery (dã man) of Vietnam, Tân intends to flee to France and abandon Huyền. When confronted by Huyền, he refuses to consider alternative possibilities for the relationship or compromise his views of modern love. Instead, he offers two rings so that Huyền can support herself. Here, the "civilized," modern male lover submits payment to Huyền, washing his hands of their relationship. Tân's sexual freedoms do not apply to Huyền. The protagonist notes, "It was a humiliating life in a kitchen corner. It was not of equality or liberation, nor was it decadence."[48] Eventually, she runs out of the money she got from selling the rings and other personal items, and she turns to prostitution. The heady romantic and sexual ethos during colonial modernity liberated men; however, for women the allure of modernity's sexual freedom was an illusion—as all paths for women with a sexual past seemed to lead to one of two colonial institutions, the colonial dispensary or a brothel.

Phụng's project of merging art and life illuminates an unresolved aspect of Rancière's thinking: the centrality of women to aesthetic modernity. As Rebecca Karl asks, what does it mean that the political and aesthetic presentation of the prosaic is precisely that of a male intellectual examining social problems through the private life of a modern woman?[49] This was the modern woman who emerged from abrupt changes of colonial modernity—a new and inclusionary educational system, a more accessible print culture, a growing consumer market, and colonial sex—and expanded the scope of literary representation. Rancière's examples of aesthetic modernity revolve around women, specifically, women readers—from Emma in Flaubert's *Madame Bovary* to Veronique in Balzac's *Le curé de village*. But what does it mean that aesthetic modernity—realism's "law of universal equivalence" that erodes the hierarchies of aesthetic content and form—is contingent on the private lives of women?

Vũ Trọng Phụng's 1936 novel, *Số đỏ* (Dumb luck), a satirical narrative about an urban vagrant, Red-Haired Xuân, who emerges as a national hero, offers an answer to this question. Phụng employed satire to critique a utopian narrative of modernity's democratization, of the disintegration of art into life and life into art, in the colonial context. The novel demonstrates that women's sexuality is a central factor in both aesthetic modernization and nationalism. It illuminates men's and women's divergent experiences of modernity, suggesting that it is precisely this difference—dumb luck for the national hero and doomed fate for the sexualized woman—that makes the rise of nationalism possible.

Like *Làm đĩ*, the structure of *Số đỏ*, translated into English as *Dumb Luck*, integrates the everyday world into the novelistic realm. However, it is not structured by reportage that frames a fictional account but rather by newspaper headlines that organize and label each chapter, indicating that daily stories of newspapers make up the content of the novel. Phụng also blurs the fictional and nonfictional worlds by giving this novel a title whose literal meaning is "red number." In the novel, the phrase's semantics evolve from the red addresses of the legalized brothels that signal the doomed fate of women under colonial rule to the "dumb luck" of Phụng's male protagonist, who is able to benefit from the transformations of colonial modernity.

Modernity's fate for the male protagonist is the dumb luck of national heroism, but on the flip side, for the novel's female characters who help Xuân
achieve national status, modernity merely provides the ill fate of sexual
identity and reputation. These two meanings signify the mirrored fortunes
of Vietnamese men and women's experiences during colonial modernity. Yet
the term's connotation derived from the male national heroism that remains
embedded in Vietnamese culture to this day, whereas the denotation of
the legal brothels under French colonialism no longer registers. In the par-
lance of contemporary Vietnamese, what initially referenced the fortune of
a modern man eclipsed the term's original context: the policing of women's
sexuality.

The transformation is embodied by the protagonist's red hair, for which
he is named: Xuân tóc đỏ (Red-Haired Xuân). His hair color indicates poverty: either a life toiling in the sunbaked streets or a deficient diet turned
his hair red. Despite this identity marker, Xuân manages to transcend his
life as a street urchin—going from ball boy and street hawker to doctor to,
ultimately, national tennis hero. Throughout this journey, he becomes the
object of desire for women who have embraced the sexual liberties afforded
by modernization. The protagonist owes much of his fortuitous success to an
instinctive ability to adapt to the radical transformations of colonial modernity, the very conditions central to the rise of the post-mandarin: the dissolution of art into life and life into art; the radical shift from the mandarinate
to print capitalism; and the emergence of the modern indigenous woman.

Xuân thrives in a modern world where, as Rancière has argued, the separation of art and nonart no longer exists, where everyday, ordinary facets of
life are aestheticized and represented. Both men's and women's clothes are
fetishized as modern aesthetic objects. Xuân first lands a job at a tailor shop
specializing in European fashion. He peddles stylized clothing that enables
women to embody the modern progress of sexual liberation—with outfits
such as "Puberty," "Women's Rights," and "Resolute Faithfulness."[50] The very
romanized letters on the clothing store's sign have been so stylized that Xuân
fails to read them. The alienating sign indicates the shifting ground of art
and language toward the everyday consumer world, and its most successful
practitioner, Xuân, is versed in its rhetoric of advertising and sales pitches.

Xuân emerges as an admired savant because of his rhetorical abilities with
the language of commercialism: "In the past he had always been extremely
helpful using his voice to conquer, oppress, and move the hearts of the
masses—whether selling roasted peanuts, working as an advertising boy at
the theater, or making loudspeaker announcements for the Cochinchinese
King of Venereal Disease Treatment."[51] Xuân receives his social credentials

not from any formal education but from his experiences as a peddler of common goods. His words appeal and pertain to the masses, even going so far as to address the social ills of venereal disease. His silver tongue allows him to capitalize on modernity's opportunities—from gainful employment to the courtship of modern women to his reputation as a man of science.

Salesmen and entrepreneurs, not the mandarinal intellects of the past, dominate the modern society of *Dumb Luck*. Xuân's boss, Victor Ban, has amassed a fortune by selling fraudulent treatments for sexually transmitted disease. Further capitalizing on the sexual trends of modern Vietnam, the businessman opens up the Fairyland Hotel—a site for couples to live out the modern ideals of sexual liberation, extramarital affairs, and their desire to "defile the honor of respectable girls."[52] As a man of the times, Xuân brings to the Fairyland Hotel Miss Snow, a young woman he is trying to woo. As Xuân and Miss Snow aim to legitimate their relationship in modern terms, flirting with the possibility of premarital sex, the couple encounter Miss Snow's various suitors. One is the "privileged son of a famous mandarin"; the other is a Europeanized intellectual and poet. Both men lose out to Xuân, the modern Vietnamese man of sport and advertising. The protagonist handily beats the mandarin's descendant in a game of tennis. Xuân also spars with the pretentious intellectual wearing a "European-style suit, and his pants were cuffed in the so-called elephant style."[53] Meanwhile, the mandarin's son offers lyrics that have no bearing on the contemporary world.

> The fairy's feet were light as air.
> Ashamed, young buds fell everywhere.
> Beauty envies rival beauty.
> She tramples flowers underfoot—alas.[54]

Not studied in the composition of verse, Xuân has no option but an improvisational performance based on his experiences as a street hawker.

> No matter if you're young or old,
> Avoid the sun, the wind, the cold.
> Beware fevers, headaches, and the flu;
> Dry skin and heat rash make you blue.
> Day and night you'll rant and rave.
> Your feet won't walk, your hands won't wave.
> For you I have these words to say:
> Buy our ointment, don't delay.[55]

While the European intellectual bows down to Xuân, citing his mastery of "satirical poetic genres," Miss Snow delights in the quasi-scientific rhetoric of advertising: "Yours is the poetry of a man of medicine."[56] It is at this moment that the protagonist wins over the young Miss Snow, who becomes his fiancé.

However, it is not Xuân's relationship with Miss Snow that allows the protagonist to achieve fame as a national hero. Rather, the most significant relationship for Xuân's maturation as a modern man is the one he has with Mrs. Deputy Customs Officer. She is introduced as a *me tây*, an idiomatic term for the wife of a Westerner. In the previous chapter I suggested that the *me tây* was a central figure of modernity. To push this claim further, I argue that Mrs. Deputy Customs Officer's sexual desires catalyze Xuân's social ascent as a national hero.

The novel explains Mrs. Deputy Customs Officer's sexual past as beginning on Armistice Day, when she was still a teenager. She was traveling from her village to the provincial capital to take part in the festivities. On the way, she encountered a European soldier who raped her, and "this unlawful rape [was followed] with years of lawful rape—he married her."[57] On the one hand, the legal domestication of rape as marriage legitimates the sexual violence of the colonial encounter. On the other hand, the assault leads to "those rare and semiconscious sensations—sensations that were strange and very difficult to describe—they had become her obsession. She desired to be ravished again, but the opportunity never arose."[58] With the backdrop of the Allied forces' glorified and triumphant military might, the dominance of Western Europe's presence is translated into sexual violence that is then transformed into new marital and domestic norms, producing new forms of sexual desire.

Shortly after the sanctioning of rape as marriage, the European soldier dies, and the widow marries an indigenous Deputy Customs Officer, who also dies and leaves her a sizable estate. A widow twice over, Mrs. Customs Deputy Officer gains a reputation for her sexual prowess. Although she cannot explain or articulate her urges, she acts on them by trying to seduce Xuân. It is precisely Mrs. Customs Deputy Officer's sexual desire that sets off the chain reaction that propels Xuân into the national spotlight.

At the beginning of the novel, Xuân loses his job as a ball boy for peeping at a French woman in a locker room. This offense is not so different from the investigative work on colonial sex by *phóng sự* writers and the genre's visual connotations, as discussed in the previous chapter. The protagonist spies on a woman during a private moment, and he is admonished for his curiosity about sex, in the same way that Phụng and his fellow observers of colonial sex were accused of masking perverse curiosity under the guise of investigative journalism. Although Phụng's hero initially looks at European women, his future, like that of post-mandarin authors, is connected to Vietnamese women affected by the crisis of colonial sex. Frustrated by being fired, Xuân roughs up a fortune teller who had predicted a promising future for him. But unknown to Xuân, Mrs. Customs Deputy Officer bails him out of jail, and the widow's sympathy for Xuân's sexual perversity sets him on the path to fulfilling his fate. However, it is neither astrology nor physiognomy, which are both referenced in the novel, that determines Xuân's future but rather Mrs. Customs Deputy Officer's generosity toward him, motivated by a sexual appetite traced to her past as a *me tây*.

Mrs. Customs Deputy Officer gets Xuân a job at the European tailor shop, where the protagonist comes to the realization that his mastery of advertising and sales has tremendous value in a modernizing Vietnam. The widow also allows Xuân to use her tennis court, where he hones and displays his athletic skills. The chain of dumb luck that led Xuân to national fame was triggered by Mrs. Customs Deputy Officer, whose own identity and fate, despite her wealth, never change; she cannot escape her sexual past.

Phụng's novels describe the realities of a world torn asunder by the shifting sexual norms of colonialism. Whereas *Làm đĩ* melds literary realism with reportage to produce a realistic account of these transformations, *Dumb Luck* satirizes the pretensions of a modernizing generation that worships European social norms without self-reflection. His satirical novel has a specific agenda: to highlight how the sexual violence of colonialism and modernity's material transformations affected men and women differently. While Xuân is afforded social mobility without limitation, despite his class position, the women in the novel suffer the humiliations of sexual violence and are held to more traditional social standards. Unlike Xuân, their social mobility and their ability to adapt to the modern world are hampered by their gender. Phung's *Dumb Luck* complicates the post-mandarin embrace of European ideas, methodologies, and modes of knowledge. There is no doubt that Phụng's perversion of the Vietnamese novel opened the genre's form and content to the ordinary world. But this was part of the greater post-mandarin turn toward the prosaic that even his bitter rivals, the Self-Strengthening Literary Group, took part in. Unlike Phụng, however, Self-Strengthening authors took a sociological approach to the novel in order to analyze and transform colonial society.

CHAPTER 3

The Sociological Novel
and Anticolonialism

Let it be known that Confucianism is no longer befitting of the times.

—Nhất Linh, "Thanh niên và công việc xã hội" (Youth and the work of society)

At the end of Nhất Linh's *Đoạn tuyệt* (Breaking away), Nguyện Thị Loan, the novel's heroine, is on trial for her husband's murder. The prosecutor accuses Loan of murdering her husband to escape an unhappy marriage. Rather than defend herself against these charges by describing the accident that led to her husband's death, she proclaims her innocence, speaking out on behalf of *chị em gái mới* (new women) who, like herself, suffered under Vietnam's traditional system of marriage: "It is not my intention to ask the court to exonerate me, since I have already been serving the sentences decreed by society."[1] Loan's defense attorney builds on her testimony and tries to prove her innocence by framing the husband's death as the tragic outcome of the conflict between *xã hội cũ* (old society) and *chị em gái mới*. Loan is ultimately acquitted of the charges because, according to the judge's interpretation, she was acting in self-defense.

Nhất Linh's novel stages the conflict between familial tradition and modern subjectivity through the travails of a female protagonist who violates social norms and codes. The novel emblematizes Nhất Linh's anticolonial project to analyze and challenge French colonialism through a sociological critique of the Confucian familial structures and practices that the French colonial regime exploited in order to maintain order and suppress native social and political agency. In the novel the author focuses on the new Vietnamese woman as the site of political resistance to the Confucian family structure and therefore to the French colonial regime. In order to overcome the mutualism of European imperialism and Confucianism, Nhất Linh turned to the critical rationality of European sociology as a tool of critique.

This chapter examines how Nhất Linh's relentless assault on Confucianism constitutes an important political form of masculine post-mandarin writing. Like the ethnographic reportage and realist novels discussed in the previous chapters, Nhất Linh's sociological novel, Đoạn tuyệt, focuses on the social norms and rituals that determine women's roles and social positions. Like other post-mandarin authors, Nhất Linh adopted European forms of knowledge for the purposes of anticolonial nationalism and premises his vision of a new Vietnamese society on modern Vietnamese women such as Nguyện Thị Loan. The similarities that I am suggesting here between the "romanticist" Nhất Linh and a realist such as Vũ Trọng Phụng challenge the central narrative of Vietnamese literary history, which sees a sharp division between realism and romanticism. Contrary to this narrative, I want to emphasize how Nhất Linh and his literary group used the tools of sociological analysis to investigate the social and gender rules of Vietnamese Confucian society.

Although they embraced different approaches, these post-mandarin writers were engaged in a shared literary project to diagnose and critique the condition of everyday life under colonial rule. Tam Lang's and Thạch Lam's reportage writing, Vũ Trọng Phụng's "pornographic" realism, and Nhất Linh's novels signal the turn toward the prosaic in modern Vietnamese literature, an aesthetic and political response to the social transformations of modernity. Even when these post-mandarin writers insisted on the differences they saw among themselves, all of them focused on the prosaic details of everyday life that arose from their shared post-mandarin background. Although Vũ Trọng Phụng chided Nhất Linh and his colleagues for their idealistic and sexless representations of romantic relationships between revolutionary young men and modern Vietnamese women,[2] both authors were committed to exposing, through the lens of gender and sexuality, the everyday practices and norms that determined the social world—practices and norms that would otherwise be taken as natural and self-evident. Whereas Phụng ventured into the demimonde to write about colonial sex, Nhất Linh placed his faith in sociology's ability to abstract, evaluate, and transform society.

Self-Strengthening authors embraced a European ideal of romantic love as an affirmation of individual liberation and sovereignty. They championed the free union between two lovers as a means of overcoming the constrictions of the Confucian family structure. Their emphasis on romantic love echoed a similar phenomenon in China. In Revolution of the Heart, Haiyan Lee argues that affect and sentimentality served as the basis for a new social order in China.

> The modern nation is first and foremost a community of sympathy. In dwelling on the brooding, melancholy lover, romantic fiction invents the individual as a self-centered, self-coherent, and ethically autonomous monad. It thus supplies the most ideal subjects for the nation that distinguishes itself from particularistic solidarities such as the family by subscribing to a universalist concept of humanity. In other words, the national community is where ascriptive differences and social hierarchies are, in theory at least, nullified.[3]

Lee claims that the discourses on modern "love," particularly as represented in twentieth-century Chinese romantic fiction, offered models for ideal individual citizens and the collective identity of a modern nation. Similarly for Self-Strengthening authors, the compassion between young lovers would serve as a model for intersubjective relationships—a new basis for a more rational and humane national community.

Nhất Linh's novels attempted to extricate women from the social facts that determined the Confucian family's gendered hierarchies and expectations. His sociological approach to the novel provides another example in which Europe's literary history—in this case, the divergence of sociology from the genre of the novel—is inverted. Wolf Lepenies has argued that in the nineteenth century sociology and literature had an antagonistic relationship because of their overlapping goals of understanding and explaining industrial society and the individual's relationship to it. As sociology tried to assert itself as a specialized discipline, Lepenies writes, "there arose a competition between a literary intelligentsia composed of authors and critics and a social-scientific intelligentsia. The problem of sociology is that, although it may imitate the natural sciences, it can never become a true natural science: but if it abandons its scientific orientation it draws perilously close to literature."[4]

Under the post-mandarin conditions of Vietnam, however, sociology and the genre of the novel converged. Nhất Linh's *Đoạn tuyệt* illuminates this confluence of literary and social scientific characteristic of post-mandarin literature. Nhất Linh's generation of French-educated writers extracted from, condensed, and reconstituted the pluralism of Europe's literary developments and movements. The present chapter demonstrates how this sociological approach to the novel is specific to Vietnam's post-mandarin condition by situating Nhất Linh in his debate with Nguyễn Công Hoan, who would later emerge as a prominent figure in the Communist Party. This debate brings into sharper relief the ways in which the representation of modern women was such a controversial subject for post-mandarin writers, particularly the plausibility of romantic plots that involved heroines negotiating the norms of tradition and modernity.

Unlike Vũ Trọng Phụng's perverse realism and authorial biopolitics, which diagnosed the crisis of colonial sex and the modern woman's doomed fate, Nhất Linh employed the novel as an instrument of social science to make visible the self-evident social forces that determine gender norms and expectations. This sociological method opened the novel up to the everyday practices and rituals that perpetuate social facts,[5] harnessing social science's aim of understanding the social world in order to remake it. Nhất Linh's insistence on Westernization and his sociological method illuminate how Self-Strengthening authors adapted European modes of critical reflection while disavowing *tout court* the Confucian familial structure and its per-petuation under French colonialism. Their rejection of tradition in favor of European modes of critical reflection gives reason to rethink the affinities, often assumed in postcolonial studies, between the colonized subject and tradition and between the colonizer and modernity.

Nhất Linh (born Nguyễn Tường Tam, 1907–63) initially received a Chinese-language education, but in 1920 he began attending the Lycée du Protectorat de Hà Nội, near Hanoi's West Lake. After three years of study, he received his high school diploma and then worked for the Bureau of Finance. During his time there, he pursued his literary ambitions, publish-ing a series of essays about *Truyện Kiều* (The tale of Kiều) in Phạm Quỳnh's journal, *Nam phong* (Southern wind). In 1925 he quit his administrative post and briefly studied at the École de médecine (trường Cao đẳng Y khoa), before entering the newly established École supérieure des beaux arts de Hà Nội to study painting and drawing. Still unsure of his vocational call-ing, in 1926 he traveled south to Cochinchina, where he played a minor role in radical national politics. A year later, he successfully applied to study in France at the Université de Montpellier, earning a bachelor's degree in sci-ence. Upon returning from France in 1932, Nhất Linh took over the journal *Phong hóa* (Customs) and turned it into a successful weekly satirical journal. At the same time he founded the Self-Strengthening group.[6]

The Self-Strengthening Literary Group was one of Vietnam's most sig-nificant cultural movements in the twentieth century.[7] Through its liter-ary and publishing ventures, the group worked to modernize Vietnamese society and transform Vietnam into a sovereign nation. Its foremost prin-ciple was to "be absolute in following the new, without hesitation."[8] The Self-Strengthening Literary Group's manifesto is succinctly enumerated:

(1) Modernize completely without hesitation, and modernization means Westernization; (2) Have faith in progress, believe that things can get bet-ter; (3) Live according to ideals; (4) Work for the good of society; (5) Train your character; (6) Encourage women to go out in the world; (7) Acquire a

scientific mind; (8) Value real achievement, not careerism; (9) Exercise and strengthen your body; (10) Learn to organize your work methodically.[9]

The Self-Strengthening group's promotion of modernization through Westernization was a direct challenge to the previous generation's conservative view of Europe, particularly those published in *Nam phong*, a journal spearheaded by the neotraditionalist Phạm Quỳnh.[10] This literary movement premised its unbridled modernization on the "scientific mind" and positivist paradigms imported from the West, conflating modernization with Westernization.

As the group's leader, Nhất Linh embraced rationality, individual rights and liberties, and a spirit of youthful optimism. Convinced of the "scientific mind," he employed the slogan "change = improvement" to express his indiscriminate belief in the new and modern. Of the post-mandarin generation, Nhất Linh was the most radical in his campaign for modernization and his denunciation of Vietnam's Confucian tradition. The resolve to modernize with the "new" stemmed from the determination to extirpate the "old"—the root of which, according to Nhất Linh, was Vietnam's Confucian tradition. He viewed Confucianism as a monolithic system of social practices that reified and perpetuated repressive social structures. His understanding of Confucianism as a system of social practices revealed an indifference to both Confucianism's textual basis and its relationship to other discourses, such as Buddhism, that guided its social practice. Uninterested in its written and intellectual traditions, Nhất Linh and the Self-Strengthening Literary Group approached Confucianism neither from a philosophical nor from a moral standpoint: "We do not want to discuss the principles of Confucianism; we only recognize that in reality it has brought our society to a state of stagnancy and darkness."[11] They limited the scope of their attack on Confucianism to social practices: how traditions and obligations dictated the conduct of social life. Nhất Linh was particularly interested in examining how Confucian ritual practices perpetuated women's social roles.

In his calls for modernization, Nhất Linh directed his strongest critique against village life, where, for him, the oppressive social effects of Confucianism were most acutely felt. However, he did not eschew village life for the sake of urbanism or cosmopolitanism. Instead, he repeatedly emphasized that change must take place through *xã hội*, a neologism in the Vietnamese language at the turn of the century that emerged as the Vietnamese equivalent to the French term *société*. It also appears in translations of European terms such as sociology (*xã hội học*), social science (*khoa học xã hội*), and socialism (*chủ nghĩa xã hội*). Nhất Linh embraced the term *xã hội* as a modern, scientific counterpart to the traditional Confucian social order and its *lũy tre xanh* (bamboo hedges), which for him signified the premodern social structures and units at the foundation of Confucian life. Nhất Linh understood society as inherently capable of critique and regeneration, unlike the stagnancy behind the bamboo hedges. He proclaimed, "I am always standing from the vantage point of society [*xã hội*]," singling out *xã hội* as the primary vehicle of transformation: "The work of society that I want to discuss is work that changes society, raises society to a greater level and greater beauty." He went on to explain that "only if society changes can the lives of the common people improve. And if society is to change, then it must change for the new."[12] Nhất Linh embraced society as a modern concept that enabled him to imagine Vietnam's social transformations beyond the Confucian village and clan.

Nhất Linh and the members of the Self-Strengthening group employed literature and print culture to pursue their agenda of representing and reconfiguring society. In doing so, they established themselves as pioneers in the development of modern Vietnamese poetry, literary publishing, journalism, and, above all, the genre of the novel. For the Self-Strengthening leader, the novel served as a site to modernize the world through new social constructs and relations. *Đoạn tuyệt* pits Confucian tradition against modern subjectivity. Such conflicts are often depicted through the tribulations of young heroines, like Loan, whose amorous desires transgress social conventions and familial expectations.

Taking the Self-Strengthening Literary Group as romanticism's cynosure, critics have berated the group for its uncritical and unapologetic embrace of all that was new, modern, and Western.[13] They have accused the group of irreverently dismissing Vietnam's intellectual past and ignoring the potential revolutionary roles of the working and peasant classes. Among the chorus of antiromantic voices, the vociferous Marxist critic Trương Tửu has attacked Nhất Linh's vague and feckless use of "an uninformed sociology [*xã hội học*] as the basis for his theories, forgetting the realities of society."[14] He would prefer to see Nhất Linh argue that class struggle is the primary cause of fundamental schisms within the capitalist order and the primary means of moving toward a more equal social system. Accusing the Self-Strengthening author's haphazard system of analysis and ideological thought, Trương Tửu derided his sociological proclamations. Nevertheless, Trương Tửu's use of *xã hội học* to characterize Nhất Linh's work points to the sociological concerns central to Nhất Linh's agenda of modernization and to his literary oeuvre, especially *Đoạn tuyệt*. Nhất Linh's embrace of the "new," along with his belief in modernization and Westernization, must be understood and defined in terms of the reflexive knowledge afforded by the sociological agency of the novel. Nhất Linh applied sociological inquiry in his descriptions and analysis of Confucian norms, rituals, and everyday practices that dictated women's social roles. His focus on women differentiates him from previous political and social theorists, particularly those from the 1920s, who saw male scholars as the "transmitters (and embodiments) of moral teachings" during French colonial rule in Indochina.[15] For Nhất Linh and Self-Strengthening writers, the proper behavior, actions, and appearance of women signified the ways in which cultural and moral tradition continued to be legitimized and transmitted in the 1930s.[16] Nhất Linh examined the social dynamics and practices that perpetuated Confucianism's established order so as to advance his vision of modernity—a vision that critically examined and questioned the limits of the traditional world through a consciousness of that world's divisions and categories. His novels analyze gender as a social category that, reproduced by patriarchal sociocultural institutions and practices, had the illusion of being natural and self-evident. Nhất Linh's literary sociology sought to transform the immutable laws and beliefs of Confucianism's worldview into social facts.

For the Self-Strengthening Literary Group, Confucianism permeated all aspects of social life, from ritualized events to personal habits and behavior. Self-Strengthening authors viewed it as an institution of doctrines and principles enforced by the familial collective: Confucian beliefs condition, saturate, and organize social life, in particular, through the reinforcement of gender differences. From their perspective, Confucianism is limited neither to the erudite traditions of the civil service examination and its mandarin candidates nor to the realm of religious doctrines to which followers adhere for moral or spiritual guidance. They did not understand Confucianism as a repertoire of ideas and principles that individuals referred to for specific situations[17] but instead as a ubiquitous and accepted social force that compelled individuals to act and behave accordingly, unaware of the imposed rules, roles, and norms.

The Self-Strengthening group saw the provincial and subordinated mindset promulgated by Confucianism's hegemonic social order as preventing individuals from forming or even imagining any social polity, such as a modern nation, beyond the family clan.[18] The perpetuation of these atomistic social practices behind bamboo hedges helped maintain the French colonial state. Thus, in order to revolutionize this "feudalistic order of colonialism,"[19] Nhất Linh based his vision of modernization on sociological knowledge that renews and reconstitutes social relations—and thus society itself.

It is not merely Nhất Linh's argument for newness that proved groundbreaking, for surely, throughout Vietnam's intellectual and literary history, neither Self-Strengthening writers nor their leader were the first to argue for the new over the old. Rather, the radicalism of Nhất Linh's promotion of the "new" derived from its underpinning logic: the potentialities of the future are contingent on the evaluation and reevaluation of the present. The reflexive relationship between sociological knowledge and social life is endemic to modernity, as Anthony Giddens has argued in *The Consequences of Modernity*:

> Modernity is constituted in and through reflexively applied knowledge, but the equation of knowledge with certitude has turned out to be misconceived. We are abroad in a world which is thoroughly constituted through reflexively applied knowledge, but where at the same time we can never be sure that any given element of that knowledge will not be revised.[20]

To support this claim, Giddens gives a nuanced account of the relationship between social sciences and reality.

> Sociological knowledge spirals in and out of the universe of social life, reconstructing both itself and that universe as an integral part of that process.
>   This is a model of reflexivity, but not one in which there is a parallel track between the accumulation of sociological knowledge on the one side and the steadily more extensive control of social development on the other. Sociology (and the other social sciences which deal with extant human beings) does not develop cumulative knowledge in the same way as the natural sciences might be said to do. Per contra, the "feed-in" of sociological notions or knowledge claims into the social world is not a process that can be readily channeled, either by those who propose them or even by powerful groups or governmental agencies. Yet the practical impact of social sciences and sociological theories is enormous, and sociological concepts and findings are constitutively involved in what modernity is.[21]

The modern world is both the product and object of social scientific interrogation. As Giddens has suggested, this cyclical feedback not only is characteristic of modernity; it is modernity itself. The promise of the "new"—thus a worthy investment in the future—is found in the infinite cycle of renewal and relegitimization that questioned the social forces behind Vietnam's Confucian society.

The reflexive sociology central to Nhất Linh's anticolonial modernization is not only a compelling reason to rethink the supposedly apolitical dimensions of the Self-Strengthening sociopolitical vision and its "romantic" literature. It is also cause to revisit some of postcolonial studies' assumptions. The Self-Strengthening critique of the colonial order, by rejecting Confucian tradition, calls into question the role played by cultural tradition in anticolonial protest.

In sharp contrast to the argument forwarded by the Subaltern Studies group, the relationship between tradition and colonialism in Vietnam is one not of contestation and antagonism but rather of mutualism and collaboration in which Confucian tradition buttressed French colonialism. From the vantage point of the Subaltern collective's analysis of Indian colonial historiography, postcolonial nationalism in the hands of indigenous bourgeois elites fails to realize any real Indian sovereignty. National elites merely substitute for colonial elites, and as a result the subaltern continues to be defined by and is thus locked into a Hegelian dialectic with colonial or national elites. Therefore, even the historical narratives of Indian nationalism cannot escape the colonial discourse that Gyan Prakash terms "post-Orientalist historiography."[22] For Dipesh Chakrabarty, the nation-state as the political imperative and geopolitical basis of decolonization overrides the historical difference that preceded colonialism and thus fails to achieve its liberatory goals.[23] According to this logic, precolonial tradition has been displaced yet remains untainted by European dominance; modernity is wholly homologous with European imperialism.

Nhất Linh's unabashed critique of Confucian tradition and embrace of Europeanization provide a crucial counterpoint to the Subaltern collective— who do not consider the role that tradition plays in shoring up colonialism. The Self-Strengthening leader adopted a sociological approach not merely to mimic European ideology, but rather to make a crucial distinction between instrumental reason and critical reason. This discernment was necessary for colonized intellectuals who, as Pheng Cheah has reminded us, Horkheimer and Adorno discussed in *Dialectic of Enlightenment*.[24] Through reflexive sociology, Nhất Linh exercises critical rationality to overcome colonialism's instrumental use of rationality. To overcome the collusion between precolonial tradition and the colonial enterprise, he conceptualizes society— represented by the liminal position of the female paramour—as a world constantly evolving from the feedback loop of evaluation and reevaluation.

Spivak has elaborated and revised some concepts of the Subaltern Studies group in ways that are salient for the present discussion of Nhất Linh. She locates Guha's definition of the subaltern within the master-slave dialectic: "Their text articulates the difficult task of rewriting its own conditions of impossibility as the conditions of its possibility."[25] She shares Guha's concerns about the perpetuation of colonial discourse by the national elites. But like Self-Strengthening authors and unlike other Subaltern thinkers, she cautions against resorting to an idealized subaltern tradition, a tradition that has already been appropriated by patriarchy and colonialism. Moreover, she analyzes—not through class, but through gender—how the subaltern is disenfranchised by colonial and then national elites. Spivak identifies the subaltern as the question of the third world woman, pointedly asking, "Can the subaltern speak?," amid the elitist nationalist discourses. She says no.

> Within the effaced itinerary of the subaltern subject, the track of sexual difference is doubly effaced. The question is not of female participation in insurgency, or the ground rules of the sexual division of labor, for both of which there is "evidence." It is, rather, that, both as object of colonialist histo- riography and as subject of insurgency, the ideological construction of gen- der keeps the male dominant. If, in the contest of colonial production, the subaltern has no history and cannot speak, the subaltern as female is even more deeply in shadow.[26]

For Spivak, all nationalist discourses constitute the subaltern as a discursive figure that cannot represent or speak for herself. Representations of third world women do not faithfully or authentically translate, do not carry over the gendered divide between the subaltern and the elite.

While the post-mandarin configuration of national literature and dis- course centers on women but does not give voice to women—resonating with Spivak's claims about the subaltern as women incapable of self- representation—the post-mandarin intellectuals' masculine anxiety dis- cussed in previous chapters disrupts the presumed gendered pattern of dominance. Their masculine vulnerability creates an opening whereby the multiple facets of the feminine, even if they may not be articulated in an authentic voice of self-representation, determine the modality, form, and content of Vietnam's modern, national literature.

For Nhất Linh and the Self-Strengthening Literary Group, it was impera- tive to reveal the everyday practices that authorized the exclusion of women from the social world beyond the domestic realm, foreclosing the promise of modernity. In order to reveal the social forces that constricted female agency, Nhất Linh investigated, through sociological inquiry, the complicit relationship between patriarchy and colonialism.

Sociology has rarely been associated with the colonial setting, and even less with colonial subjects' agency. During its disciplinary formation, the purview of sociology was limited to European modernity: to understand how European modernity began and how to intervene in its development. And though the colonial project was integral to European modernity, "the dynamics of empire were not incorporated into the basic categories, models of explanation, and narrative of social development of the classical sociolo- gists."[27] In order to address this blind spot, scholars have persuasively argued that contemporary sociological paradigms should engage with postcolonial studies to include non-Western modernities.[28] Nevertheless, these scholars conflate their methodological approaches (postcolonial) with their object of study (colonial modernization). As a result, thinkers who have combined sociological and postcolonial thought have failed to give adequate attention to colonial subjects' assertion of their own agency through sociology. Nhất Linh, for one, employed sociology in order to give epistemological value to the colonial alterity of Vietnam while attempting to move beyond its Confucian past.

Published in 1935, *Đoạn tuyệt* tells the story of a young woman torn between tradition and modernity. Nguyễn Thị Loan, a young, modern woman, is forced into marriage to a man from a traditional family. Her biological parents arrange the marriage in exchange for money that they need to pay off a debt. Thân, Loan's new husband, is more despondent than nurturing. His actions and words are bent toward the will of Loan's callous mother-in-law. Lurking in the background of Loan's difficult life as a new bride and daughter-in-law is an unfulfilled relationship with Dũng, a former classmate. The heroine pines for Dũng, imagining the life that she could have had with him. Accepting her marital fate, she could only consider herself "a wife in spirit with Dũng."[29]

To compound the grief caused by her biological father's death, Loan's first child becomes sick and dies because bà Phán, the mother-in-law, insists on traditional medicine for her ailing grandchild. After the grandson dies, Thân marries a second wife, Tuất, whom he hopes will give the family another grandson. The tensions that arise from the polygamous arrangement erupt into an argument one night when Loan accidentally kills her husband with a knife. She is tried in a colonial court and is exonerated on the premise that she was acting in self-defense. But she is only truly free after her father, husband, and son die, enabling her break with the social bonds of Confucianism. This trinity represented a woman's "three obediences" (*tam tòng*) throughout her life: obedience to her father as daughter, to her husband as wife, and to her son as widow.

Both Loan and her star-crossed lover, Dũng, struggle against the established sociopolitical order. The two characters, however, take different paths of resistance, occupying different social spaces. Dũng is involved with political, armed activities on the front lines of an anticolonial struggle. He moves from town to town, crossing one border after another. During a discussion about Loan's murder case, Dũng says to a male friend, "We were born as boys, so we can escape to the outside."[30] Men have the mobility to go "outside," to go beyond, to abandon the home. Meanwhile, Loan is confined to her in-laws' home in a Vietnamese hamlet (having left her parents' home in Hanoi). Loan's inability to leave the domestic space signifies women's immobility, while Dũng's political missions outside the home indicate men's mobility.

The gender difference in mobility is most evident the night the couple splits up: Loan gets married, and Dũng embarks on his revolutionary activities. The narrative shifts between each character's respective vision of the same night sky as a way to emphasize their connected but divergent paths. (This is the only moment in the novel when a dual perspective is presented.) It is Loan's wedding night and her marriage is being consummated with a man she barely knows:

> Suddenly Loan felt a light hand upon her shoulder. She did not turn around, lifting her eyes to look out the window where she saw an image of Dũng appear vividly in her imagination as if he were before her eyes. The stars in the sky disappeared, and her eyes were open, but unable to see anything clearly. She only saw a color that was as dark as ink.[31]

Loan's mind becomes separated from her body. Even as her husband rests his hand on her shoulder, presumably beckoning her to their marital bed, her bond with Dũng proves resilient. The two lovers seem to connect telepathically while looking at the same stars. Then, just as quickly, the ensuing sexual encounter with her husband blinds her: Loan keeps her eyes pinned open, but she is unable to see or to comprehend what is before her.

Meanwhile, Dũng is traveling in modernity's emblematic machine: the train. The world now moves at an accelerated pace, with the exterior landscape rapidly running by him: "At that moment on a night train to Yên Bái, Dũng sat looking at a crisp spring moon running behind one dark forest after another, on the horizon."[32] Dũng experiences the mobility afforded by modernity, while Loan is being sexually initiated into the traditional social order of a Confucian family. Dũng is the modern traveler: he is capable of overcoming greater distances in less time, yet his interaction with the landscape is limited by modern technology—restricted and made unnatural by his stationary position in a train compartment.[33]

This is a rare instance when we know Dũng's destination: Yên Bái. But throughout the novel, he comes to and goes from Hanoi, constantly leaving for mysterious destinations, as if disappearing into the horizon. He never knows where he is going or what his next mission will be. He has forsaken all familial ties; he is mired in abject poverty. To readers, he is merely an elusive, shadowy presence. We never know his exact whereabouts or his specific role in the anticolonial movement. We do know, however, that he has residual feelings for Loan.

Critics have questioned such romantic representations of revolutionary characters. Phan Cự Đệ asserts that the Self-Strengthening group's revolutionary figures like Dũng lack a true national spirit: "That is the situation with a group of young men after the failed Yên Bái uprising. The defeated have become heroes lost in fantasy. *The revolutionary's persona is now an amalgam of the colonized's bitterness and the romanticist's infatuation with pure beauty and a bohemian life.*"[34] For Phan Cự Đệ, the Self-Strengthening group's militant characters belong to a genre of men, particularly those of the Việt Nam Quốc Dân Đảng (Vietnamese Nationalist Party), too demoralized by their unsuccessful 1930 military uprising against the French, who quickly stamped out the Yên Bái movement. According to Phan Cự Đệ, these men were overcome by romanticist malaise in their search for idealized notions of beauty, love, and life—a malaise that compromised them militarily and politically.[35]

Phan Cự Đệ restricts the parameters of political revolution to the battlefield while ignoring the domestic front as a site of political resistance. He lionizes the combatant and dismisses the wife and mother as figures in a social struggle for liberation. In contrast to Phan Cự Đệ, Nhất Linh pairs a rebellious heroine with a militant figure to bridge the gender divide while pointing to the different sets of revolutionary questions and circumstances for those on each side of the gender divide. In the novel, for example, Dũng's ideological intentions are aimed at liberating the popular masses, particularly the peasantry.

> Dũng could sense the soul of the nation, but that nation is not represented by those who have been in power. Rather, it was the lot of the humbled masses, nameless and ageless. The people are the nation. To love the nation is to love the people, to think of the suffering of the common people.[36]

However, Dũng realizes that class uprising can only be achieved if the masses are able to realize and articulate their adversities.

> Perhaps they have become too accustomed to suffering to know what that change is? Or if they do know, they cannot convey it. . . . We have to convey it for them to see; we have to convey what we want for them. Somehow they have to want what we want. I still hope that the peasantry will no longer be oppressed or exploited. We have to believe that our hopes will be realized, so that the peasantry will desire change with our fervor.[37]

The goal is, quite problematically, not just to improve the lot of the peasants but also to enlighten them so that they will be cognizant and reflect on their own situation. Dũng believes that self-awareness of one's disadvantaged position leads to an indefatigable quest for social transformation.

Dũng's political vision, however, is divorced from Loan's situation, causing her to wonder if his revolutionary work even considers women like her. She assumes that her revolutionary lover does not reciprocate her feelings because "there are more significant issues he has to worry about, rather than the petty quandaries of a woman like me."[38] Not only is Loan justified in her doubts about the exclusion of women from Dũng's political intentions, but she is the missing link between Dũng's revolutionary vision and the actualization of that vision. She is the disenfranchised figure who acquires the self-awareness and self-expression necessary for revolutionary social change and mass mobilization. Such social transformation, however, does not fall solely along class lines, but also gender lines. It does not concern only peasants, but also women.

Social transformation in the novel, then, is actualized through Loan's critique of her own social circumstance. Not only does she reject her role as a domestic woman, but she also questions how her social position is predetermined by tradition. Building up to the confrontation that leads to the husband's death, the narrator comments on Loan: "Only recently did she realize that she was cowering under her life of customary practices, not courageous enough to break away from those practices, but her education convinced her that they should be abandoned, that they should be destroyed."[39] In order to emphasize how Loan's life is structured by customary practices, Nhất Linh fills his short novel with an overabundance of ceremonial rituals (lễ).[40] The rituals include Loan's engagement ceremony, her wedding, ancestor worship, initiation into a husband's family, New Year's practices, offertory ceremonies at a Buddhist temple, death anniversaries, and a mistress's marital rites into the family. Throughout the novel, both Loan and the narrator refer to these social rituals as invisible strings that bind her to certain obligations, effectively manipulating her deeds and even thoughts: "She thought of the countless pleasures waiting for her at some remote place. She was tightly bound by invisible strings that kept her here, incapable of any escape."[41] Loan anticipates the obligations that will confine her within her husband's family. As a newlywed, these invisible strings restrict her movement and script her responsibilities and actions. The engagement ceremony and all subsequent ritualized practices make up a complex system of controls masterfully manipulated by traditional society. She becomes a stoic figure obliged to mechanically fulfill the duties of daughter-in-law and wife, from daily chores to sex and childbirth. Loan sees herself merely as an object, exchanged between two families to settle debts and acquired as a "birthing machine" (máy đẻ): "She did not have to know about love: she had the responsibilities of a birthing machine, and she had to understand that that was her role. Her husband's deeds always reminded her of that role and only that role."[42] The functions and identity already determined for Loan preempt free will or even an authentic self.[43]

The bonds of ritualistic practice become more profound as they mediate Loan's social capital, social relations, and gender roles. After the death of Loan's son, her husband marries his mistress, Tuất, who is pregnant with his child. Loan feels conflicted about her new position as an elder wife. She sees no difference between the two wives' situations: both are subject to the tyrannical expectations of the husband's family. But her mother-in-law explains the need to establish hierarchies and boundaries between the elder and younger wives during the second wedding ceremony:

> You should just sit there so she can kowtow to you. If that's not what you want, then that's your decision. But rituals should be rituals. Superiors should be superiors, inferiors should be inferiors. [She] will live with us for a long time, and if there is no [official] acknowledgment, [she] will become suspicious [of your status], and then there will be problems.[44]

According to the mother-in-law, the ceremony is necessary to legitimize Loan's authority and privilege as the elder wife. Without the official ceremony, the newest member of the family would fail to respect the eldest wife, since both women are supposed to be jealously vying for the husband's attention. These ceremonies and the symbolic acts entailed, like kowtowing, are meant to position women in a familial order premised on and stabilized by hierarchical power relations.

In one scene, Loan's status as the elder wife obliges her husband to hide his sexual preference for the new wife. This tension between the husband's sublimated sexual desire and Loan's legitimacy as the elder wife comes to a breaking point in the argument that leads to the husband's death. The couple has moved to Hanoi, and later that night the second wife arrives in the city. The husband feels obligated to sleep next to the elder wife but wants to be with the second wife. Loan is reading a novel, using a letter knife to cut the pages of her book. Loan's husband wants her to turn off the lights so he can sneak out of the room. His intentions are obvious to Loan, and she refuses to relinquish her novel. A loud and violent argument ensues, prompting the mother-in-law to enter the room. The mother-in-law shouts directions in an attempt to restore order, but Loan refuses. She confronts her mother-in-law: "You are a person, I am a person. No one is better or worse than the other."[45] Appalled by her daughter-in-law's brazen disobedience, the mother instructs her son to kill Loan, and the son dutifully obeys. He picks up a bronze (đồng) fixture to assault Loan, who dodges her husband's blow. She falls onto the bed, holding the letter knife, upon which her husband then fatally impales himself.

This scene's symbolism is too blatant to ignore. The bed is the site of the marriage's consummation. The letter knife, which the heroine uses to cut the pages of her book, allows for Loan's engagement with European literature. Loan's use of a letter knife makes her akin to nineteenth-century novelistic heroines, like Emma Bovary or Anna Karenina, quixotically inspired by novel reading to romantically rebel against a domestic world that confines them. The letter knife also works metonymically to signal that the novel is a weapon in Nhất Linh's literary project of social transformation. Rather than view this murder as an accident in a romantic plot gone awry, I view this episode as a metaliterary moment that reveals Nhất Linh's investment in the genre of the novel. The author sees the novel as a means to reconfigure the Confucian patriarchal order—to kill off the husband, the son, and the father. Đoạn tuyệt's sociological rendering of Confucian social order, its goal of social transformation, and its metacommentary on the genre of the novel come together to allow the heroine, and by extension all readers of the novelistic genre, the possibility of being liberated from the Confucian trinity of the father, the husband, and the son. By making visible the "strings" that determine and constrain women's social positions, Nhất Linh's Đoạn tuyệt attempts to explain and displace the accepted social practices and power of Confucian rituals. The novel is a tool for sociological analysis that deepens and broadens the reader's knowledge beyond his or her field of immediate experience. In turn, the novel and its sociological work play a role in changing society. The mutual relationship between the genre of the novel, sociological analysis, and society elucidates Nhất Linh's vision of modernization and Westernization through xã hội and newness.

While Communist critics do not deny Đoạn tuyệt's significance as one of the touchstones of modern Vietnamese literature, they view Nhất Linh's representation of revolutionary and nationalistic characters, his dismissal of the proletariat class in the countryside, and his instrumental use of the heroine as a mouthpiece for bourgeois ideology as politically shortsighted and even reactionary.[46] One of the more sustained and pointed attacks against Nhất Linh's novel came from Nguyễn Công Hoan. Initially, the Self-Strengthening group had accused Nguyễn Công Hoan of plagiarizing Đoạn tuyệt to write the novel Cô giáo Minh (Miss Minh, a schoolteacher).[47] Responding to the accusations, Nguyễn Công Hoan explained that the impetus for writing Cô giáo Minh was the failure of Nhất Linh's work as a luận đề (thesis) novel. He felt that Nhất Linh's novel had a transparent message: through the travails and outcome of the modern heroine's struggles against the traditional

family, one can understand the superiority of the "new" over the "old." However, according to Nguyễn Công Hoan, the Self-Strengthening protagonist
never takes a firm position against traditional familial structures because, by
the author's design, her husband dies accidentally. Therefore, Loan dissoci-
ates herself from the traditional family by chance and not through her own
agency (*hành động*).

> [Nhất Linh] dares not allow his Loan to be so new that she leaves her fam-
> ily to marry her old lover, that she abandons her in-laws with no choice but
> divorce. He dares not allow his Loan to be so audacious that she kills off her
> husband, and he dares not allow his Loan to be pathetic enough to kill her-
> self. He dares not even allow her to be so cunning as to file for divorce.[48]

The husband's random death makes for an unnatural and unrealistic circumstance, dictated by the author's message. Nguyễn Công Hoan continues in a facetious tone to suggest the absurdity of the death scene, directly
addressing both the female readership of the novel and Loan.

> If your husband fights with you and a sharp knife doesn't accidentally stab
> him in the chest, then I am certain that you young women, including Loan
> from *Đoạn tuyệt* as well, must "patiently obey in order to manage a peaceful
> life."
>   So what if Nhất Linh encourages "breaking away from the traditional
> family"; he does not offer a path for people to follow.[49]

In response, Nguyễn Công Hoan writes *Cô giáo Minh* to offer a more
realistic model for young female readers to emulate should they have differences with their traditional families. Rather than break from these
families, he imagines women reconciling themselves to their lives in the
Confucian order. The writer intends his compromising and selfless protagonist, Nguyễn Thu Minh, to be a didactic model: although the modern heroine experiences difficulties and frustrations as a daughter-in-law,
she sacrifices her individual will and desires in an attempt to reconcile
the "new" with the "old." She eventually settles into and fits in with her
husband's extended family. Reluctant to challenge the Confucian social
order, the novel's humbled protagonist is an antidote to Nhất Linh's haphazard approach to the "new." The differences in the two heroine's fates
are striking. Whereas Nhất Linh liberates his heroine, Nguyễn Công
Hoan tries to reimagine and improve her plight within the family clan
system.

The novels resolve the conflict between tradition and modernity in
contrasting ways. Nguyễn Công Hoan presents and addresses the conflict
between the new and the old primarily by means of characters' dialogue and

thoughts. For example, in a scene where Minh is trying to counsel her sister-in-law, who is having her own marital doubts and problems, the heroine discusses her process of self-reflection to come to terms with, rather than rebel against, her role as a wife: "I should say that I often blame myself first before I blame others. Perhaps you have done something to frustrate or sadden him [your husband]."[50] Minh's transformation from a reluctant, modern woman to a compromising, selfless wife is captured by such thoughts. Social transformation depends on the modern individual adapting to preexisting social norms and practices. However, realism in this sense is a mere code word for the gendered status quo. Unlike Nguyễn Công Hoan, Nhất Linh seeks to upend precisely those gender norms central to the Confucian social order.

The debate between these two writers highlights that Vietnamese authors viewed the novel as a didactic tool that plays a critical role in social tranformation and that they were especially concerned with the position of the new modern women who was located outside of old familial structures.[51] Novelistic discourses were interrelated with intellectual and political debates as well as journalistic and biographical writing. Nhất Linh, however, employed the novel to mediate social transformation differently—that is to say, sociologically. He aimed to make visible and to restructure the underpinnings of Confucian society that determine women's social roles. Nguyễn Công Hoan's works were not more realist than Nhất Linh's; rather, they describe and restrict themselves to the existing social order and therefore refuse to imagine radical social transformation.

For Nhất Linh, the novel is an instrument for knowledge and large-scale social transformation, while for Nguyễn Công Hoan the novel serves only as a model for individual self-transformation. The Self-Strengthening author does not intend for his young characters to be mere examples. Rather, he sends them out on different, though interrelated, missions of social transformation. Nevertheless, the sociological ambitions of this post-mandarin novel for revolution are contingent on the heroine's desires for a revolutionary man. Her desires, then, are interconnected with and mediated through the revolutionary male.

The critical establishment failed to recognize Nhất Linh's radical project. The critic Huỳnh Sanh Thông, for example, disapproved of the passionate emotions expressed by Self-Strengthening characters that forgo "sociological truth": "As we read their novels now, we may feel that those authors [Nhất Linh and Khái Hưng] stacked the deck against the family system they condemned, at the expense of sociological truth and artistic integrity." Huỳnh Sanh Thông singles out "Nguyễn Công Hoan's style of writing as epitomizing the best in the realistic, leftist movement, drawing freely on the lore and idiom of the common people, and more accessible to readers with little or no knowledge of French."[52] In contrast to Nguyễn Công Hoan and other Marxist critics, I argue that the novel served as a vehicle for sociological observation and the dissemination of that information. Novel reading then becomes complicit with social science's dual objective of analyzing and transforming the world.

We can address Trương Tửu's doubts about Nhất Linh's faith in the "new" and the Western-educated by considering the constant renewal of reflexively applied knowledge. The critical reflexivity here is the intellectual organ necessary for the assessment of the past and present, with the hope of reordering the future social world. This is a good example of what Giddens has called the "institutionalisation of doubt" that is inherent in modernity.[53] It is worth remembering here Hoàng Đạo's association of critical reason with Western thought: "Not until Western civilization spread over to us did we see a sense of skepticism emerge. Only then did we gradually perceive the negative aspects of the old society."[54]

In the same way that Nhất Linh's belief in Western-educated intellectuals was rooted in the Enlightenment notion of critical reason, his endorsement of newness was premised on the constant evaluation of the present. The promise of the "new" then was found in the limitless cycle of renewal and relegitimization that questioned social forces. Nhất Linh's understanding of the new and attacks on Confucianism prove to be more complex than the "romanticist" categorization allows. The same can be said of his Self-Strengthening colleague and collaborator, Khái Hưng. Khái Hưng did not incorporate sociology into his novels; rather, he focused on the Confucian sociolinguistics that structure the Vietnamese language. We now turn to Khái Hưng's novelistic analysis of language through post-mandarin women's liminal position at the disjuncture between Vietnamese, a noninflected language, and the impositions of French, an inflected language.

CHAPTER 4

I Speak in the Third Person

Women and Language in Colonial Vietnam

The first day—who knows when—that the word "I" [tôi] appeared in Vietnamese poetry, it was truly surprising. It was as if "I" was lost in a strange land. This is because it brought with it a perspective not yet seen in this country: the individual perspective. Since ancient times there was no individualism in Vietnamese society. There was only the collective: the large one being the country, the small one, the family. As for the individual, its unique characteristics were submerged in the family and in the country, like a drop of water in the sea.

—Hoài Thanh and Hoài Chân, cited and translated in David Marr, "Concepts of 'Individual' and 'Self' in Twentieth-Century Vietnam"

In the opening scene of Khái Hưng's 1934 *Nửa chừng xuân* (In the midst of spring) Dương Thị Mai, the novel's protagonist, walks toward the gates of a French colonial school in Hanoi. A security guard confronts the young woman:

—You there, what do you want?

The young woman stutters:

—Sir, I . . . I . . .

The guard snaps again:

—What?

—Sir . . . nothing.

—Then leave. What are you standing there looking at? Or are you waiting for some man? Dressed in those clogs![1]

Recently arrived in the city of Hanoi, the young woman wants to see her brother, Dương Huy. The guard's snide remark about her clogs is an intentional misreading of her clothes as being provocative; her white head scarf and shirt split down the sides indicate a person in mourning (her father has recently died). Once Mai gets past the guard and enters the administrative office, the schoolmaster asks her to identify herself. She responds, "I [*Tôi*] am Dương Thị Mai."[2] The schoolmaster is not interested in her name but rather her familial relationship with the student she wants to see. The official then turns to an assistant to discuss Mai's request, deliberately leaving her out of the conversation by speaking in French. The schoolmaster assumes that as a woman the protagonist has not been educated in French.

In both instances, the school authorities are suspicious of Mai's intentions because she does not identify herself by familial association but instead uses the self-reference forms of the first-person singular pronoun *tôi* and her proper name. Both forms are independent of the Vietnamese language's person-reference system based on the kinship relations that structure Vietnamese Confucian society. During the interwar period, the gender-neutral first-person singular pronoun *tôi* emerged in literature as an expression of individualism, the result of the influence of European ideas that was antithetical to familial and social collectivism.[3] However, the heroine's struggles to employ the first-person singular pronoun point to a disjuncture between the individualistic *tôi* and the collectivism of Vietnamese Confucian society, between individualism and Vietnam's Confucian sociolinguistic order. Mai must negotiate European notions of individualism and the sociolinguistic structures still prevalent in modern Vietnamese society.

With the post-mandarin transformations of print, language, and education, women became the new subjects and target audience of print journalism,[4] and male authors and intellectuals appropriated the figure of the Vietnamese woman in their discussions of nationalism and modernization. Despite women's presence as subjects of discourses and as readers of print culture, there were few female authors of literature at the time.[5] Addressing the relationship between male authors and represented female subjects, critics and historians have argued that cultural representations of women serve as symbols in masculine articulations of morality and nationalism.[6]

While I am sympathetic to these arguments about the instrumental use of female representations, I want to shift away from figurative readings since they risk subsuming women's diverse relations with and reactions to modernity under a monolithic representation of femininity. Such readings reify the symbolic myth they seek to critique. Instead, this chapter examines Mai's social practice of language within and against the sociolinguistic structures reproduced in the genre of the novel, revealing the limitations and subversive potential of the heroine's language. Mai's necessary manipulation of self-references in the novel, embedded in the sociolinguistic structures of Vietnam's Confucian society, shows that the transition from collectivism to individualism was an incomplete process fraught with the discrepancies between tradition and modernity, as well as the differences between men and women's experiences of modernization. The novel also reveals the disparities of social power within Vietnam's post-mandarin literary field and between female literary subjects like Mai and male literary authors. As in post-mandarin reportage, fictional realism, and the sociological novel, women are excluded from yet revealingly frame the process of modernization. Taking on another facet of the post-mandarin condition, the present chapter explores how the paradoxes and incompleteness of colonial modernity are manifested in the sociolinguistic structures of the novel.

Born in 1896, Trần Khánh Dư, who later used the pen name Khái Hưng, was the eldest child of a provincial governor in colonial Indochina. He first earned a degree in Sinology and then, later in his twenties, a French baccalaureate. After a brief interlude as a schoolteacher, in 1932 he wrote his first novel, *Hồn bướm mơ tiên* (Butterfly soul dreaming of an immortal), which established him as one of the leading novelists of his generation. The author quickly gained a reputation for his portrayals of romantic relationships as ways of liberating women from the demands of Confucian society; but his detractors, as discussed below, claimed that his romanticism was delusional if not harmful to women (figure 5). That same year Khái Hưng began collaborating with Nhất Linh to form the Self-Strengthening Literary Group. The Self-Strengthening group quickly emerged as pioneering authors, editors, and publishers of modern Vietnamese literature. They published *Phong hóa* (Customs) (1932–36) and *Ngày nay* (Today) (1936–40, 1945), weekly periodicals that emerged as important arenas of cultural production. The group's publishing endeavors had a profound influence on modern Vietnam's burgeoning post-mandarin literary field. The Self-Strengthening members were the primary advocates for the Thơ mới, or New Poetry, movement, which broke away from Vietnam's thousand-year-old poetic tradition. They also helped revolutionize the honored tradition of autobiographical writing by publishing Nguyên Hồng's *Những ngày thơ ấu* (Days of childhood). Their publications played a significant role in the development of the reportage genre, the new mode of journalistic writing that gained significance and appeal for its ability to critique social reality.

One defining characteristic of Vietnam's modern poetic, autobiographical, and reportage genres is the use of the term *tôi* as the articulation of an individual's autonomy, interior depth, psyche, and self-consciousness. As suggested in the Hoài brothers' epigraph above, the term *tôi* is a definitive marker of modern Vietnamese poetry, signaling the sociocultural shift from Vietnamese collectivism toward Western-influenced individualism. The

Figure 5. Caricature of Khái Hưng. Published in *Loa*, August 1, 1935.

New Poetry lyricists were more concerned with their own subjectivity than with conventional form and content. The term *tôi* functioned as the linchpin for a subjective or lyrical voice no longer subsumed under established social or poetic orders.

Critics who address this imported perspective and its literary presence through the term *tôi* have made their claims through the genres of autobiography and reportage. In an introduction to the collected English translations of Vũ Trọng Phụng's reportage *Cơm thầy cơm cô* (Household servants), Tâm Lang's reportage *Tôi kéo xe* (I pull a rickshaw), and Nguyên Hồng's autobiographical *Những ngày thơ ấu* (Days of childhood), Greg Lockhart focuses on the term *tôi* to explain the social and cultural changes taking place in Vietnamese urban spaces during the 1930s. He argues that modernization transformed Vietnamese society from the traditional vertical orientation of the family and state to a democratically horizontal orientation of the renewed "political, social, and literary consciousness."[7] For example, the reportage writer Tâm Lang employs *tôi* to indicate self-reflexivity as he assumes the role of a rickshaw puller. The narrator's role-playing position blurs the line between the learned, narrating subject and the plebeian, narrated subject, forging a new type of social interaction.[8] For Lockhart, such interchangeable identities signal emerging "democratic-social" relations. He argues that the semantics and contexts of *tôi* shifted from the representation of passive "subjects" or "people" under a monarchy toward a representation of the working class and "the people" who could constitute a nation:

> At least loosely, old concepts of "I" and "people" were thus associated in a semantic field that was dominated by a sense of monarchy and moral hierarchy. And so with the monarchy destroyed, we have the implication of a democratic revolution in which the rise of the active "I" is associated with the rise of "the people" and the "nation," as well as "class."[9]

Lockhart describes the more "horizontal" social interactions and self-awareness as "democratic." However, his idealistic anticipation of the modern, atomistic subject not only attributes abstract autonomy and equality to the individualistic *tôi* but also obscures Confucianism's and French colonialism's structured systems of social differences—in particular, as will be discussed shortly, those of gender and class—that continue to affect and shape the individual.

Unlike Lockhart, David Marr takes a skeptical approach to individualism, claiming that it was at odds with the familial structures at the foundation of Vietnamese society.[10] Tracing the development of nascent individualism in twentieth-century Vietnamese intellectual history and cultural production, Marr takes Nguyên Hồng's autobiographical *Những ngày thơ ấu* as an exemplary text that merges individualism with the *tôi*—an unorthodox self-exploration in the genre of autobiography.

> Although many reviewers of *Những Ngày Thơ Ấu* have emphasized the social criticism inherent in Nguyên Hồng's description of traditional family customs and attitudes, most notably in relation to marriage and the inferior status of women, far more original and compelling it seems to me, is his sensitive evocation of a young boy growing up buffeted by emotions arriving

from many directions. . . . We feel we have come to know this street-wise kid
as an individual, in a way not achieved in Vietnamese literature before or
since.[11]

Marr goes on to discuss the use of *tôi* by this generation of writers: "Young
writers like Nguyên Hồng often employed words to startle readers into rethinking comfortable assumptions. We see this with their use of pronouns,
especially the first-person singular *tôi*." The use of *tôi* was common in 1930s
literature, yet for Marr, its oppositional stance against familial and state col-
lectives was too foreign and estranged to have a lasting effect, thus account-
ing for its "fragile, contested status."[12] He suggests that, as a Western concept,
individualism was too foreign and therefore too threatening for a society
rooted in collectivism.

Marr concludes his discussion about the first-person singular *tôi* thus:

> As it turned out, *tôi* failed to achieve the status of *moi* or *je* in French,
> although it remains important and can still be observed as a marker of indi-
> viduality in certain circumstances. . . . All in all, however, *tôi* was like a lusty
> adventurer who had accumulated partners in various ports, but then grown
> old without finding his true equal.[13]

His comparison of *tôi* to a traveler accurately captures the cross-cultural
migration of the first-person grammatical category. However, I want to
reconsider Marr's claim about *tôi*'s shortcomings, as well as his personifica-
tion of *tôi* as a "lusty adventurer." On the one hand, Marr's explanation of
the *tôi* as a failed presence begs for a more accurate assessment of the term's
linguistic nature. On the other hand, the claim that the *tôi* is a promiscuous male traveler demands more scrutiny for its gendered presumptions.
To see individualism as a passing phenomenon is to dismiss too quickly the
struggles between the individualistic self and the outer world. Moreover, it
is precisely the struggle to make sense of the self and the world through gendered subjectivity that is the central problem for Self-Strengthening novels.

Even though *Nửa chừng xuân* focuses on the heroine's individualistic
struggle,[14] the *tôi* is muted in this work, particularly when compared to the
literary genres discussed above. Despite critics' attribution of individualism as a theme in Self-Strengthening novels, these novels have third-person
omniscient narrators who do not refer to themselves as *tôi*. These narrators
are not named and do not enter the novelistic space and time as bodily characters. Neither the narrators nor the characters use the term *tôi* as a mode of
narration; it is employed primarily by characters in dialogue.

The *tôi*'s absence in Self-Strengthening novels is inconsistent with the
period's most significant literary developments and works, even those

published by the Self-Strengthening Literary Group. The New Poetry movement and its breakthrough first-person lyrical voice gained its initial momentum from the pages of the group's journal *Phong hóa* in 1932, and Nguyên Hồng's *Days of Childhood* was published serially in the group's journal *Ngày Nay* in 1938 to much acclaim for reworking the genre of autobiography through the first-person voice. Yet for all the accusations and characterizations of Self-Strengthening's overemphasis on individualism, the *tôi* was relatively absent in their novels, particularly in their most well-known and most scrutinized works. Why is the first-person *tôi* not present in their novels? Why did Self-Strengthening novelists not have their narrators or characters embody the *tôi* in order to promote the social consciousness found in reportage writing? Or to express the personal desires and passions of New Poetry? Or to underscore the individualism implicit in the first-person utterances of Nguyên Hồng's autobiographical voice? I contend that the answers to these questions lie in the post-mandarin turn toward the prosaic in the novelistic genre. Self-Strengthening novels, particularly Khái Hưng's *Nửa chừng xuân,* presuppose a world ordered by everyday sociolinguistic structures embedded in language, and female speakers, such as Mai, cannot sidestep the sociolinguistic structures of Vietnamese society to take on an autonomous subjectivity.

In *Translingual Practice*, Lydia Liu offers a linguistic approach to first-person narratives that conceptualizes the formation of subjectivity through language without taking European languages as the universalizing norm. She invokes Émile Benveniste's claim that subjects are formed through language and discourse due to the shifting, deictic characteristics of personal pronouns. Benveniste has shown that each utterance of "I" only refers to the moment of speech: "*I* can only be identified by the instance of discourse that contains it and by that alone. It has no value except in the instance in which it is produced. But in the same way it is also as an instance of form that *I* must be taken; the form of *I* has no linguistic existence except in the act of speaking in which it is uttered."[15] Benveniste's theory on the deictic qualities of the first person draws attention to "language's empty place markers, particularly the personal pronouns," which are occupied by an individual speaker's position.[16]

Liu engages with Benveniste for several reasons. On a general level, the French linguist's work on the first-person pronoun has had a profound influence on contemporary theory's focus on the formation of the subject through language, particularly through the grammatical category of the first person. At a more specific level, she observes that Benveniste's universalizing claims about language and subjectivity are based on European languages and their inflected grammar.[17] Taking this as her point of departure, Liu highlights the differences between noninflected and inflected languages: "Not all languages privilege the personal pronouns as a primary deictic category. For instance, what about those non-inflected languages that do not resort to conjugation and do not always emphasize the importance of personal pronouns?"[18] These differences are significant precisely because the grammatical category of the first person has crossed linguistic boundaries from inflected to noninflected grammatical systems, from Indo-European to Asian languages, and most pertinent to the present discussion, from French to twentieth-century Vietnamese.

Liu claims that "deictic constructions [of modern vernacular Chinese fiction] no longer reflect a purely linguistic reality that Benveniste identifies in inflected languages, but offer themselves up as *literary tropes* that cut across linguistic boundaries. They are deictic tropes, so to speak, of gender, subjectivity, time, and space that are constructed as such to represent the Chinese experience of the modern while never ceasing to make reference to non-Chinese languages and literature."[19] But whereas Liu considers the abstract, deictic characteristics of the first-person pronoun as translated literary tropes, this chapter takes a pragmatic approach to examine the relationship between the Vietnamese first person and the larger contexts of sociolinguistic structures—the relationship between the utterances of an individual's speech and macrosociological contexts. Within a pragmatic framework, as Wittgenstein has suggested, language is not reduced to the grammatical properties of the first-person singular pronoun but rather is a medium of social practice.[20] The term *tôi* is one of many person-reference forms in the Vietnamese language that are linked to broader social contexts and structures. In the Vietnamese colonial context, I would argue, the formation of the subject was no longer based on universalized European languages. Instead, it was premised on the disjuncture between the European cultural paradigm framed by the first-person grammatical category and the Vietnamese sociolinguistic system, with its pragmatic functions of person-reference forms, particularly kinship terms.

The Vietnamese language's complex person-reference system of kinship terms denotes the hierarchies of the Confucian social order beyond one's immediate family.[21] The most obvious and popular example of Vietnamese speakers using a kinship term in reference to a nonrelative is "Bác Hồ" (short for "Uncle Ho Chi Minh").[22] One's relationship to a family member—with respect to seniority, age, gender, and marital status—extends to the social realm. Therefore, speakers who are not genealogically related use kinship terms ubiquitously. In his insightful *Discursive Practices and Linguistic Meanings*, Hy Văn Lương discusses the interconnected relationship between Vietnamese kinship terms and social structures. Notice here the deemphasis of the deictic qualities of pronouns.

> The pervasive use of kinship and "status" terms for person reference—terms which transcend the here-and-now and shifting reference nature of personal pronouns—constantly highlights the supposedly stable and hierarchical nature of social relations in the system. In other words, the organic unity framework emphasizes the paramount importance of the collectivist orientation of individual members toward sociocentric rules—rules which supposedly transcend individual membership and to which members' conformity contributes to the survival and prosperity of the organic whole.[23]

Given the relationship between the linguistic web of kinship terms and non-genealogical relations, personal pronouns are used less frequently than kinship terms in Vietnamese person reference. In most cases, personal pronouns in the Vietnamese language negate solidarity, deference, and formality—making ambiguous the social differences reproduced by language.[24] Therefore, as a nonkinship term often associated with individualism, *tôi* appears to be exempt from the organic web of social relations predicated on kinship relations.

Nevertheless, the term *tôi* is still deeply connected to a linguistic system marked by social differentiation and hierarchies. Almost without exception, the modern individualistic *tôi* has been translated as if it were synonymous with the French *je* or *moi* or the English "I" or "me." This translation pattern, which continues today, presupposes that the Vietnamese first-person grammatical category has an equivalent Western counterpart.[25] Initially, the term *tôi* was not a pronoun but a common noun meaning "subject-of-the-king."[26] Although the modern *tôi* is a nonkinship term that denotes individualism, it does not signify an abstract subject—formed, as Benveniste suggests, at an instance of utterance—exempted from collective identity or social relations. Contrary to its modern resemblance to *je* or "I," it pairs up with other kinship terms or status terms—not other pronouns. Hy Văn Lương notes that "the term *tôi/tui* ('subject-of-the-king') in its self-referring use co-occurs not with any of the second-person pronouns *mày, mi*, and *bay* [toi/you], but only with other common nouns."[27] *Tôi* does not follow a first- and second-person pattern between a subject pronoun and an object pronoun, as expected in French or English in such constructions as "I" and "you"; rather, it matches up with other nouns, particularly kinship terms. For example, a middle-aged man using *tôi* when addressing a younger woman could refer to her as *cô*, a common noun that primarily means "paternal aunt," specifically, the younger sister of one's father. Thus *cô*'s secondary meaning, used beyond familial circles, refers to a young woman and can function as the prefix to a young woman's proper name. This kinship term suggests age and gender disparities between the male addressor and female addressee, and both speakers must be mindful of these differences.

Given the inextricable relationship between the term *tôi* and the Vietnamese sociolinguistic web, a pragmatic approach is necessary to examine how the Vietnamese forms of self-reference structure and reproduce the power relations and differences of the colonial period and how this translates in Khái Hưng's modern novelistic world. The author employs the genre of the novel to represent, in Pierre Bourdieu's words, the "relationship between the structured systems of sociologically pertinent linguistic differences and the equally structured systems of social differences."[28] The female protagonist of *Nửa chừng xuân* is inscribed in a world of prose, where the individualistic self must discursively relate herself to and against others and utterances of *tôi* that assume autonomous individualism are impossible. The novel situates the heroine in the everyday pragmatics of language so as to reinforce the complex disjuncture of sociolinguistic forms of address. This is a form of the prosaic turn in the post-mandarin novel but specifically toward sociolinguistic structures. Her agency in language reflects, as Tanabe and Tokita-Tanabe have argued, non-European women's agency in socio-communal interactions.

> Women can assume critical perspectives on the present social relations with a reflexive mind, and develop a body of practice embedded in socio-communal interactions at the same time. They seem to negotiate their positions through both reflexive self-liberation and embedded/embodied self-fulfillment. Here the agency of women is achieved not by liberating individuals from the community as is often assumed. Rather, there is an opening of new possibilities of action precisely through shaking and loosening conceptual dichotomies such as individual:community. The embodied person with critical reflexivity in the context of social relationships neither simply abandons the community nor just remains embedded there.[29]

Khái Hưng's novel opens with the death of a Confucian scholar, who leaves his daughter, Dương Thị Mai, the novel's protagonist, responsible for her younger brother, Huy. With her mother long deceased, Mai must now see to it that her brother finishes his education. But given the family's depleted fortune, this task proves difficult. She tries to sell the family estate to a landowner in a neighboring province. Attracted to Mai, the landowner tries to strong-arm the young woman into a different sort of agreement—that she become his concubine in exchange for financial support. Prior to

her visit with the landowner, Mai had run into Lộc, one of her father's former students. Upon learning about Mai's predicament and the landowner's coerciveness, he moves Mai and Huy into a Hanoi apartment and pays
for Huy's tuition. The altruistic relationship between Lộc and Mai soon
becomes an intimate one. As the couple's love continues to blossom, Lộc
convinces a woman to stand in as his mother in order to stage a matrimo-
nial ceremony. The couple consummates the supposed marriage, and Mai
becomes pregnant.

But, as Lộc had anticipated, his biological mother refuses to allow him to
marry a fatherless and impoverished woman. To ensure the failure of Lộc's
relationship with Mai, the mother visits and chastises Mai for compromising
her son's future marital prospects with the daughter of a province chief. The
mother also leads Mai to believe that she speaks on her son's behalf. After
this visit, Mai and her brother move out of Lộc's apartment. The brother and
sister fall back into financial despair. Convinced by his mother that Mai is an
adulterous woman, thus an unworthy wife, Lộc proceeds with the arranged
marriage. Meanwhile, Mai gives birth to their son. Out of loyalty to Lộc,
she also rejects both the financial and amorous advances of various men.
Five years pass, and Lộc becomes a high-ranking civil servant. During this
time, his legitimately married wife has yet to give birth to a son. The disap-
pointed grandmother tries to wean the child from Mai and take him back to
the patriarchal home, but Mai defiantly resists. Lộc finally becomes aware of
his mother's manipulation and learns that she thwarted his relationship with
Mai. In an attempt to revive his relationship with Mai, he proposes three
scenarios: (1) that she become his second wife; (2) that they remain apart
in order to preserve their past love; or (3) that they run away together. Mai
chooses the second option, encouraging Lộc to be mindful of his lawful wife
and to act selflessly.

The heroine's decision to respect Lộc's relationship with his legal wife has
prompted critics to characterize her as selfless, idealistic, and naive. Moreover, since she puts aside her personal desires and sentiments, the love
between the two transcends to a realm of idealism.[30] Critics therefore con-
clude that the novel's protagonist, like the story's ending, fails to address
adequately the conflict between the individual and the family that lies at
the heart of the novel. Myopically focused on Mai's ideal character traits,
critics have ignored *how* Mai rejects traditional values and expectations:
through different forms of linguistic self-reference. As a result, they have
also overlooked one of the novel's key themes: language and its relationship
to the changing sociohistorical contexts of colonial Vietnam, particularly
the changes in educational systems.

Mai and Lộc come from two different systems of indoctrination: Confucianism and European thought, respectively. Although Mai's wretched financial situation began with the death of her father, a Confucian scholar, he had convinced her that a person can cultivate himself or herself through Confucianism—but without the *lễ nghi* (rituals) or *hiếu* (filial piety). Meanwhile, Lộc espouses the Western individualistic paradigm as a means toward self-cultivation: "Since childhood, I [older brother] have been Western-educated; my mind has absorbed Western ideologies. I [older brother] understand, I [older brother] am fond of . . . I [older brother] appreciate the value, the right of individualistic freedom."[31] Mai, however, realizes that despite Lộc's Western education, he cannot escape the profound influences of Confucianism. Lộc understands Confucianism as a monolithic tradition that, contradicting his European education, hampers his individualism. The male character's wholesale dismissal of Confucianism reveals his ignorance of Confucianism as a set of social practices that—enacted through rituals and reinforced through language—forced individuals, particularly young women like Mai, to conform to a social hierarchy structured on kinship relations. Khái Hưng and his fellow members of the Self-Strengthening group believed that Confucianism's ability to dictate the behavior and beliefs of individuals had been ingrained in Vietnamese society and in individual psyches. Unlike Lộc's tenuous claims that a European education allowed him to escape the collective mind-set of Confucianism—as if it were merely an intellectual paradigm—the novel's heroine, as well as the Self-Strengthening authors, grapples with rituals and language that determined social order. Lộc's idealization of Western individualism does not account for the social effects of Confucianism for both him and his mother. For example, his self-references during this discussion on the "right of individualistic freedom" reveal that he still operates within the sociolinguistic structures based on familial relationships. He employs the familial term *anh* [older brother] while discussing individualistic freedom. Although the term is commonly used by a male speaker in an intimate relationship with a woman, it denotes an older brother and implicates Mai, the addressee, as *em,* or a younger sibling.

As Mai suggests in her rebuttal, Confucian rituals and practices are not easily displaced by one's formal education because they are inculcated into one's very being.

> But all the principled rituals in Confucianism have barely flashed through your intellectual mind, though for your mother they have been sown into her psyche, blended into her blood vessels. . . . You have been influenced by the Western spirit, Western pedagogy since childhood, but you are still constrained within the boundaries of Confucianism. There is not much more to

say. It is the word "piety" that prevents you from taking pleasure in our love. Because we have to follow the rituals, we have to place the word "love" below the word "piety," but "love" and "piety" are words we barely understand, or perhaps we have no choice but to try to understand them.[32]

Lộc's mother dogmatically believes that Confucian rituals are necessary in everyday life, and in turn, her belief in rituals is perpetuated by the son's filial obligations to fulfill his mother's wishes. Consequently, ritualistic form and filial piety take precedence over the couple's emotions and desire for each other, disrupting the relationship. Lộc's Western education has resulted in his avowal of individualism, yet he is blind to the social forces of Confucianism that would ruin his relationship with Mai. The conflicting perspectives on individualism are linked to gender, particularly to the differences in the educational privileges of the male and female characters. Unlike Lộc's hypocritical embrace of individualism and his uncritical submission to Confucianism, Mai's position as a woman—excluded from a Western education while being held to the gendered expectations of Confucian tradition—forces her to negotiate her position within traditional social structures.

Mai concludes her counterpoint to Lộc's idealized notions of Western individualism by emphasizing language's ability to set the order of things: "Because we have to follow the rituals, we have to place the word 'love' below the word 'piety,' but 'love' and 'piety' are words we barely understand, or perhaps we have no choice but to try to understand them." In the context of the novel, words are spoken for the sake of being spoken, just as rituals are performed for the sake of being performed—even when their meanings are emptied out. Both language and rituals dictate one's behavior, position, and mind-set. Language, then, like rituals, enforces and reproduces order. As Hy Văn Lương has noted, this is fundamental to the Confucian notion that language, particularly names and titles, must be in accordance with social hierarchies.[33] The interrelationship of the structured system of language and the equally structured Confucian social order is precisely where Mai wages the struggle between her subjective views and orthodox Confucianism; this struggle thus becomes the novel's focal point.

Throughout the novel, characters are measured and judged by their *ngôn ngữ* (language). How a character speaks determines not only his or her identity but also his or her legitimacy and relationship in regard to others. This is apparent in a scene where Mai tries to resolve the family's financial problems. The family's financial problems begin with the changes in the educational system from the traditional mandarin system to the French colonial system. Not only does her father's career as a Confucian scholar go into decline, but the family's problems are compounded by the financial demands of her brother's French education. Mai has little choice but to try to sell the family estate to a wealthy landowner, the only person in the province who can afford the land. A pasty, overweight man with a pointed mustache, Nguyễn Thiết Thanh comes from the old socioeconomic order: the feudalistic practices of landownership and polygamy. During the negotiations, the landowner becomes attracted to Mai and tries to coerce her into his familial order as his third wife.

The person-reference forms throughout the scene at first establish the differences in age and gender between Mai and Thanh. But as the landowner tries to seduce the heroine, he narrows the age gap through different kinship terms, terms that Mai refuses to use or acknowledge. The awkwardness of the situation brings Mai to tears, and the landowner asks:

—*Why* are you [*em*] crying?

Mai saw Thanh standing next to her [*mình*], and immediately backed up. Mai pretended to smile—a smile that was more painful than tears—and replied with a stutter:

—Dear *cụ* . . .

—Dear *ông*, dear *mình* . . .

—Dear *ông*. I [*tôi*] think of my father, and so I [*tôi*] am crying.

Thanh pretends to miss the old teacher:

—It's a shame that the old man is no longer here to celebrate his daughter's new status as gentry.

After a moment of thought, Thanh looks at Mai with a smile and says:

—So I [*tôi*] will give you [*cô*] a thousand right now so that *cô*, so that *em* will have some capital, and *em* will just have to counterfeit a promissory note for the house and land, to trick the rest of the world, to be paid next June. . . . And then . . . next June . . . and I [*tôi*] will draft another contract for *em*, for *cô* . . . . Do you [*cô*] think this will work?

—Dear *cụ*, *cụ* should let *cháu* go home to think about this.

—What's there to think about? It's only a piece of paper, *cô* just needs to write down a few words, and that's it—right, *cô*?

Mai comes up with a plan, a delay tactic:

—Dear *cụ*, I [*cháu*] am illiterate.

—Just use the romanized alphabet.

—I [*cháu*] don't know the romanized alphabet either.[34]

In this brief exchange between the two characters, there are a total of nine different person references: seven kinship terms—*cụ, ông, con, bà, cô, em, cháu*—and two nonkinship common nouns—*mình, tôi* (the translations of the nine references are discussed below). Both Thanh and Mai employ an array of person references to establish, undermine, and reestablish different social frames. The passage begins with Thanh addressing Mai as *em*, which, as a gender-neutral term, has the primary meaning of younger sibling or cousin—but it is also commonly used by a husband to refer to his wife. In this context, the landowner is using the term to imply future intimacy with Mai. The heroine, however, distances herself by using the term *cụ*, which as a gender-neutral kinship term denotes great-grandfather or great-grandmother and in extrafamilial contexts connotes a person of elderly, respectable age and status. This is the same term used by the landowner in reference to Mai's father. Mai's use of the term casts Thanh as a man of her father's stature and age, subtly suggesting that the generational difference should discourage the possibility of marriage. In response, Thanh tries to revive the romantic possibilities by eschewing the fatherly associations through self-references other than *cụ*. Saying, "Thưa ông, thưa mình" ("Dear *ông*, dear *mình*"), he tries to correct Mai's person references. Although the primary meaning of *ông* is grandfather, the word connotes a gentlemanly status. Unlike *cụ*, however, the term *ông* has extrafamilial connotations that allow the landowner to replace the fatherly association with a nobler image. In singular constructions, the term *mình* refers to the self, its literal meaning. In plural contexts the term refers to a collective, often an intimate one that includes addressor and addressee. Thanh, by uttering the term, assumes an intimate bond with Mai. Moreover, the landowner's use of *tôi* is quite cunning. At first it allows him to keep a distance, to appear businesslike. Once he tries to seduce the younger woman, the term neutralizes the difference in age between him and Mai. He does not have to refer to himself as *cụ*, which is Mai's term of address for him.

Similarly, Mai at first uses the term *tôi*, but once the landowner makes his advances, she switches to the term *cháu*, which has a range of meaning: grandchild, niece, nephew, or children. The latter self-reference suggests that Mai is too young and naive to participate in marital discussions. For both speakers the neutrality and egalitarianism connoted by *tôi* fail to represent their social differences. Assuming the advantageous position afforded by his social and financial capital, the landowner cunningly experiments with person-reference forms, knowing that his attempts at seduction through language will cost him little social capital. Meanwhile, Mai's vulnerability and predicament necessitate the manipulation of language. It is not *tôi* but the kinship terms that the characters jockey over. Linguistically, *tôi* does not pair up with a pronoun but rather with a kinship term: *tôi/cô; tôi/ cụ; tôi/em; tôi/ông*. Mai uses language in order to disrupt the social structure at large and the marriage system at its foundation.

In her attempts to elude the patriarch's polygamous arrangement, Mai takes advantage of the landowner's assumptions about women's illiteracy. When the landowner asks her to draft a contract, she lies about her inability to write in character-based script. The landowner is not surprised when Mai claims that she cannot read (which is untrue, since she studied with her father). The landowner then suggests that she draft an agreement using the romanized alphabet, hoping that Mai is versed in this new written language. However, Mai quickly defuses this possibility by again lying about her literacy. Though he had just assumed that Mai should be able to use the romanized alphabet, Thanh does not question Mai's second lie because he does not know whether a woman in Mai's position should, given the changes in language and educational system of the time, be literate or illiterate. Mai uses her position—at the post-mandarin threshold of linguistic and educational transformation during the French colonial period—to delay the marriage proposal indefinitely, excusing herself from the landowner's house. Mai is exluded from the processes of modernization, yet she reveals the contradictions and disjuncture of colonial modernity. Moreover, she shrewdly evades the dichotomy of the lingering Confucian gender norms and colonial modernity's circumscribed possibilities. Thanh's presumptions about Mai's linguistic competence are predicated on social differences of gender and education—that is, the literacy of men and the illiteracy of women as a result of their exclusion from the educational system. Meanwhile Mai's linguistic trickery hinges on generational and educational differences—those who are educated in the romanized script (Mai) and those who are not (Thanh). In both instances, language gains value from structured systems of social differences.

Throughout the novel, characters are constantly shifting to different forms of person reference either to frame or to reframe an established social situation. They have no choice but to take part in language's reproduction of social relations. There is, however, one exception: Ái, Mai's young son. The name Ái is deceptive here, due to its multiple meanings and uses. At a semantic level it means "love" when paired with other words. For example, the most common construction is *ái tình*, which means "love" or "passion." Therefore, it seems that the name Ái reaffirms his identity as the product of Lộc and Mai's love. But this is not the term's only significance. When not coupled with any other term to form a compound word, *Ái* is an onomatopoeia that, as defined in Vietnamese-language dictionaries, imitates the sudden

cry of someone shocked by surprise or pain. When this secondary significance is taken into consideration, the child's name stands in contradistinction to other Vietnamese forms of person reference because it does not place
him in any social order.[35] The name, an imitation of a sound, is befitting for
the child since he is educated in the modern, romanized alphabet and thus
sheltered from the patriarchal sociolinguistic structures particular to Confucian Vietnam. His initiation, however, into the extant linguistic order and
its social implications is inevitable.

Once Mai's brother graduates and finds work as a schoolteacher, the sib-
lings, along with the child, enjoy a stable life. This amounts to an unconven-
tional family comprising an unwed mother, a single man, and a fatherless
child. The alternative family isolates the child, now a toddler, from the patriarchal social and linguistic structures.

All of this, however, changes when *bà* Án, Lộc's mother, arrives at their
home in an attempt to bring the child back as the male heir to her son. To
accomplish her goals, the grandmother must choose her words carefully and
appropriately. At first, she must address her son's former lover and child—
both considered illegitimate—so as not to disclose her brash intentions, but
eventually she must speak in a manner that pragmatically implies that Mai
is her daughter-in-law and Ái her grandson. This provokes anxiety for *bà*
Án, particularly when she asks the brother, Huy, about Mai's whereabouts.

Bà Án pondered a bit. She wanted to ask about Mai, but she did not know
how to address her. To call her *bà tham* or *bà huyện* would be awkward,
and she was afraid Huy would laugh. But to call her *cô* would be inappropriate. There was little else to talk about, and Huy leaned against a chair,
silent and staring. Suddenly, *bà* Án found a term of address she deemed
appropriate, and immediately raised her voice to ask:

—Sir, did *lệnh tỉ* step outside?[36]

The social footing here is slippery, making it hard for the elderly woman
to find the appropriate term of address. She immediately wants to associ-
ate Mai with Lộc, mentally considering the term *bà*. Its primary meaning is
grandmother, but it can also denote a madam or lady. Here, the term would
act as a gender prefix to her son's title as a high-ranking civil servant (*tham*,
short for *tham biện*) or district chief (*huyện*), designating Mai as Lộc's wife,
the wife of a public official. This form of reference is inappropriate for the
grandmother, because it would also place her in a position of lower status
than her son's former lover—drawing ridicule from Mai's brother. But to
call her *cô*, a more conventional term (as seen in the passage above with the
landowner), would imply a more distant, nonfamilial relationship. Unlike

Mai's use of language as subversion, the elderly woman uses language to preserve the existing social order. After a moment of awkward silence, she finds
an appropriate but outdated term of address: *lệnh tỉ*, which literally means
"your respectable older sister." Although this term denotes a familial relationship, its connotations are formal and nonthreatening because it is outdated. By using an anachronistic term, *bà* Án does not reveal her intention
to imply a familial relationship with Mai, while she does maintain appropriate degrees of respectability.

Bà Án experiences the greatest difficulties in forging a relationship with
the child. Even though there is a genealogical connection, the child has
never met her. She must somehow overcome their estrangement and bring
him into the linguistic fold. When the grandmother first sees the child, he
is pretending to be a car, making onomatopoetic horn noises, "Bí bo! Bí
bo."[37] The child takes on the identity of the sounds' referent, *ô-tô*, which
is a transliteration of *auto*, short for automobile—a symbol of modernization: "Excuse me! The auto [*ô-tô*] is blowing its horn, get out of the
way."[38] The child's self-appellation, *ô-tô*, draws parallels to the first-person
grammatical category in two ways: not only does the term's etymological root, "self," suggest self-constitution but it also points to Western, particularly Greek, origins. Nevertheless, the grandmother plays along and
says, "Such an obedient auto! Let me give it a kiss now."[39] Although the
grandmother follows the child's linguistic footing, the child rebuffs her
affection. He chastises her for taking literally his onomatopoetic noises
and for personifying an automobile: "Auto? An obedient auto? When is an
auto ever kissed!"[40] *Bà* Án employs the wrong figures of speech, even when
she enters the child's imaginary world. In this instance, the grandmother
does not try to impose a genealogical relationship through a kinship term,
instead calling him by his own self-reference. Nevertheless, her attempts
at linguistic flexibility scare the child away. Their generational difference
makes them linguistically incompatible.

The child is acutely aware of the linguistic differences. As his uncle sits
with the elderly woman, the child wants to communicate his hunger in such
a manner that the stranger would not understand. He shyly tiptoes behind
his uncle and spells out his thoughts in romanized script, as if it were a foreign language, to exclude the woman from his thoughts.

—*O-h* u-n-c-l-e. . . . I a-m h-u-n-g-r-y.

The spelled-out message that the child thought was code made the guest
and homeowner laugh. *Bà* Án asked Huy:

—The child goes to school?

—Yes *cụ*, the child studies entirely in the romanized alphabet.

—The child is very good. . . . Ái, come over here with me.

But Ái remembered the guest's earlier actions and dared not approach her, timidly hiding behind his uncle.

—*Bà* is calling for Ái.

Bà Án heard Huy call her *bà* and took the term to mean the grandmother of a child. *Bà* was elated. Her cheeks turned red, and her eyes closed with laughter. Huy saw that the child was still hesitant to approach, and immediately led the child to *bà* Án.[41]

Despite the child's attempts to keep a linguistic and physical distance from *bà* Án, his uncle circumscribes him into a position of obligatory deference through the term *bà*. Although the term connotes an elderly woman who, beyond familial contexts, should be treated with deference, the woman understands the term in the most literal manner: biological grandmother. Taking her cue from Huy's term of address, she assumes that her role as the child's biological, paternal grandmother had been reestablished. Again, the legitimacy of the patriarchal home is recognized and organized by language. Once she has been sanctioned linguistically as grandmother, the child is forced into a behavior pattern appropriate for a respectful grandchild. In the same way that the individualistic *tôi* is not abstract or autonomous from the larger social structures, *Ái* is no longer exempt from the sociolinguistic order.

Although Ái is not exempt from the Confucian order, Mai strategically finds a way to manipulate language to provide for her son an alternative social order. The custody argument continues once Mai returns home. As it approaches an unfavorable ending for *bà* Án, she resorts to one last point of contention: the child's surname. She reasons that since Ái carries on his father's last name he belongs in his father's home: "My grandson bears my husband's family name, my son's family name."[42] The mother-in-law's claim is premised on the Confucian notion that names and titles determine the order of things. However, Mai had already given the son *her* family's last name, Dương—not the name of the child's father or grandfather. *Bà* Án views Mai's decision as blasphemy: "Is that how you teach him? How dare you teach my grandchild principles that violate religious, moral beliefs?"[43] According to the grandmother, family names do not merely suggest an association with one familial line or another, but the act of naming also has didactic implications. According to her way of thinking, to align a child with his patriarchal lineage is to teach a child proper behavior. Language not only dictates social order; it also molds a person's moral conscience and judgments. The occupants of specified names and roles (e.g., grandson, father, or son) must act according to "behavioral patterns constitutive of the definitions of these roles."[44]

By naming her son after the matrilineal line, Mai breaks away from the patrilineal norms and hierarchies. She resists the prescriptions of the patriarchal linguistic and social order. Her decision provides an alternative to this Confucian male collectivity, forging a different type of familial lineage, a different social formation for her son. She employs language to challenge effectively the male-oriented sociolinguistic order. Therefore, Mai is neither naive nor idealistic—in contrast to critics' claims—when she decides to remain separated from Lộc.

Caught in the radical transformations from Vietnamese collectivism to Western-influenced individualism, the protagonist challenges the social hierarchies and differences produced by the sociolinguistic structures of Vietnamese society while attempting to establish a social foothold as a female speaking subject. Although the cultural translation of Western individualism and its literary manifestation through *tôi* have been acknowledged as an indelible mark of Vietnamese modernity, the disparate realities, experienced especially by women, between Vietnamese sociolinguistic structures and Western individualism have been disregarded. As the foundational structures of Vietnamese society were being transformed, Mai's use of spoken language draws attention to language's ability to reflect and structure social hierarchies and differences while disrupting the idealistic conceptions of a Westernizing society. Mai's linguistic interpellations are neither complicit with masculine nationalist imaginations and their symbolization of the female figure, nor with the abstract understandings and appropriations of Western paradigms or modes of thought.

Mai's role as a novelistic speaking subject provides her with agency to resist and even subvert Vietnam's sociolinguistic order. The heroine reveals language's ability to produce social order in the novelistic writing of a male author, and her agency is circumscribed to the novelistic world as colloquial dialogue. The literary field in which Khái Hưng's *Nửa chừng xuân* was produced and published lacked such agency by women. Mai's relationship to language must be distinguished between the possibilities of colloquial language and her exclusion from written language.[45] As a modern novel focused on a woman at the threshold of modernization, Khái Hưng's *Nửa chừng xuân* replicates the gendered complexities at both the textual level and the institutional level of literary production—neither of which allowed for the feminine first-person narrative voice of *tôi*.

CHAPTER 5

Queer Internationalism and Modern Vietnamese Aesthetics

In 1928 Pierre Do-Dinh, a young Indochinese emigrant living in Paris, wrote to André Gide, asking for permission to translate *La porte étroite* (Strait is the gate) into Vietnamese. To justify his request, the aspiring translator made the following observations about the literature of colonial Annam, which consisted of the three eastern regions of French Indochina that today make up the nation of Vietnam:

> As you know, Annam is a French colony. Of all the countries in the Far East, it is most influenced by French culture. It is not rare to hear people speak of Victor Hugo or of Lamartine with great seriousness and precision . . . . But contemporary literature, I would not go so far as to specify modern literature, is completely ignored.
>
> We are belated. Do our contemporary writers have little chance of success? Are we impermeable to modern thought? I do not believe so. I believe, to the contrary, that insofar as it [modern thought] is preoccupied with the mystery of interiority, which reverberates in the anxieties and darkness of our subconscious, it is even nearer to us.[1]

For Do-Dinh, the contemporaneous formations of modern Vietnamese literature and French literature appear disjointed and asynchronous. It is Vietnam's presumed belatedness that compels him to contact Gide in the hope of translating his work.

Later, in 1939, Do-Dinh compared modern Vietnamese literature's belatedness to Homais, the philistine character in Flaubert's *Madame Bovary*. When introducing Vietnamese literature to a Western audience, Do-Dinh writes, "That from the West which appeals to the Annamite is the philosophy of Monsieur Homais and all the inferior, pretentious forms of Western life."[2] Do-Dinh's reference to Homais likens the cultural transmission from metropole to colony to that from city to province. In Flaubert's novel, ideas of art, fashion, love, and science flow from the urban center to the provincial outskirts, where they are received by unfit imitators like Homais. Thrown into sharp relief by the rigor of Flaubert's style, Homais, the pharmacist who cobbles together scientific information from unreliable journals and pamphlets, derives his ambitions as a reader and writer from dilettantish intellectualism. Convinced of Vietnam's cultural lag and the need for "modern thought," Do-Dinh completed and published his translation of Gide, who during the mid-1930s was emerging as one of the most influential contemporary French authors in colonial Vietnam.[3]

Do-Dinh's observations and speculations regarding Gide's significance in Vietnam raise a number of fundamental questions. How is the relevance of a modernist French writer of Gide's stature in Vietnam to be explained and characterized? Given the emergence of Vietnam's modern literature under French colonial rule, what are the literary forms and discourses that take shape as a consequence of modernity and modernism's cross-cultural transmission? Why did the contemporaneous formations of modern Vietnamese literature and French literature appear disjointed and asynchronous? Unlike Do-Dinh, I am not concerned with explaining or correcting the supposed shortsightedness of modern Vietnamese writers by taking French literature as the new, twentieth-century standard. Nor do I intend to appropriate modern Vietnamese literature to the paradigmatic category of European modernism. Colonial Vietnamese intellectuals' engagement with Gide exceeded Do-Dinh's assumption of belatedness. Indeed, Gide's significance for Vietnamese writers had more to do with the literary politics that stemmed from his idiosyncratic convergence of left-wing activism and sexual politics—which resonated with post-mandarin authors—than his modernist forms, style, or narrative techniques.[4]

By examining Vietnamese intellectuals' reception of Gide, I want to revisit the question of engagement between European modernists and colonial writers during the post-mandarin period. This chapter argues that through Gide's "queer internationalism"—an internationalism premised on same-sex politics—post-mandarin intellectuals found a suitable expression for the particularity of their post-mandarin condition and colonial predicament, particularly with regard to their masculinity. The male reserve of the literati had become transformed into a strained triangulation between the male native intellectual, the European male colonial, and the modern indigenous woman. As discussed in previous chapters, not only did post-mandarin intellectuals have to assert their authority through European forms of knowledge while adjusting to the demands of print capitalism, but the post-mandarin transformation of gender and sexuality compelled them to reflect on their own sexuality and masculinity. They did so by writing for and about women readers. I further examine the post-mandarin adaptation to the feminizing literary world by looking at literary works in which male authors pose as women writers and women readers. This post-mandarin masquerade leads to homoeroticism that, exceeding the boundaries of sexual heteronormativity, expresses a nonnormative desire. The articulation of nonnormative sexuality is a culmination of the various facets of the post-mandarin condition discussed thus far: how the shifting gender and sexual dynamics, compounded by masculine anxiety about the emergence of the modern Vietnamese woman, leads to the manifestation of a nonnormative identity. And to extend the significance of this argument, the particularity derived from Vietnam's specific post-mandarin condition took on the significance of a national literature and identity. Gide appealed to post-mandarin intellectuals because of his idiosyncratic combination of sexual and aesthetic politics—a combination at the basis of his cultural and political vision, the derivation of international universality from national particularity.

André Gide's influence on Vietnam was profoundly felt during the *Nghệ thuật vị nghệ thuật* (art for art's sake) versus *Nghệ thuật vị nhân sinh* (art for life's sake) debate, which, lasting from 1935 to 1939, was one of Vietnam's most significant literary exchanges during the interwar period. Readers of Anglo-European modernism will be familiar with how the debate played out on the continent.[5] In Vietnam, however, it turned out differently: both sides appropriated Gide's ideas of individual and national particularity, which, as discussed below, originate in his politics of homosexuality. The debate's interlocutors interrogated modern Vietnamese literature's purpose, as well as its content and form, while engaging with post–World War I literary discourses about the relationship between art and social reality, particularly their manifestations in Soviet cultural politics.[6]

Because of Vietnam's colonial relationship with France, Soviet cultural and aesthetic thought was first channeled through "French sensibilities and concerns" before reaching Annam.[7] For Vietnamese intellectuals, Gide was the most significant mediator of Soviet cultural aesthetics' circuitous route through Paris. He proposed a literary system based on particularity as a viable means of reaching "internationalism." Gide's conception of internationalism underscored a nation's sovereignty and interdependence with other nations rather than the transcendence of the particular that is central to models of modernism's transnational circulation, as well as paradigms of world literature.[8] Frantz Fanon has suggested the significance of national particularity in relation to internationalism: "It is at the heart of national consciousness that international consciousness establishes itself and thrives."[9] Likewise, modern Vietnamese writers aimed to reach an international universality through national particularity.

Although they embodied European knowledge, post-mandarin intellectuals were relegated to a circumscribed educational and intellectual world. Confined to these inferior parallel spheres, these intellectuals resembled European men—but were never to be European. This was a masculine difference premised on racial and cultural differences. But rather than view their situation as inferior, they understood it as a nonnormative particularity that—if realized in the form of nationalism—would assimilate into and redefine the universal. Post-mandarin authors envisioned a universalism that was "constitutively open to being affected by *other particulars* and, hence, by alterity and particularity in general."[10] Therefore, they turned to Gide for his sexual politics more than his class politics. Beyond communism's critique of objective material conditions, Gide's proposed interpolation of nonnormative sexuality and particularity appealed to Vietnamese intellectuals as they grappled with the inequalities and unevenness of colonial modernity.

At the 1935 International Writers' Congress for the Defense of Culture, Gide argued for the particularity of the nation and of the individual.[11] Serving as cochair, Gide opened the meeting by refuting fascism's suffocating grip on culture.

> There are, for people as for individuals, certain indices of particular refractions, and this is precisely the great interest of our cosmopolitan meeting: it allows us to understand the different aspects of these dangers, different ways of comprehending and confronting them. It is necessary to begin from this point: the culture that we aspire to defend is the sum of the particular cultures of each nation. This culture is our common good. It is common to all of us. It is international.[12]

Gide argued for the enunciation of the particularity of different cultures and individuals rather than a subordination of the particularistic perspective—what he called *désindividualisation*—to the interest of the masses. In his "Défense de la culture" speech to the International Writers' Congress, he reiterated his rallying cry for the "triumph of the general in the particular, of the human in the individual."[13] Envisioned as a system premised on the "refractions" of different cultures as well as individuals, Gide's international model was intended to counteract fascism's agenda of national supremacy, imperial aggression, and aesthetic censorship. According to Gide, national and individual particularity would flourish, respectively, under a system of internationalism and communism. Particularity and social collectivity mutually define each other: "For my part, I claim to be strongly internationalist while remaining intensely French. In like manner, I am a fervent individualist, though I am in full agreement with the communist outlook, and am actually helped in my individualism by communism."[14] For Gide, the free development and articulation of the individual can only be realized by the free development and articulation of all.

Gide went on to suggest that human universality is mediated through the literary aesthetics of the particular. He invoked individualism and nationalism together as if the shared attribute of particularity canceled out their differences. To substantiate these claims, the French author declared, "What could be more *particularly* Spanish than Cervantes, what more English than Shakespeare, more Russian than Gogol, more French than Rabelais or Voltaire—at the same time what could be more general and more profoundly human."[15] These exemplary authors managed to reach a level of human universality by particularizing their own personal individuality and capturing the specificity of their respective national cultures. Here, the most forceful literary expression of individual particularity is seen as congruent with national identity, which, in turn, transcends to a level of universality. Gide's insistence on the specificity and sincerity of individual expression meant that he repudiated most of nineteenth-century French literature, which he deemed artificial, decadent, bourgeois, and, ultimately, devoid of social significance.

Calling for an engaged cultural aesthetics, Gide wanted the literary author to be in perfect union with the masses and fully committed to a new reading public: "The only remaining possibility is to write for the unknown reader of the future." The author is not only to communicate with the new reader but also to help this unknown, future reader "form and project himself." For literature to accomplish this communion—as was, supposedly, the case in the Soviet Union—the writer must effectively address and engage with the reading public, creating a new, more inclusive community. With the division between high and low, elite and popular cultures dissolved, literature would then take on new social meaning as it fosters a radically new society. The aesthetics of the particular gains the political power of emancipation as it disrupts and reconstitutes the established social body.

All of the issues taken up by Gide—the relevance of literary tradition, the social role of the contemporary author, and a new reading public—were of immediate concern for post-mandarin writers and intellectuals confronted with the uncertain future of colonial modernity and the displacement of Vietnam's intellectual traditions. Within this cultural and intellectual milieu, the participants of Vietnam's art-versus-life debate argued over the direction and purpose of modern Vietnamese literature, drawing Gide into the fray. Attentive to his call for individual and national particularity, they echoed Gide's reconceptualized literary aesthetics concerning the destabilization of established hierarchies of aesthetic subject and forms, the address to and transformation of the masses, and the formation of a new collective ethos through individual expression. Thiếu Sơn, Hoài Thanh, and Lưu Trọng Lư were the main proponents of the *duy tâm chủ nghĩa* (idealist) position, while Hải Triều was the most impassioned voice of the *duy vật chủ nghĩa* (materialist) camp.

One of the earliest critics to advocate for a Western-influenced literature, Thiếu Sơn initiated the art-versus-life debate when he published an article titled "Hai quan niệm về văn học" (Two literary perspectives) and sided with Art for Art's Sake. He outlined Vietnamese literature's two paradigms: the first belonged to the previous generation of classical moralists who, still mired in Confucianism, doggedly viewed literature as a vehicle for didacticism and social obedience; the second emphasized and celebrated authorial creativity and self-expression. He identified the former literary perspective as "Eastern" and the latter as "Western." Thiếu Sơn claimed that within the Confucian framework literature had the primary purpose of cultivating a compliant subject in Vietnamese society's hierarchical structures. If, Thiếu Sơn feared, such use of literature carried over to the 1930s, a period when nationalist and socialist political parties were gaining traction, then ideological paradigms would function as blinders for writers and readers. For him, social or political proselytization through literature subordinated aesthetic form to political considerations while continuing Confucianism's authoritative use of literature. The most effective way to break from the instrumental use of literature was to develop an aesthetics derived from creative imagination and personal expression.

Thiếu Sơn advocated for an individual's liberation and self-realization. In his view, literature had the capacity to incite the sensibilities and conscience of ethically autonomous individuals, making way for a renewed social community and ultimately a renewed nation. He emphasized that creative imagination and personal expression were necessary if Vietnamese literature was to "rise" to the level of other national literatures: "Given the rules of evolution, Vietnamese literature will develop like the literatures of other nations."[16] Implicit in Thiếu Sơn's critique of Confucianism is an attack on French colonial cultural policies, which sought to stabilize Vietnamese society by buttressing its Confucian culture. The aesthetic experience should be independent of any ideological system, and art's social purpose and meaning are contingent on this autonomy and its role in the formation of individual subjects for a "more beautiful, more dignified world."[17]

In an immediate response, Hải Triều, one of the most ardent Marxist critics of the time and a member of the *duy vật chủ nghĩa* camp, dismissed Thiếu Sơn's dichotomy of East and West. He refuted the claim that only Eastern literature was socially engaged and pragmatic. It was not a matter of East or West for Hải Triều; it was literature's engagement with social reality, an engagement epitomized by realist fiction. Hải Triều defined art as a product of social life and as a means for social reform. To make his point, he provided myriad examples, including Dickens, Dostoevsky, Kuo Mo-jo, Maxim Gorky, the older Tolstoy, and Upton Sinclair. Writing in a bellicose tone, Hải Triều accused Thiếu Sơn of identifying subjective expression as art's sole purpose and telos while himself proclaiming the opposite—that art's natural trajectory worked toward social progress. He went so far as to announce the death of "impressionism, neoimpressionism, futurism, cubism, etc.," associating these movements with capitalism, which would, he predicted, come to an end in the twentieth century.[18] Dismissive of avant-garde movements, Hải Triều advocated for an aesthetic movement grounded in realism—a more pragmatic medium for social critique and reform. If Vietnamese literature were to develop in a meaningful way, then it had to thematize material conditions in order to mobilize the masses.[19] Otherwise, Hải Triều warned, authorial self-expression would result in saccharine, effeminate romance or psychological novels.

Hải Triều's stand against Thiếu Sơn established the debate's polar extremes: art as a pure and transcendental exercise versus art as a social and political practice. However, Hải Triều's accusation of self-indulgent, autonomous aesthetics obscured Thiếu Sơn's wish to overthrow the hierarchies endemic to precolonial aesthetics. Thiếu Sơn was concerned with replacing the thesis-driven *văn có ích* (pragmatic literature) with the more prosaic *văn chơi* (literature of leisure).[20] He wanted to democratize literature, to break down the barriers that separated the *quân tử* (scholarly gentry) from the *tiểu nhân* (commoners), who were all in service to the intellectual elites: "Because of that hierarchy, our past literature is a kind of cruel literature, a kind of privileged literature, with no pretensions of addressing the life, the situation, or the spirit of the common people."[21] Thiếu Sơn's advocacy for an aesthetics based on self-realization was an attempt to liberate authors from ideological confines and differences so that they could engage with the masses and form a community premised on a more universal conception of humanity rather than political or intellectual allegiances. Both Thiếu Sơn and Hải Triều agreed on the need to address wider reading audiences, but they were at odds about the type of literature that would most effectively do so: either a literature that emphasized individual expression and self-realization or a literature that represented and addressed the social masses.

The literary critic Hoài Thanh, famous for his writings on the significance of individualism in modern Vietnamese literature and another proponent of the *duy tâm chủ nghĩa* position, stepped in to reconcile the divide by arguing for the relationship between individualism and the social masses. He did so by excerpting Gide's "Défense de la culture" speech: "It is in being the most particular that each person most effectively serves a community."[22] Moreover, Hoài Thanh underscored and explained Gide's understanding of the compatibility between individualism and communism.

> Gide expresses his complete commitment to individualism. Individualism does not contradict communism, but rather individualism needs communism in order to reach complete fruition. The more an individual develops his character, the more the collective benefits, Gide claims. The same is true for each national culture: the more each enunciates its distinctiveness, the more mankind benefits.[23]

By introducing Gide into the debate, Hoài Thanh provided a reference point that was relevant to Thiếu Sơn's concerns for subjective expression as well as Hải Triều's demand for literature's political engagement.

For their main textual example, the interlocutors of Vietnam's art-versus-life debate focused on a popular 1935 collection of short stories, *Kép Tư Bền* (Tư Bền the actor), by Nguyễn Công Hoan, a prolific writer of realist, and later socialist realist, short stories and novels. *Kép Tư Bền* depicts a range of characters and social situations that reflect the rapid, often disorienting changes of modernity: educated or fashionable women who do not conform to familial expectations; the dual realities of the lower classes and urban elites; the diminishing filial piety between the nouveau riche and their parents. Hoài Thanh attributed the success of *Kép Tư Bền* to the "estranged style that Nguyễn Công Hoan meticulously worked into plots of nothing."[24] He argued that the collection's aestheticized style, as a formal element, takes precedence over the stories' realistic content. Accordingly, Nguyễn Công Hoan's privileging of style produced eternal aesthetic qualities rather than attending to the political urgencies of the time.

In a direct rebuttal of Hoài Thanh, Hải Triều proclaimed Nguyễn Công Hoan's collection of short stories one of the earliest manifestations of the Art for Life's Sake movement in Vietnam, praising the author as a writer not only of the people but also of the "wretched" (*khốn nạn*).[25] The critic favored the representation of characters toiling in the decrepit underside of urban, colonial life—from rickshaw pullers to petty thieves. According to Hải Triều, the stories provide an accurate cross section of Vietnamese society, exposing the inequalities of everyday life. Hải Triều considered the collection at the forefront of Vietnamese realism,[26] attributing its aesthetic merit to Nguyễn Công Hoan's subject matter and content: his representation of the lower classes and thus his engagement with the reading public. Hải Triều explained the value and power of such art: "The sentiments of art do not derive from any one individual, but precisely from the synthesis of social sentiments. When an artist presents any sentiment on a piece of paper or a stone . . . there is the intention for each person in society to see and to feel."[27] Influenced by Nikolai Bukharin's and Tolstoy's aesthetic ideas, Hải Triều viewed literature as an effective means to "socialize sentiments" or to "emotionally infect" readers.[28] For Hải Triều, Nguyễn Công Hoan had created a literature in which content derived from and engaged with the social. He stressed that this type of realist literature was part of the Art for Life's Sake movement then gaining momentum worldwide, in part through its broad appeal to the masses.[29]

Evident in his praise of *Kép Tư Bền*, Hải Triều wanted literature to aspire to universal and equal representation. This ideological and aesthetic position was the seed of his future advocacy for socialist realism; however, his later views of literature were strikingly less inclusive and more orthodox—calling for literature to focus strictly on the working class. In his discussions of critical and socialist realism, Hải Triều specified the type of characters that should populate realist works: "In discussions of social or popular literature there is only mention of beggars, orphans, rickshaw pullers, thieves, or prostitutes. There is no representation, no observation, no mention of the most important class, the class that is most exploited now, the class that will lay the foundation for a new society, namely, the working class."[30] Hải Triều contradicted himself. The character types that he dismissed in favor of the working class are the very characters he had lauded in *Kép Tư Bền* when arguing for realist literature as the appropriate medium for Art for Life's Sake.[31] He initially praised *Kép Tư Bền* for its representation of the "wretched"—not its representation of the working class.[32] In this respect, Hải Triều first qualified *Kép Tư Bền* as a pioneering work of Art for Life's Sake for its democratic representation of social characters. His ordination of Nguyễn Công Hoan's *Kép Tư Bền* as one of the inaugural moments of Vietnam's Art for Life's Sake movement precedes the stringent guidelines of socialist realism that would become dominant in the late 1930s and ultimately gain state sanction after the August Revolution of 1945. In his discussions of *Kép Tư Bền*, Hải Triều's exaltation of the egalitarian and objective approach to social types had yet to conform to Vietnamese socialist realism's moralistic tendencies, including the denouncement of literary representation of prostitutes and thieves.

Hải Triều's initial interest in literature's democratic possibilities, as opposed to a magnified focus on the working class, is evident in one of the debate's slight but consistent undercurrents: allusions to the law of equivalence in Flaubert's aesthetics. Hải Triều's reference to Flaubert is a decontextualized misreading that favors democratization of literary content over class politics. Unlike Do-Dinh's use of Homais to convey a sense of belatedness, Hải Triều cites Flaubert to argue that art and social life should constitute each other: "I believe in Form and Content[,] . . . two entities that would not exist without the other."[33] Although the quote supports Hải Triều's claim that content and form are interdependent, the line's context, an ongoing correspondence with George Sand, suggests the opposite. Flaubert had declared to Sand his aesthetic credo to pursue beauty above all else.[34] With some similarities to Hải Triều, Sand encouraged Flaubert to "maintain [his] worship of form, but be more concerned with content," and to instill in his readers a sense of morality through ethically "good" literary characters.[35] Hải Triều mistook Flaubert's aesthetics, suggesting that his focus on social content determined his literary form. On the contrary, Flaubert's *suprême impartialité*, to borrow Sand's term, sought to nullify the opposition between form and content through his writing style. Flaubert was indifferent to content and thus stylized and aestheticized all content under a law of democracy and equivalence.[36]

By contrast, when discussing *Kép Tư Bền*, Hoài Thanh ascribed to Nguyễn Công Hoan Flaubert's ambitions to aestheticize everything and thus to write about nothing.[37] Hoài Thanh exalted Nguyễn Công Hoan's prioritization of an "estranged" style and its entwinement with "plots of nothing."[38] Meanwhile, to punctuate his call for the pure aesthetic experience disconnected from any pragmatic function, Thiếu Sơn quoted Flaubert, emphasizing the author's principle of pure art: "Occasionally, I sense a spiritual state that transcends reality."[39] The quote corroborates Thiếu Sơn's opening argument that an author is omniscient yet transcendent in his work, not imparting personal ideologies or predilections.[40] In Flaubert, Thiếu Sơn found the epitome of an authorial, transcendent self-expression that provides the absolute sensation of an aesthetic experience, when art "skillfully allows for readers to see as if looking, to hear as if listening."[41] For Thiếu Sơn and Hoài Thanh, Flaubert's allure was his *suprême impartialité*—his indifference to, respectively, ideological biases and content. The political impetus of equality translates into the literary democratization of subject matter, form, and readership.

Central to the art-versus-life debate, these egalitarian approaches to subject matter, as well as arguments for an author's personal writing style, hinged on an unspoken queerness—both in Gide's political agenda and in Nguyễn Công Hoan's collection of short stories. Gide's homosexuality was an open secret in Vietnam at the time, and the politics of particularity that made Gide relevant for these Vietnamese thinkers derived from the politics of this unspoken queerness. Consider, for example, writings on Gide by Hoài Thanh and the poet Lưu Trọng Lư. Hoài Thanh discusses Gide's homosexuality obliquely. He comments on Gide's "desire" (*lòng ham muốn*) while emphasizing Gide's physical attributes and tics to suggest a natural yet repressed sexual energy. Gide is a person of "strength" (*khỏe mạnh*), "restless energy" (*bứt rứt khó chịu*), with the "inclinations to run and jump" (*ưa chạy nhảy*); such a person is bound to feel hemmed in by "walls" (*bức tường*).[42] Further employing coded language, Hoài Thanh claims that Gide made a commitment to the Communist Party less out of political conviction than the desire to liberate himself from "his aristocratic inclinations, the inclinations that have since betrayed his natural self. His inclinations toward the people offer a new world, an infinite amount of resources still untouched by literature."[43]

Lưu Trọng Lư also drifts into coded language about sexuality while defending Gide's about-face and critical writings against the Soviet Union— *Retour de l'URSS* (Return from the USSR) and *Retouches au retour de l'URSS* (Afterthoughts on the USSR)—in a 1939 essay, "Con đường riêng của trí-thức" (An intellectual's own path). The Vietnamese lyricist describes Gide's personal path as "alternative" and "discreet" (*một cách khác, lặng lẽ*).[44] According to Lưu Trọng Lư, Gide is an intellectual who aimed for the realization of the "truth" (*sự thực*) and "potential from within" (*sức tiềm-tàng ở trong mình*). He explains Gide's allegiance to communism more as a commitment to "humanity" (*lòng nhân đạo*) than as a narrowly ideological stance. In order to understand the efficacy of Gide's communism, Lưu Trọng Lư continues, "We must take off all the yokes: the yoke of the past, of the present, of prejudices, of rules, of ideologies, to have people return to their natural character."[45] Hoài Thanh's and Lưu Trọng Lư's recognition of personal expression as political thought and action dovetails with Michael Lucey's observations on Gide's relationship to the Soviet Union: "Not that the expression of sexuality is the expression of some truth. Rather, it is the quality of interruption that marks Gide's writing of sexuality, often the interruption of an ideology that passes for truth, an interruption that refuses truths about sexuality, that offers perhaps unattainable politics of sexuality 'itself' as a possibly curious, radical openness."[46] Both Hoài Thanh and Lưu Trọng Lư sensed the sexual politics behind Gide's Communist activism: the act of articulating, in Lưu Trọng Lư's phrase, one's "natural character"—that is, one's sexuality—offered liberating political possibilities.

In "Nhân tình tôi" (My love), a story from the collection *Kép Tư Bền*, Nguyễn Công Hoan relates individual literary enunciation to the development of a national literature—specifically through the possibility of a homoerotic relationship between a reader and a writer. Trần Văn Căn, the first-person narrator and protagonist of "Nhân tình tôi," is an aspiring writer who, educated in the Franco-Vietnamese system, writes in the romanized alphabet and has a particular interest in *quốc văn,* or national literature. Căn's dedication to and interest in national literature, developed within the realm of the romanized alphabet and print, is in stark contrast to his father's career as a mandarin. As the protagonist attempts to contribute to a national literature, he also seeks to fulfill his personal desires. He begins to write to female columnists, hoping to flirt with and possibly seduce one of them. Kim Chi, a newspaper columnist discussing gender equality, catches the protagonist's attention, and he begins to correspond with her by posing as a fellow woman columnist. He signs his articles "Minh Châu, Female Author." During their correspondence, Căn falls for Kim Chi. Soon he pens personal letters to her and eventually reveals his male identity. They begin to plan face-to-face meetings, but Kim Chi never appears at the predetermined times and places. Still persistent in his efforts to meet Kim Chi, Căn then writes a romantic comedy for the stage and asks Kim Chi to play a leading role with him. The play is never realized, yet Kim Chi boldly writes a letter to invite Căn to visit her house while her family is away in the country. When Căn arrives, the house is dark, and Kim Chi hides her face.

Kim Chi speaks in furtive whispers, as if concealing something about herself. But Căn proudly declares that he has keen ears and can clearly understand the mumbling. Kim Chi says that she is hard of hearing, so Căn offers to switch ears with her. Kim Chi, however, refuses a simple exchange and requests the ears as a gift. Căn complies and tells Kim Chi to go ahead and cut off his ears, which the protagonist deems insignificant: "So you want me to 'sú-vơ-nia' my ears for you? I thought there would be something else since ears belong to the era of obedience."[47] ("Sú-vơ-nia" is a transliteration of the French term *souvenir,* used here to mean "to give as a keepsake.") After trading flirtatious whispers and gestures, Kim Chi reveals herself to be a man. The unmasked Kim Chi raises a glimmering knife and says, "Here's a knife, please 'sú-vơ-nia' your ears for me."[48] Hinting at (self-)castration, Kim Chi's line, the story's penultimate, takes literally Căn's suggestion that ears are no longer relevant once their literary and epistolary correspondence has reached its culmination.

The sociocultural context of modern Vietnam's literary production serves as the story's backdrop: the shift away from the literary figure of the mandarin, new social relations premised on individual sentiment and desire, and, above all, new gender roles and relations in modernizing Vietnam. The fluidity of sexual identity in the story is a result of print culture's revolutionary developments, namely, the possibility of women as both writers and readers. This is evident at an extradiegetic level, through the narrator's male voice, and in the story's plot. Nguyễn Công Hoan initially published the story in *An Nam tạp chí* (Annam journal) under the nom de plume "Hà Thành—nữ sĩ" (Hà Thành—female author). The male narrator addresses an implied male audience through his vocative call, *các ngài* (your excellencies); however, the assumed homosocial relationship between narrator and reader is undermined by a plot that develops around a female readership and concludes with a scene of homoeroticism. The story's protagonist encroaches on the cultural sphere of, as it is called in the story, *nữ văn giới* (world of women's literature). Căn tries to initiate a heterosexual relationship by forging a feminine writing persona and homosocial bond. Yet his attempts to veil male desire for a female object turn out to be desire between two men.

The anxieties of the transition from the male literary world of mandarins to the inchoate realm of *nữ văn giới* play out through the story's suggestive castration, when the two characters flirtatiously consider cutting off their ears. The lovers' first attempt to share with each other, to trade their sensual experiences, quickly turns into a suggestion of violent deformation. These men of modern letters, who must pose as female writers and readers to adapt to the evolving literary market, ultimately propose physical mutilation of each other. Their agency and legerdemain reflect a troubling historical paradox specific to modern Vietnam: a literary market orienting itself to women readers, yet still lacking female literary writers.

The story's aural theme also signals the material development of print culture, as well as the sphere of privacy provided by reading. Căn's aesthetic and personal interests depend on the development of *quốc ngữ* newspapers as a public forum. The story juxtaposes the privacy of the written word to the public performance of theater, which proved to be ineffective during Căn's courtship of Kim Chi. When Kim Chi jokingly suggests that Căn cut off his ears as a gift for her, the protagonist dismisses the relevance of ears as anachronistic. Căn equates them with Confucian instruction and conformity. Unlike the aural channels of direct, face-to-face communication, the private world of print makes possible the characters' expression and pursuit of personal desire, and within print culture individual sentiments and relationships between readers and writers are as revealing as they are unexpected.[49] Căn's aim of fulfilling his personal desire is inextricably tied to his interest in national literature. In Nguyễn Công Hoan's "Nhân tình tôi," as in

Gide's notion of particularity, the enunciation and revelation of sexual desire through personal, literary expression allow for both individual and national particularity while radically reconfiguring the community of readers.

André Gide's relevance to Vietnamese critics resides in the synthesis of his sexual politics, Communist leanings, and the subsequent vision of a literature *engagé*. The unspoken queerness—the paradigm of sexual particularity—at the heart of Gide's politicized aesthetics not only reflected modern Vietnam's shifting sexual and gender roles, inextricably tied as they were to the practices of writing and reading and the material development of print, but also served as the paradigm for addressing and examining the relationship between art and social reality. For the idealists, the politics of sexuality led to the articulation of individual desire that destabilized the established social order while fostering new social relationships. For the materialists, Gide's politicized aesthetics allowed for the literary representation and legitimization of social types previously unacknowledged. As a site of modernism, Vietnam was a contentious locale in the international circuit of Art for Life's Sake versus Art for Art's Sake. The debate, however, over literature's function and value was never about the autonomy of art but how literature would affect, address, and shape the reading masses, specifically, a national reading audience.

Conclusion

My conceptualization of the post-mandarin rethinks Vietnamese aesthetic modernity and anticolonial nationalism through the radically transformed gender and sexual dynamics of colonial modernity. The book began by establishing the post-mandarin predicament of deracinated intellectuals as French colonial policies reconstituted intellectual and literary fields. By 1919 the French colonial regime had overhauled Vietnam's thousand-year-old civil service examination system. This imposition of a colonial education alienated post-mandarin generations from their fathers' intellectual traditions. Educated in French and in *quốc ngữ*, the Vietnamese romanized alphabet, both of which had no corresponding literature referencing Vietnamese society, post-mandarin writers attempted to fill this void and establish a national literature. At the same time, the French-educated intellectuals had to adapt to altered gender boundaries: the all-male mandarinate had been dissolved, while a new educational system and print culture allowed women access into the world of letters. The book illustrates how post-mandarin intellectuals founded this modern literature by turning to Vietnamese women as protagonists, readers, and potential addressees of an emergent national literature and political discourse. The writers were drawn to these women because they experienced colonial modernity's paradoxical nature most acutely. Women were affected by the sweeping spread of capitalism's material changes and consumerism, yet they had to negotiate moral, social, and linguistic codes that continued to regulate female—more than male—expressions of gender and sexuality. *Quốc ngữ* literature, therefore, did not fulfill the meaning embedded in its etymology—"national script"—until women occupied a more prominent place in the post-mandarin literary address and female readers became a crucial demographic in the mutual development of a national literature and a national audience.

Colonial education imbued native intellectuals with a double consciousness that allowed them to understand their peripheral situation through the revelations of the European metropole.[1] This lens of comparison brought into sharper relief the political and social differences that shaped their national identity. Benedict Anderson has pointed out that new modes of communication and the acceleration of long-distance travel accentuated the double consciousness of the colonized by scaling the world down to a more accessible and comprehensible form in which everything was comparable, resulting in what he calls the "spectre of comparisons." As Pheng Cheah notes, Anderson emphasizes how material change provides "quotidian universals that make everything comparable for everyone, and cause everyone to compare everything."[2] Colonized intellectuals in Southeast Asia had greater knowledge about European metropoles than adjacent cities or regions.[3]

Clearly, post-mandarin intellectuals set their sights on the Parisian capital, but my discussion here of the post-mandarin also suggests that the anxious outward look, as a way of measuring one's self, was also cast more locally at modern native women. The inseparability of post-mandarin masculinity and femininity lies at the crux of Vietnamese aesthetic modernity. The chapters in this book have explored how the various complexities of this local specter of comparison were problematized in language and literature as post-mandarin authors attempted to grasp the "truth" about Vietnamese society. The post-mandarin representations of women not only registered the writers' concerns about shifting gender roles and relationships during colonial modernity, but they were also an occasion to reflect on their burgeoning national identity: what it meant to be Vietnamese.

The Vietnamese women represented in post-mandarin literature were caught amid the hypocrisies of colonial policies and Confucianism's residual social effects that characterized Vietnam's colonial modernity: the legalization yet failed policing of commercial sex; sexual progressivism undermined by persistent sexual taboos; the lingering gender codes of Confucian society despite the dismantled all-male examination system; and the sociolinguistic structures of kinship terms cutting against the promised universalism of the first-person pronoun *tôi*. Post-mandarin male authors' representations of women were not merely exercises of power and authority that mediated their discussions of modernity and nationalism through the private lives of women. They did not view Vietnamese women in essentialist terms as either representative of Vietnamese tradition or wholly reborn figures of European modernization. Instead, they examined how women's social positions were produced at the particular historical disjuncture of colonial modernity. The dynamic is more complicated if we consider the deracinated male intellectuals' estrangement: cut off from precolonial intellectual and cultural history and defined by a masculinity that may be likened but never equal to the European male colonial master. Indeed the colonized intellectual's uncertain masculinity—to borrow Pheng Cheah's words, "an a priori vulnerability, the a priori opening-out of itself onto something other"[4]—upends our assumptions about the roles of masculinity and femininity in the colonial situation. I suggest that the male colonized intellectual, rather than masculinizing the discourses of nationalism and modernization by denying women's agency, in fact feminizes discourses of nationalism and modernization by representing the prosaic settings in which women exercised their agency.

The chapters here have traced the various post-mandarin representations of women negotiating the everyday terrain of modernity.[5] The reportage works of Tam Lang and Thạch Lam are autoethnographies in which the narrators immerse themselves in the social milieus occupied by women, empirically conducting research as participant observers. Vũ Trọng Phụng not only challenged the established boundaries of literary representation with the private and graphic details of sex workers' lives but also blurs the distinction between fiction and nonfiction by folding reportage-style investigative journalism of the everyday into the structure of the novel form. The leader of the Self-Strength Literary Group, Nhất Linh, aimed to demystify the rituals that structured the gender hierarchies of Vietnamese Confucian society. In his novel *In the Midst of Spring*, Khái Hưng based his plot on the discrepancies in the Vietnamese language's person-reference system and the imported, presumably universal first-person pronoun, reflecting on the sociolinguistic pragmatics of language. That novel's modern heroine is hemmed in by the grammatical structures of language, but she also manipulates language and its post-mandarin sociohistorical context to establish a family outside patrilineal lineage and its sociolinguistic structures.

Post-mandarin authors made the genre of the novel analogous with Vietnamese society. As Anderson has argued, the analogous relationship between the cultural artifacts of the newspaper and the realist novel and a given social space creates the conditions of simultaneity, or homogenous, empty time necessary for readers to imagine themselves as a part of a community beyond face-to-face interactions. For Anderson, *technē* is necessary for the self-actualization of the nation. While it is clear that print culture, through its mechanical modes of reproduction and transmission, catalyzed nationalism, its effectiveness, I argue, had greater dependence on the reconfigured systems of representation—the flattening of hierarchies of representation—to include all subject matter. The representation of all prosaic subjects—including marginalized characters and their everyday conditions—makes visible all common forms of life. As the democratic representation of the prosaic broke down the barriers between "subject matter and mode of representation" in post-mandarin Vietnam,[6] the revolution in aesthetics contributed to a revolution of political representation.

As I bring the book to a close, it has become more apparent that the case of Vietnam's post-mandarin literature gives reason to reiterate a distinction that Raymond Williams made in his 1987 lecture, "When Was Modernism?": the distinction between modern and modernist. Williams points to this difference because the canonization of modernism had been narrow to the point of neglecting history.

> After modernism is canonized, however, by the post-war settlement and its complicit academic endorsements, the presumption arises that since modernism is here, in this specific phase or period, there is nothing beyond it. The marginal rejected artists become classics of organized teaching and of travelling exhibitions in the great galleries of the metropolitan cities. "Modernism" is confined to this highly selective field and denied to everything else in an act of pure ideology, whose first, unconscious irony is that, absurdly, it stops history dead.[7]

Williams captures how the canonization of modernism takes the form of an afterlife, no longer situated in the history of modernity, and fails to consider how authors grappled with and responded to modernity. He goes on to suggest it is necessary to recover the "modern" from the aesthetic category of modernism. The insistence here on analyzing modernism in its modern contexts is particularly salient—perhaps more urgent—for the setting of colonial modernity, where aesthetic modernity may develop in ways that are wholly unfamiliar with its contemporaneous strains in Europe and elsewhere. The defining development of Vietnamese aesthetic modernity was not an appropriation of European modernism. Instead, it was literature's turn toward the prosaic everyday—as a way of writing and reading the modern—that generated the form and content of a national aesthetic modernity.

The imperatives of prose to grapple with the everyday experiences of colonial modernity and to capture the complex and shifting dynamics of gender and sexual relations explain how and why Vietnam's modern authors extracted and employed imported literary forms and styles in counterintuitive ways.

What had developed over decades in Europe arrived in French Indochina as condensed "packages."[8] Post-mandarin intellectuals broke down and reconfigured European forms of knowledge and methodologies in ways that often inverted the genealogy of French and, more broadly speaking, European literature. The post-mandarin integration of ethnography, investigative journalism, and sociology with the novel came at a time when, in Europe and in America, those modes of investigations were becoming, if not already so, more professionalized in institutions such as the university system or the newspaper profession and thus farther removed from the fields of literary production. We have seen, for example, how post-mandarin authors employed the reportage genre as the basis for the realist novel, reversing a literary history in which French realism gave way to naturalism and reportage. The imperative to report external reality in a scientific fashion overrode any concern that such documentation was based on personal testimony, producing a realist aesthetic that bore little resemblance to European modernism's defining attributes of fragmentation, stylistic defamiliarization, the denunciation of verisimilitude, and medial reflexivity. In this sense, European modernism's medial reflexivity was intransitive, while the prosaic turn in Vietnamese literature was transitive. The latter assumed the efficacy of language to recode and transform the referents of society and thus society itself.

Recently scholars have read modernism through the significance of the prosaic and its affective counterpart of boredom. For Liesl Olson, the ordinary is antithetical to literary modernism's moments of transcendental understanding, such as James Joyce's "epiphanies" or Proust's involuntary memory.[9] For Saikat Majumdar, whose scope is Anglophone modernism, the prosaic and boredom starkly contrast with the violence, trauma, and other historical events of decolonization—which in turn dominate colonial and postcolonial narratives. For Majumdar, the aesthetics of prose emerge from a weariness toward the "obvious spheres of struggle and suffering, be they wars, riots, genocide, or other headline-grabbing political upheavals, but also to articulate vocally a theoretical polemic against the enslavement of the novelistic imagination to such spectacles."[10] These two studies illuminate how the literary aesthetics of banality and the affect of boredom resist the spectacle and eventfulness of modernity and postcolonialism. And specifically for Majumdar, the prosaic captures colonialism's quotidian inadequacies—a reality at the colonial periphery that has received insufficient attention when compared to decolonization's spectacle of violence and suffering.[11]

While also attempting to rethink modernism through the prosaic, *Post-Mandarin*'s claims differ from the above studies in a number of ways.

Contrary to understanding colonial modernity through banality and boredom, I have examined its accelerated transformations. The seismic shifts in
language, material culture, cultural and intellectual fields, educational institutions, and gender relations produced vertiginous changes that pitted the
precolonial past against the colonial present. As Harootunian has suggested,
this coevality manifests in the everyday,[12] and from this tension, I argue,
aesthetic modernity developed. The case of Vietnamese aesthetic modernity
reverses Majumdar's temporal sequence, giving us reason to locate the political efficacy of aesthetic modernity's prose not after the anticolonial struggle,
from the postcolonial perspective, but *prior* to decolonization as a necessary
condition of possibility. Post-mandarin prose did not follow and respond
to the violence and trauma of anticolonial struggle. It emerged as the revolutionary aesthetics of signs that made the realm of literary representation
indistinguishable from social reality. The radical democratic representation in post-mandarin prose expanded the scope of political representation,
making it possible for the imagination of an anticolonial, national movement. This literary turn toward the prosaic—the turn toward the address
and representation of women, toward *nữ văn giới* (the world of women's
letters)—defined Vietnam's aesthetic modernity and its political ambitions
and accomplishments.

   To consider modern Vietnamese literature and its politics through
questions of gender and sexuality is to challenge Vietnamese Marxist
criticism that was made orthodox and inflexible by the machinations
of state power and partisan politics. This is an attempt, as Fanon has
suggested, at stretching Marxism[13]—specifically here, beyond the state's
dominant historiography. Legitimating the Communist insurgency and
its rise to state power, this foundational narrative explains the emergence
of modern Vietnamese literature as the fulfillment of Vietnamese socialism, the teleological end of anticolonial revolution. Marxist Vietnamese
literary criticism canonized works that advanced the Communist movement and writers who were Party members while systematically deval-
uing authors who did not politically align with the Communist Party.
Since the perestroika policies of the 1980s and 1990s that merged Vietnam's socialist economy with global capitalism, critics and historians
have begun to chip away at this myopic evaluation of literary works and
authors. This book has aimed to contribute to this reassessment with its
primary arguments: that the post-mandarin engagement with and representation of colonial sex and gender fostered an inclusive field of cultural
representation and, more broadly speaking, a democratic national culture from which Vietnamese Marxism emerged. Vietnam's anticolonial

national movement during the twentieth century was not the singular Marxism narrated and codified by the state but was rather conditioned and formed in conjunction with modernity's sociohistorical transformations, various political ideologies, and, most pertinent here, an aesthetic modernity attending to questions of gender and sexuality.

ACKNOWLEDGMENTS

The origins of *Post-Mandarin* can be traced to my Fulbright Fellowship at the Trường đại học khoa học xã hội và nhân văn (University of Social Sciences and Humanities) in Ho Chi Minh City, under the tutelage of Võ Văn Nhơn. During this time I met Hoàng Thị Mai, who remains an interlocutor. My understanding of Vietnamese culture was greatly influenced by Phan Thị Vàng Anh's intellectual capaciousness and rigor. Throughout my time in Vietnam, I benefited from colleagues and friends who generously offered suggestions and inspiration, including Lại Nguyên Ân, Nguyễn Quang Thiều, Nguyễn Quốc Chánh, Nguyễn Quyến, Trà Phạm, and Trần Tố Loan. Nguyễn Quí Đức has been the consummate mentor and friend. The École française d'Extrême-Orient and Viện văn hoc (Institute of literature) in Hanoi generously provided me with invaluable resources.

This project is much indebted to Karl Britto for his unfailing support and vigilance; to Michael Lucey for his perceptive theoretical insights; and to Peter Zinoman for his attention to history and its footnotes. Rebekah Collins, Tom McEnaney, Nguyễn Nguyệt Cầm, Jenny White, and Karen Zumhagen-Yekplé have been dear friends and colleagues.

I have had the opportunity to present my research in draft form at the Asian/Pacific Studies Institute at Duke University, the "Comparative Modernisms, Medialities, Modernities" conference sponsored by New York University and Fordham University, the MacMillan Center at Yale University, and the Centre for Cultural, Literary and Postcolonial Studies at the School of Oriental and African Studies (SOAS), University of London. The comments and questions I received from the audiences helped shape this book. I am especially grateful to Toral Gajarawala, Shai Ginsburg, Erik Harms, Aimee Kwon Nayoung, and Jini Kim Watson. Working with Fordham University Press has been an incredible experience. I am indebted to Helen Tartar, who believed in *Post-Mandarin* from the beginning, and to my editor,

Thomas Lay, for seeing the project to fruition. I am also deeply indebted to Chris GoGwilt, who, in addition to being an intellectual and professional model, provided generous and thorough feedback that helped me improve the manuscript. Lisa Lowe has been a constant source of support throughout the publishing process. Through the years Tony Day, Janit Feangfu, Rachel Harrison, Sarah Weiss, and Jack Yeager have engaged with much of my work and thinking. Mariam Lam commented on parts of the manuscript and offered help and advice. I thank Chris Goscha, Agathe Larcher-Goscha, Martina Nguyen, and Shaun Malarney for sharing sources with me. Richard Hermes and Chris Kowalski, my fellow publishers of *bluemilk* magazine, have always been there to remind me of the significance of art and literature.

Chapter 4 was previously published in *positions: asia critique* (Summer 2013): 579–605 and is reprinted by permission of Duke University Press. Chapter 5 was previously published as "Queer Internationalism and Modern Vietnamese Aesthetics," in *The Oxford Handbook of Global Modernisms* (2012), edited by Mark Wollaeger and Matthew Eatough, and is reproduced by permission of Oxford University Press. I am grateful to the journal and publishers.

Many colleagues and friends have made Vanderbilt an intellectual home. I am grateful to Ruth Rogaski for her advice. Rob Campany provided thoughtful and incisive feedback on the manuscript. Dana Nelson stepped in at the last minute with sharp and helpful suggestions. I thank Mark Wollaeger for his constant guidance, comments, and advice; without his persistence the Gide chapter may have never come to life. Jen Fay and Scott Juengel have always pushed and inspired my intellectual thinking. I thank Colin Dayan for conversations, including the one that led to the title. I offer a special expression of gratitude to Chris Benda, who thoroughly and patiently combed over the manuscript. Much gratitude also goes to Andy Hines, Amanda Lehr, and Hoang Phung Ly for their help with the manuscript. Much of my research for this project and future ones would be impossible were it not for Jim Toplon, Yuh-Fen Benda, and the other members of Vanderbilt's library staff. I am humbled by all that I have learned and will continue to learn from the members of the Contemporary in Theory working group at the Robert Penn Warren Center. I am grateful for support from Vanderbilt's College of Arts and Sciences and the office of the Vice Provost for Research.

I am deeply indebted to my parents, who were my first teachers of literature. I am grateful to Laura Schachter for her support and willingness to share a bourbon when needed. My brother, Benny Tran, and my sister, Linda Hinh, have always been unconditional with their love and support. And finally, I want to thank Allison Schachter, who makes the prosaic come to life with meaning.

NOTES

INTRODUCTION

1. Vietnam's Lý dynasty (1009–1225) was the first to administer civil service exams. In 1010 officials founded Thăng Long (present-day Hanoi) as the capital. They established the Temple of Literature in 1070 and held the first recruitment exams in 1075. (Thăng Long would remain Vietnam's political and cultural capital until the beginning of the nineteenth century, when the Nguyễn dynasty came to power and moved the capital, along with the national university, Quốc Tử Giám, to Huế.) Lý Đạo Thanh, the monarch's highest-ranking official, conducted exams to recruit officials to aid Lý Càn Đức, a child king, in maintaining the state, particularly amid fears of Chinese invasions. See Keith Taylor, "Authority and Legitimacy in 11th-Century Vietnam," in *Southeast Asia in the 9th to 14th Centuries*, ed. David Marr and Anthony Crothers Millner (Singapore: Institute of Southeast Asian Studies, 1986), 152–55. Along with Buddhism and Taoism, Confucianism was influential to various degrees during the Lý and Trần dynasties from the eleventh to the fifteenth century. It became the official state ideology of the Lê dynasty (1427–1789). Examination Chinese became the primary language for government and scholarly inquiry practically until 1919, when the French abandoned the mandarinal exams.

From the Lê through the Nguyễn dynasty, Vietnamese scholars deepened their knowledge of Confucian texts. However, this did not necessarily mean the universal spread of Confucianism to the detriment of other belief systems in Vietnam. As Shawn McHale has acutely argued: "[Vietnam's Confucian literati] were a highly eclectic and constantly shifting assemblage about which it is difficult to generalize" (406). He goes on to question claims about the primacy of Confucianism in Vietnam, attributing such perceptions to discourses that substantiated Vietnamese culture as rooted in Chinese and Confucian heritage. These discourses were a response to French colonialism: "Faced with the traumatic impact of French colonization, Vietnamese intellectuals in the 1920s and 1930s searched for what they believed must have held Vietnam together in the past. French repression of political discussions and writings meant that, in the search backwards, Vietnamese were pressed to find cultural answers to Vietnam's strength in the far past as well as its more recent failure to stand up to the West in the near past. Searching for their origins, the Vietnamese came up with Confucianism and all its 'strengths' and 'weaknesses.'" Shawn McHale, "Mapping a Vietnamese Confucian Past and Its Transition to Modernity," in *Rethinking Confucianism: Past and Present in China, Japan, and Vietnam*, ed. Benjamin A. Elman, John B. Duncan, and Herman Ooms (Los Angeles: UCLA Asian Pacific Monograph Series, 2001), 428–29.

2. Alexander Woodside, *Lost Modernities: China, Vietnam, Korea, and the Hazards of World History* (Cambridge, MA: Harvard University Press, 2006), 17.

3. Woodside compares the Vietnamese and Chinese mandarinates, particularly the nineteenth-century Nguyễn emperors and the Ch'ing dynasty. See Alexander Woodside, *Vietnam and the Chinese Model* (Cambridge: Council on East Asian Studies, 1988).

4. Trinh Van Thao, *Vietnam du confucianisme au communisme: Un essai d'itinéraire intellectual* (Paris: L'Harmattan, 2007), 359.

5. Based on the Latin alphabet, this writing script was initially developed in the seventeenth century by Jesuit missionaries for the purposes of transcription, learning Vietnamese, and proselytizing. Besides using Latin, the first practitioners of *quốc ngữ* relied on their own national languages, predominantly Portuguese and Italian, while borrowing diacritics from the Greek language. This transliteration project of the Vietnamese language into a romanized alphabet was modeled after efforts in Japan. In the nineteenth century *quốc ngữ* was normalized according to French standards.

6. Sarraut coordinated a series of policies to modernize Vietnam according to Republican principles of equality and freedom. He signaled his faith in the indigenous population's potential for development by investing in the colonial infrastructure so as to stimulate the economy, trimming down the colonial bureaucracy, allowing for symbolic and restricted political representation for the native population, and expanding the educational system. For Sarraut's Republicanism, see Gilles de Gantès, "Protectorate, Association, Reformism: The Roots of the Republican Policy Pursued by the Popular Front in Indochina," in *French Colonial Empire and the Popular Front*, ed. Tony Chafer and Amanda Sackur (New York: St. Martin's Press, 1999), 103–30; Peter Zinoman, *Vietnamese Colonial Republican: The Political Vision of Vũ Trọng Phụng* (Berkeley: University of California Press, 2014), 22–26. However, Sarraut's educational agenda was not the education of the masses but rather the promotion of a French-educated class that would supersede the native elite. The governor-general designed a system to replace one generation of collaborators with another, walling off future generations from Vietnam's Sino-centric intellectual history. Moreover, the colonial school system offered a second-rate education comprising "Vietnamese-appropriate" vocational subjects, more conducive to farming than clerkship or commerce. The Franco-Vietnamese curriculum and language instruction prevented indigenous students from integrating into the French educational or bureaucratic track. The school system turned the French colonial education system into a two-track system: one track for the French elite and the other for the indigenous population. See Gail Paradise Kelly, "Colonial Schools in Vietnam: Policy and Practice," in *French Colonial Education: Essays on Vietnam and West Africa*, ed. David H. Kelly (New York: AMS Press, 2000), 3–132; and Pascale Bezancon, *Une colonisation educatrice? L'Experience Indochinoise (1860–1945)* (Paris: L'Harmattan, 2002), 117–65.

With precolonial education and the civil service examination system delegitimized and the French schools exclusively reserved for French children, higher education in the Franco-Vietnamese system was resuscitated and expanded. Hanoi's Indochinese University, which had been closed in 1908, only a year after its inauguration, due to an anti-tax protest, was reopened with the added departments of Medicine and Pharmacy, Veterinary Science, Education, Watercourses and Forestry, Commerce, Finance, Law, and Administration. Nevertheless, the system filtered out the majority of students at the upper primary and secondary levels, before they could reach the university level. See Pierre Brocheux and Daniel Hémery, *Indochina: An Ambiguous Colonization, 1858–1954*, trans. Ly Lan Dill-Klein (Berkeley: University of California Press, 2011), 221, 223; also see Bezancon, *Une colonisation educatrice?*, 118–22.

7. Albert Sarraut, "Discourse prononcé le 27 avril 1919 au Van-Mieu." I thank Chris Goscha and Agathe Larcher for providing me with a copy of this speech.

8. Sarraut's campaign was part of France's efforts to establish an extensive educational system in what is now present-day Vietnam. The system was more expansive in Vietnam than in other parts of the French Empire, even more than Cambodia and Laos, where traditional Buddhist schools were preserved and then modernized. The aim was to draw Vietnamese students away from private Sino-centric instruction and study abroad in France, which gave students a modern education and, more dangerously, political ideals.

9. Sarraut, "Discourse prononcé le 27 avril 1919"; my translation. Hereafter, all translations are mine unless noted otherwise. Sarraut consistently employed the metaphor of father or even older brother to describe and justify France's supposed guiding role in Vietnam until it came of age as a mature society. For further discussions of this metaphor, see David Marr, *Vietnamese Tradition on Trial* (Berkeley: University of California Press, 1981), 6; Hue-Tam Ho Tai, *Radicalism and the Origins of the Vietnamese Revolution* (Cambridge, MA: Harvard University Press, 1992), 37–38.

10. The speech marked the end game for the Vietnamese mandarinate. Sarraut declared his intention to extirpate the Confucian examination curriculum, yet employed the Temple of Literature as a vestige of a past gone awry to be renovated by French guidance. Analogously, the French government rendered the mandarinate powerless, yet preserved the Confucian literati figure as a relic of indigenous intellectual authority. The French colonial government's instrumental use of Confucianism worked in various ways. As an intellectual history, Confucian tradition had been the epistemological grounding of Vietnamese society. Yet after French colonial appropriation, Confucianism as the basis for Vietnam's political structure became the tradition against which intellectuals at the beginning of the twentieth century reacted. As Phan Châu Trinh sharply noted in his critique of the mandarinate, French colonial rulers understood that "Vietnamese society cannot change overnight; the Vietnamese people are helpless as long as the entire country has been taken over, yet the Vietnamese government continues to capitulate. Continue to use the mandarinate, give it orders, and let it do the work of taxation." Phan Châu Trinh, "Thư gửi Toàn quyền Đông Dương" [Letter to the governor-general of Indochina], in *Toàn tập* [Collected works] (Da Nang: NXB Đà Nẵng, 2005), 2:54. Vietnam's mandarinate had been disgraced by the time Sarraut made his speech since a majority of the scholar-gentry had collaborated with the French and compromised Vietnam's position when confronted with imperialism. David Marr has written about intellectuals who established the Reform Movement that criticized the mandarinate's collaboration with

the French; see *Vietnamese Anti-Colonialism, 1882–1925* (Berkeley: University of California Press, 1980). Emmanuel Poisson has recently challenged the history of collaboration so often attributed to the mandarinate by looking at its complex historical changes, regional differences, and the tensions between state and local powers; see his *Mandarins et subalterns au nord du Viet Nam: Une bureaucratie à l'éprueve (1820–1918)* (Paris: Maisonneuve & Larose, 2004). Wynn Wilcox has argued that the increasingly venal mandarin class did not lose its significance because of its insistence on moribund ideas. Instead, he effectively traces Vietnam's epistemological shifts in the nineteenth and twentieth centuries from the universalist ideals of the mandarinal intellectual tradition (in which Europeans were considered the barbaric others) to particularistic nationalist values. See his "French Imperialism and the Vietnamese Civil Service Examinations," *Journal of American–East Asian Relations* 21.4 (2014): 373–93. Agathe Larcher has written about Sarraut's repeated calls for Franco-Annamite collaboration and the intelligentsia's response to these efforts. See her "La voie étroite de réformes colonials et la 'collaboration Franco-Annamite' (1917–1928)" [The single road to colonial reform and the Franco-Annamite collaboration (1917–1928)], *Revue française d'histoire d'outre-mer* 82.309 (1995): 387–420.

11. The colonial paternalism takes on the role of both teacher and father, a duality denoted by the Vietnamese term "thầy." So, interestingly, colonial imposition here not only displaces but also replicates indigenous authority.

12. Before this centralization, Vietnam's structure of education comprised two systems, Confucian and Franco-Vietnamese schools, that coexisted in an unrelated and loosely organized way. For an insightful discussion of the school system's centralization and history, see Trần Thị Phương Hoa, "From Liberally Organized to Centralized Schools: Education in Tonkin, 1885–1927," *Journal of Vietnamese Studies* 8.3 (2013): 27–70.

13. The luminary Hồ Xuân Hương and the eighteenth-century poet Đoàn Thị Điểm, among others, come to mind. For profiles of Vietnam's women authors, see *Nữ sĩ Việt Nam: Tiểu sử và giai thoại* [Vietnam's female authors: Biographies and recollection], ed. Như Hiên and Nguyễn Ngọc Hiền (Ho Chi Minh City: NXB Văn học, 2006). However, I would argue that these women were exceptions to the mandarinate's all-male normative.

14. For discussions of colonial modernity, see Antoinette Burton, "Introduction: The Unfinished Business of Colonial Modernities," in *Gender, Sexuality, and Colonial Modernities*, ed. Antoinette Burton (London: Routledge, 1999), 1–16; Saurabh Dube, "Colonialism, Modernity, Colonial Modernities," *Nepanthala: Views from the South* 3.2 (2002): 197–219; Tani Barlow, ed., *Formations of Colonial Modernity in East Asia* (Durham, NC: Duke University Press, 1997); and David Scott, *Refashioning Futures: Criticism after Postcoloniality* (Princeton, NJ: Princeton University Press, 1999), 23–52.

15. Sarraut, "Discourse prononcé le 27 1919," 5.

16. Trần Thị Phương Hoa, "From Liberally Organized to Centralized Schools," 28.

17. For an account of Vietnam's multilayered linguistic history and how it was shaped by French colonization, see John DeFrancis, *Colonialism and Language Policy in Viet Nam* (The Hague: Mouton, 1977). Also see Milton Osborne, *The French Presence in Cochinchina and Cambodia: Rule and Response* (Ithaca, NY: Cornell University Press, 1969).

18. The marginalization of these character scripts began during the early stages of French colonialism. In 1869 the French colonial government declared that all government documents were to be composed in *quốc ngữ*, not in Chinese. The implementation of the romanized alphabet as the official language continued in phases. In 1878 the government decreed that from 1879 all official documents were to be written in *quốc ngữ*. Beginning in 1882, promotion and privileges, including tax breaks, were given to civil servants versed in *quốc ngữ*. In the south, a new educational policy as early as 1879 implemented *quốc ngữ* as the basis of a new pedagogical curriculum. In the years leading up to World War I, French administrators suppressed increasing anticolonial activities and the accompanying circulation of anti-French writings, most of which were composed in Chinese. Moreover, the ideas of European thinkers like Darwin, Diderot, Kant, Montesquieu, and Rousseau had been translated into Chinese. During World War I, these concerns were exacerbated by Germany's production of anti-French propaganda in Chinese and distribution of the material south of the Sino-Vietnamese border. Although such thinkers occupied the pantheon of European Enlightenment, colonial officials considered the Chinese language—the primary language, up to that date, in which European Enlightenment ideas were transmitted and translated for a Vietnamese audience—incommensurate with modern knowledge.

19. *Quốc ngữ* has always been an effective means of transmission, not only for its initial uses by the Catholic Church, but also for Examination Chinese and *Nôm*. As Hoàng Xuân Việt has argued, both character scripts actually flourished as *quốc ngữ* translations and dictionaries made them more accessible. Thus, the emergence of *quốc ngữ* as the primary writing script did not displace Vietnam's previous writing forms. Its status as a primary language was, rather, due to French colonial policies. Hoàng Xuân Việt, *Tìm hiểu lịch sử chữ quốc ngữ* (Ho Chi Minh City: NXB Văn hóa thông tin, 2007), 364–65, 428–31.

20. Shawn McHale, "Printing and Power: Vietnamese Debates over Women's Place in Society, 1918–1934," in *Essays into Vietnamese Pasts*, ed. K. W. Taylor and John K. Whitmore (Ithaca, NY: Cornell Southeast Asia Program, 1995), 173–94.

21. My use of "print capitalism" refers to the literary field's shift to a supply-and-demand market. I am as concerned about the alienation of the creative process, as prescribed by Marx's teleological historical materialism, as I am about print capitalism's potential for newly imagined communities, as outlined by Benedict Anderson. For Anderson, print capitalism's nonteleological materialism is part of a greater confluence that made possible imagined communities: the "half-fortuitous, but explosive, interaction between a system of production and productive relations (capitalism), a technology of communications (print), and the fatality of human linguistic diversity." Benedict Anderson, *Imagined Communities: Reflections on the Origins and Spread of Nationalism* (New York: Verso, 1991), 42–43. The fatality of language that is pertinent here is Examination Chinese. Pheng Cheah further elaborates the nuances: "Anderson's formal argument is clearly allied with a certain materialism. . . . [The] constellation of forces that Anderson calls 'print capitalism' is not the dialectical process of creative labor's alienation but of chance and accident. This fortuitous coupling engenders a form of community that frustrates the relentless dehumanizing logic of capitalism as well as the cosmopolitan proletarian revolution Marx envisaged. The nation-form may be a product of capitalism. But it is a product of

print capitalism, which Anderson repeatedly links to *preindustrial mercantile* capitalism and not *industrial* capitalism. This is a form of capitalism that is more "communal," capitalism with a more sociable face if you will. For instead of shattering and
vaporizing all communal bonds, the upheavals of print capitalism, which destroyed
the transnational religious communities of the pre-modern era, also led to the creation of the new imagined solidarities from below through the spectrality of vernacular print." See Pheng Cheah, "Grounds of Comparison," in *Grounds of Comparison:
Around the Work of Benedict Anderson*, ed. Pheng Cheah and Jonathan Culler (New
York: Routledge, 2013), 6; original emphasis. In *Grundrisse*, speaking about automa-
tion and machinery, Marx momentarily aligns with Anderson on possible contin-
gencies of capitalism: "[Capital] is thus, despite itself, instrumental in creating the
means of social disposable time, in order to reduce labour time for the whole society
to a diminishing minimum, and thus to free everyone's time for their own development" Karl Marx, "The Grundrisse," in *The Marx-Engels Reader*, 2nd rev. and enl. ed.
(New York: W. W. Norton, 1978), 278.

22. Prominent among these were the Self-Strength Literary Group's *Phong hóa*
(Customs) and *Ngày nay* (Today), the publisher Vũ Đình Long's *Tiểu thuyết thứ bảy*
(Saturday novel), *Phổ thông bán nguyệt* (Popular biweekly), and *Tao Đàn* (Literary coterie), as well as *Ích Hữu đổi mới* (New companion) spearheaded by Lê Văn
Trương. During this period, both fiction and nonfiction flourished, as intellectuals
vigorously engaged in debates, such as Vietnamese national literature, national education, the lingering social effects of Confucianism, the mutual imbrications of culture and political ideology, the old vs. the new, idealism vs. materialism, Art for Art's
Sake vs. Art for Life's Sake, and social collectivism vs. individualism.

23. According to Trinh Van Thao, a historical sociologist, over 50 percent of the
new intellectuals were employed in the print industry. Trinh Van Thao, *Vietnam du
confucianisme au communisme*, 128.

24. The post-mandarin cohort differed from preceding generations that also
engaged with European thoughts and letters. With the authority of the mandarinate
delegitimized by the French colonial conquest, intellectuals who came of age during
the 1880s staged a reform movement. The two leading figures were Phan Bội Châu
and Phan Châu Trinh. Although influenced by "gió Âu mưa Mỹ" (European wind
and American rain), members of the movement came from a scholar-gentry background, trained in Chinese classical texts. They engaged with revolutionary European ideas, particularly social Darwinism, and were exposed to these ideas from
K'ang Yu-wei of China and his disciple Liang Ch'i-ch'ao. Phan Bội Châu met and collaborated with Liang Ch'i-ch'ao in Tokyo in 1905. See Hue-Tam Ho Tai, *Radicalism
and the Origins of the Vietnamese Revolution*, 20–31; and Mark Bradley, *Imagining
Vietnam and America: The Making of Postcolonial Vietnam, 1919–1950* (Chapel Hill:
University of North Carolina Press, 2000), 10–44. Trinh offers a detailed account
of three generations of "conjuncture" that grappled with the encounter between
European and East Asian intellectual histories. However, the association he draws
between the Confucian intellectual and the rise of communism, particularly through
the Leninist conception of the Communist Party and the role of the intellectual, does
not consider the disruption of gender roles and norms that are, I argue, definitive
of the post-mandarin field of cultural production. See Trinh Van Thao, *Vietnam du
confucianisme au communisme*.

25. The Self-Strength group abided by a core agenda of unabashed modernization through "Westernization," inaugurating the weekly satirical journal *Phong hóa* in 1932. The group consistently assailed writers who continued to work in the Confucian tradition, which they characterized as overwrought with didacticism, allusive intertextuality, parallel constructions, rigid rhyming patterns, and a cosmological worldview. The group's core members were the novelists Nhất Linh, Khái Hưng, and Thạch Lam; the prominent lyricists of the Thơ mới (New Poetry) movement Xuân Diệu, Huy Cận, and Thế Lữ; the satirist Tú Mỡ; and the cultural and political commentator Hoàng Đạo. They gained popularity and legitimacy as pioneers in poetry, literary publishing, and journalistic publishing, as well as the genre of the modern novel.

As the Self-Strength group produced novels that reflected the particularities of Vietnamese society (escaping the tradition of Sinology, yet distinct from the influx of European influence), the publisher Vũ Đình Long abandoned his press's specialization in educational texts and martial arts fiction and, under the publishing house Tân Dân, inaugurated *Tiểu thuyết thứ bảy* in 1934 to provide entertainment for the working classes at the end of the workweek (thus the title) and to capitalize on the growing market for contemporary fiction. The weekly publication was launched without any expressed political or aesthetic conviction, yet it fostered a loosely affiliated collective of writers whose depiction of the middle and working classes, as well as subjects of the urban underworlds, differed from the Self-Strength group's bourgeois and petite bourgeois subjects. Intellectuals affiliated with *Tiểu thuyết thứ bảy* included Ngọc Giao, Lê Văn Trương, Nguyễn Công Hoan, Lan Khai, Tô Hoài, Nam Cao, Nguyên Hồng, Vũ Trọng Phụng, and Nguyễn Tuân. In 1936 Tân Dân also debuted *Phổ thông bán nguyệt*, a journal dedicated to short stories and novels, and in 1939 *Tao Đàn*, a forum dedicated to nonfiction prose that involved established intellectuals like Nguyễn Triệu Luật, Nguyễn Trọng Thuật, Phan Khôi, Hoài Thanh, Trương Tửu, Lan Khai, Lưu Trọng Lư, and Nguyễn Tuân. For a more comprehensive coverage of this rich publishing and intellectual period; see Huỳnh Văn Tòng, *Báo chí Việt Nam: Từ khởi thủy đến 1945* [Vietnamese newspapers: From origins to 1945] (Ho Chi Minh City: NXB Thành phố Hồ Chí Minh, 2000), 276–77, 307–36; Phạm Thế Ngũ, *Việt Nam văn học sử: Giản ước tân biên* [History of Vietnamese literature: A new survey], 3 vols. (1965; repr., Đồng tháp: NXB Đồng tháp, 1996), 3:414; Thanh Lãng, *Phê bình văn học thế hệ 1932*, 2 vols. ([Saigon?]: Phong trào văn hóa, 1972). See Phan Cự Đệ, *Tiểu thuyết Việt Nam hiện đại* [The modern Vietnamese novel], vol. 1 (Hanoi: NXB Đại học và trung học chuyên nghiệp, 1975). From the vantage point of a prominent critic and translator who worked in America, see Huỳnh Sanh Thông, "Main Trends of Vietnamese Literature between the Two World Wars," *Vietnam Forum* 3 (Winter–Spring 1984): 110–23.

26. Colonial policies varied in each region of French Indochina. The French directly ruled Cochinchina, the southern part of Vietnam, and began dismantling the mandarinal exam system as early as 1867, much earlier than the indirectly ruled regions of Annam and Tonkin, respectively the central and northern regions. By the 1920s the Franco-Vietnamese school system was much more established in the south, and intellectuals turned to print culture and journalism for the purposes of political activism. Philippe Peycam gives an insightful account of print culture's subsequent emergence, tying it to the rise of political journalism and an unprecedented

public sphere. See his *The Birth of Vietnamese Political Journalism: Saigon, 1916–1930* (New York: Columbia University Press, 2012). In Tonkin the legacy of Confucian intellectual history runs deeper. Therefore, the repercussions of the abrupt changes caused by the Franco-Vietnamese school system and the rapid development of print culture profoundly affected post-mandarin literature. For further discussion of these differences, as well as those within Indochina, see Bezancon, *Une colonisation educatrice?*

27. Woodside argues that mandarinal meritocracies, based on civil service examination systems, constituted a source of modernity that prefigures European modernity. His claims about the mandarinate's nonhereditary, merit-based power, meritocracy's self-awareness, welfare systems, and use of systems theories provide a convincing account of the mandarinate's modern qualities. At a revealing moment, however, Woodside writes, "[the mandarinate examinations] applied affirmative action to make sure that disadvantaged minorities (but no women) could participate." See Woodside, *Lost Modernities*, 32. Woodside parenthetically acknowledges the mandarinate as an exclusively all-male modernity, bracketing the exclusion of women. While my book aims to analyze Vietnamese modernity in rethinking modernities beyond the purview of Europe, the angle taken here inverts the bracketing of women's exclusion from the mandarinate.

28. All the intellectuals central to this project followed in their fathers' footsteps. With the exception of Vũ Trọng Phụng, all were the sons of civil servants. Trinh Van Thao has argued that this generation's intellectuals were sons of civil servants, intellectuals, or mandarins, yet they were educated under a different educational system. According to his survey, more than 85 percent were educated in the French system, and more than 50 percent were the sons of intellectuals. Trinh Van Thao, *Vietnam du confucianisme au communisme*, 121–31.

29. This phenomenon has been recently analyzed globally as "the modern girl." See Modern Girl around the World Research Group et al., eds., *The Modern Girl around the World: Consumption, Modernity, and Globalization* (Durham, NC: Duke University Press, 2008). This volume effectively examines the emergence of "the Modern Girl" within modernity's global contexts of commodity advertising and consumption.

30. Again, of the writers discussed here, Vũ Trọng Phụng is the exception, as he refused European attire.

31. Hoài Thanh and Hoài Chân, *Thi Nhân Việt Nam* [Vietnamese poets] (1941; repr., Hanoi: NXB Văn học, 1998).

32. John T. McAlister and Paul Mus, *The Vietnamese and Their Revolution* (New York: Harper and Row, 1970), 97.

33. Though in a different context, Ngũgĩ Wa Thiong'o has discussed the alienation of the colonized subject's mental universe in starker terms: "It starts with a deliberate dissociation of the language of conceptualisation, of thinking, of formal education, of mental development, from the language of daily interaction in the home and in the community. It is like separating the mind from the body so that they are occupying two unrelated spheres in the same person. On a larger social scale it is like producing a society of bodiless heads and headless bodies." Ngũgĩ Wa Thiong'o, *Decolonising the Mind: The Politics of Language in African Literature* (Portsmouth, NH: Heinemann, 1986), 28.

34. Pheng Cheah, *Spectral Nationality: Passages of Freedom from Kant to Postcolonial Literatures of Liberation* (New York: Columbia University, 2003). Horkheimer and Adorno discuss the crucial distinctions between critical and instrumental rationality in Max Horkheimer and Theodor W. Adorno, *Dialectic of Enlightenment: Philosophical Fragments*, trans. Edmund Jephcott (Stanford, CA: Stanford University Press, 2002). Also see Megan Thomas's discussion of *ilustrados* and the overlap of nationalist and colonialist thought in *Orientalists, Propagandists, and Ilustrados: Filipino Scholarship and the End of Spanish Colonialism* (Minneapolis: University of Minnesota Press, 2012).

35. Frantz Fanon, *The Wretched of the Earth*, trans. Richard Philcox (New York: Grove Press, 2004), 173.

36. Ibid. Fanon outlines this progress in three steps: the intellectual at first assimilates the colonizer's culture but then reacts against his mental subjugation by conjuring up childhood memories as if they constituted some prelapsarian nativism. Such yearning, Fanon continues, is naive and unrealistic since colonialism had violently appropriated and thus disfigured and destroyed the precolonial past. Unlike the native bourgeois who comes to corrupt the decolonized nation, leading it toward neocolonialism, the native intellectual must, finally, join the mass movements advancing national consciousness.

37. Ibid., 238. For further discussion of Fanon's ideas of nationalism and the role of the intellectual, see Neil Lazarus, *Nationalism and Cultural Practice in the Postcolonial World* (Cambridge: Cambridge University Press, 1999), 79–143.

38. For critiques of Fanon's "masculine universal," see Gwen Bergner, "Who Is That Masked Woman? or the Role of Gender in Fanon's *Black Skin, White Masks*," *PMLA* 110.1 (1995): 75–88; and Anne McClintock, "'No Longer in a Future's Heaven': Gender, Race, and Nationalism," in *Dangerous Liaisons: Gender, Nation, and Postcolonial Perspectives*, ed. Anne McClintock, Aamir Mufti, and Ella Shohat (Minneapolis: University of Minnesota Press, 1997), 89–112.

39. Gayatri Chakravorty Spivak, "Can the Subaltern Speak?," in *Marxism and the Interpretation of Culture*, ed. Cary Nelson and Lawrence Grossberg (Urbana and Chicago: University of Illinois Press, 1988), 306.

40. For a discussion of hypermasculinity in relation to colonial domination, see Ashis Nandy, *The Intimate Enemy: Loss and Recovery of Self under Colonialism* (Delhi: Oxford University Press, 1983). Mrinalini Sinha has looked at the mutually constitutive relationship between modern European masculinity and traditional Indian conceptions of masculinity in *Colonial Masculinity: The "Manly" Englishman and the "Effeminate Bengali" in the Late Nineteenth Century* (Manchester: Manchester University Press, 1995).

41. Lisa Rofel, *Other Modernities: Gendered Yearnings in China after Socialism* (Berkeley: University of California Press, 1999), 19–20.

42. Ibid., 19–20. For other discussions of gender and modernity's entwinement, both theoretically and empirically, see Akio Tanabe and Yumiko Tokita-Tanabe, *Gender and Modernity: Perspectives from Asia and the Pacific*, ed. Yoko Hayami, Akio Tanabe, and Yumiko Tokita (Kyoto: Trans Pacific Press, 2003); Rita Felski, *The Gender of Modernity* (Cambridge, MA: Harvard University Press, 1995); and Modern Girl around the World Research Group et al., eds. *The Modern Girl around the World*.

43. See Dipesh Chakrabarty, "The Difference-Deferral of a Colonial Modernity: Public Debates on Domesticity in British India," in *Subaltern Studies VIII*, ed. David

Arnold and David Hardiman (Delhi: Oxford University Press, 1994), 50–88; Partha Chatterjee, *The Nation and Its Fragments: Colonial and Postcolonial Histories* (Princeton, NJ: Princeton University Press, 1993). Also see Sudipta Kaviraj, "The Filth and the Public Sphere: Concepts and Practices about Space in Calcutta," *Public Culture* 10.1 (1997): 83–113; Tanika Sarkar, "The Hindu Wife and the Hindu Nation: Domesticity and Nationalism in Nineteenth-Century Bengal," *Studies in History* 8.2 (1992): 213–35.

44. Barbara Watson Andaya, *Flaming Womb: Repositioning Women in Early Modern Southeast Asia* (Honolulu: University of Hawai'i Press, 2006).

45. Nhung Tuyet Tran, "Woman as Nation: Tradition and Modernity Narratives in Vietnamese Histories," *Gender & History* 24.2 (2012): 411–30. For another nuanced take on gender and modernity, though in the Burmese context, see Chie Ikeya, *Refiguring Women, Colonialism, and Modernity in Burma* (Honolulu: University of Hawai'i Press, 2011).

46. Chris GoGwilt, *The Passage of Literature: Genealogies of Modernism in Conrad, Rhys, & Pramoedya* (New York: Oxford University Press, 2011), esp. 153–75.

47. Ibid.,175.

48. Marr, *Vietnamese Tradition on Trial*, 190–252.

49. Hoàng Ngọc Hiến interview, cited in McHale, "Printing and Power," 29–30.

50. McClintock, "'No Longer in a Future Heaven,'" 95.

51. Vietnamese poetry also went through dramatic transformation, particularly through the Thơ mới (New Poetry) movement, yet it is beyond the scope of this project.

52. For works that emphasize modernism's transnationalism and global dimensions, see Laura Doyle and Laura Winkiel, eds., *Geomodernisms: Race, Modernism, Modernity* (Bloomington: Indiana University Press, 2005); Susan Stanford Friedman, *Mappings: Feminism and the Cultural Geographies of Encounter* (Princeton, NJ: Princeton University Press, 1998); Douglas Mao and Rebecca L. Walkowitz, "The New Modernist Studies," *PMLA* 123.3 (2008); 737–48; and Mark Wollaeger, with Matt Eatough, eds., *The Oxford Handbook of Global Modernisms* (New York: Oxford University Press, 2012).

53. Jessica Berman, *Modernist Commitments: Ethics, Politics, and Transnational Modernism* (New York: Columbia University Press, 2011), 7.

54. See, e.g., Chris GoGwilt, *The Passage of Literature: Genealogies of Modernism in Conrad, Rhys, & Pramoedya* (New York: Oxford University Press, 2011); Simon Gikandi, *Writing in Limbo: Modernism and Caribbean Literature* (Ithaca, NY: Cornell University Press, 1992); Amie Elizabeth Parry, *Interventions into Modernist Culture* (Durham, NC: Duke University Press, 2007); Shu-Mei Shih, *The Lure of the Modern: Writing Modernism in Semicolonial China, 1917–1937* (Berkeley: University of California Press, 2001); and Chana Kronfeld, *On the Margins of Modernism: Decentering Literary Dynamics* (Berkeley: University of California Press, 1996).

55. Rey Chow, *Entanglements, or Transmedial Thinking about Capture* (Durham, NC: Duke University Press, 2012), 37.

56. Rancière has called this *le partage du sensible* (the distribution of the sensible): "[Political statements and literary locutions] define variations of sensible intensities, perceptions, and the abilities of bodies. They thereby take hold of unspecified groups of people, they widen gaps, open up space for deviations, modify the speeds

of trajectories, and the ways in which groups of people adhere to a condition, react to situations, recognize their images." Jacques Rancière, *The Politics of Aesthetics*, trans. Gabriel Rockhill (New York: Continuum, 2004), 39. The new literary reality functioned transitively, as it incarnated literary locutions in the external world through its renegotiation—the distribution of the sensible—of what is sayable and who is able to speak. Because its answers to these questions is anything and anyone, fictional realism is a "democratic" form.

57. I am thinking of Anderson's suggestion of nation-ness as "cultural artefacts": Anderson, *Imagined Communities*. Also see Amilcar Cabral, "National Liberation and Culture," in *Return to the Source: Selected Speeches of Amilcar Cabral*, ed. Africa Information Service (1970; repr., New York: Monthly Review Press, 1973), 39–56.

58. Rancière, *The Politics of Aesthetics*, 27.

59. César Aira, *How I Became a Nun*, trans. Chris Andrews (New York: New Directions Books, 1993), 64–65.

60. Jacques Rancière, *The Politics of Literature*, trans. Julie Rose (Cambridge: Polity Press, 2011), 12–13.

61. See Harry Harootunian, *Overcome by Modernity: History, Culture, and Community in Interwar Japan* (Durham, NC: Duke University Press, 2000), xvi–xvii.

62. See Nguyen Ngoc Tuan, *Socialist Realism in Vietnamese Literature* (n.p.: Vdm Verlag Dr Muller, 2008); and Kim Ngoc Bao Ninh, *A World Transformed: The Politics of Culture in Revolutionary Vietnam, 1945–1965* (Ann Arbor: University of Michigan Press, 2002).

63. Trường Chinh, *Chủ nghĩa Mác và văn hóa Việt Nam* [Marxism and Vietnamese culture] (Hà Nội: NXB Sự thật: 1974), 9–10.

64. Ibid., 17.

65. Even though Trường Chinh defines culture (*văn hóa*) in broad strokes to include "văn học, nghệ thuật, khoa học, triết học, phong tục, tôn giáo" (literature, art, science, philosophy, customs, and religion), this series of speeches only addresses literature.

66. Trường Chinh, *Chủ nghĩa Mác và văn hóa Việt Nam*, 14.

67. Trường Chinh writes, "Thực dân Pháp truyền bà văn hóa Pháp sang Đông-dương để gây ảnh hưởng về tinh thần, nắm lấy trí thức và thanh niên" (The French colonialists disseminated French culture in Indochina to influence the soul, as well to take hold of the mind of the younger generation). See Trường Chinh, *Chủ nghĩa Mác và văn hóa Việt Nam*, 35.

68. See Christopher E. Goscha, *Vietnam or Indochina? Contesting Concepts of Space in Vietnamese Nationalism, 1887–1954* (Copenhagen: NIAS Books, 1995). For an insightful discussion of Vietnamese Republicanism through the author Vũ Trọng Phụng, see Peter Zinoman, *Vietnamese Colonial Republican*.

69. For an early articulation of the dialectical relationship between literature and politics, see Hải Triều, "Sự tiến hóa của văn học và sự tiến hóa của nhân sinh" [The evolution of literature and human life], in *Toàn tập* [Collected works], 2 vols. (Hanoi: NXB Văn học, 1996),1:129–40. In the same year (1933) Hải Triều also sparred with Phan Khôi over materialists vs. idealists, in "Ông Phan Khôi là một học giả duy tâm" *Toàn tập*, 1:241–51. For a critic coming to terms with materialism and eventually aligning himself with Trotskyism (under the pen name Nguyễn Bách Khoa), see Trương Tửu, "Văn học Việt Nam hiện đại" [Modern Vietnamese literature], in *Tuyển tập nghiên cứu*,

phê bình [Selected research and criticism], ed. Nguyễn Hữu Sơn and Trịnh Bá Đĩnh (Hanoi: NXB Lao động, 2007). For Trương Tửu's exploration of romanticism's roots in Vietnam, see Trương Tửu, "Tóm tắt và so sánh *Tố tâm, Nửa chừng xuân, Đoạn Tuyệt*" [Summarizing and comparing *Pure heart, In the midst of spring, Breaking away*] in *Tuyển tập nghiên cứu, phê bình* [Selected research and criticism], ed. Nguyễn Hữu Sơn and Trịnh Bá Đĩnh (Hanoi: NXB Lao động, 2007), 114–18. Also consider Trương Tửu, "Văn-chương lãng mạn ở xứ ta," *Quốc Gia* [Nation] 1.2, Sept. 9, 1938, 2; Trương Tửu, "Cái buồn lãng mạn và các thi sĩ Thế Lữ, Lưu Trọng Lư, Phạm Huy Thông, Nguyễn Vỹ" [The sorrow of romanticism and the poets Thế Lữ, Lưu Trọng Lư, Phạm Huy Thông, Nguyễn Vỹ], *Quốc Gia*, Sept. 9, 1938, 1.2, 1.4. (I thank Peter Zinoman for pointing me to these sources.) It should be noted that Nguyễn Bách Khoa never fell in line with the Party, and after 1957 his books were not published in North Vietnam. For an early Vietnamese interpretation of Marxist-Leninism, see Đặng Thai Mai, *Văn học khái luận* [Outline of literature], in *Toàn tập Đặng Thai Mai* [Collected works of Đặng Thai Mai] (1944; repr., Hanoi: NXB Văn học, 1997), 1:87–319. Also see Đặng Thai Mai, *Vai trò lãng đạo của Đảng trên mặt trận văn học ba mươi năm nay* [The Party's lead in the cultural front in the past thirty years], in *Toàn tập Đặng Thai Mai* (1960; repr., Hanoi: NXB Văn học, 1997), 2:671–724. For self-criticisms against taking part in romanticist movements, particularly the Self-Strength Literary Group, see Thế Lữ, "Những sợi dây trói buộc tôi" [The ropes that bound me], *Văn Nghệ* [Literature and the arts] 41 (1953): 14–20; and Xuân Diệu, "Dứt khoát" [Without question], *Văn Nghệ* [Literature and the arts] 41 (1953): 21–27.

70. See Nguyễn Huệ Chi, "Đổi mới nhân thức lịch sử trong nghiên cứu khoa học xã hội nói chung, nghiên cứu văn học nói riêng" [To renovate the truth in social scientific research in general, literary criticism in particular], *Tạp chí Văn học* [Journal of literature] 6 (1990): 1–9; and Vũ Tam Giang, "Bàn thêm về đổi mới nhận thức lịch sử" [Further renovating the historical truth] *Tạp chi Văn học* 3 (1991): 1–5. For a more sustained critique of the political overtones of Vietnamese socialist realism, see Tuan Ngoc Nguyen, *Văn học Việt Nam dưới chế độ Cộng sản* [Vietnamese literature under the Communist regime] (Stanton, CA: NXB Văn Nghệ, 1996).

CHAPTER 1: AUTOETHNOGRAPHY AND POST-MANDARIN
MASCULINITY

1. Vũ Trọng Phụng, "Cơm thầy cơm cô," in *Phóng sự Việt Nam 1932–1945* [Household servants], ed. Trọng Thưởng Phan, Nguyễn Cừ, and Nguyễn Hữu Sơn (Ho Chi Minh City: NXB Văn học, 2000), 3:769. My translation here differs from "Household Servants" in *The Light of the Capital*, trans. Greg Lockhart and Monique Lockhart (Kuala Lampur: Oxford University Press, 1996), 156.

2. Or to borrow from Henri Bergson, this is a "synthesis of pure memory and pure perception, that is to say of mind and matter" (Henri Bergson, *Matter and Memory*, trans. N. M. Paul and W. S. Palmer [New York: Zone Books, 1988], 244). For a helpful discussion of literary impressionism, see Jesse Matz, *Literary Impressionism and Modernist Aesthetics* (Cambridge: Cambridge University Press, 2001).

3. Vũ Trọng Phụng summarizes the shift to experiential knowledge in the following manner: "So now I would like to become a sociologist, a psychologist, a philosopher, but first I should become a humble servant! A rickshaw puller knows all the

cruelty of human beings far better than a scholar. A room-boy knows more about the debauchery of humanity than a surgeon. A servant understands more clearly the behavior of human beings than a realist writer." This citation is from Lockhart's translation, "Household Servants," 154.

4. See John Carey, introduction to *The Faber Book of Reportage*, ed. John Carey (London: Faber and Faber, 1987).

5. V ũ Ngọc Phan understands *phóng sự* as the "firstborn child" of newspapers. Vũ Ngọc Phan, *Nhà văn hiện đại* [Modern authors] (1941; repr., Saigon: NXB Thanh Long, 1960), 3:557.

6. See Charles Laughlin, *Chinese Reportage: The Aesthetics of Historical Experience* (Durham, NC: Duke University of Press, 2002); Rudolph Wagner, *Inside a Service Trade: Studies in Contemporary Chinese Prose* (Cambridge, MA: Council on East Asian Studies, Harvard University, 1992); Georg Lukács, "Reportage or Portrayal?," in *Essays on Realism*, trans. David Fernbach (London: Lawrence and Wishart, 1980), 45–75.

7. See Phan Trọng Thưởng, introduction to *Phóng sự Việt Nam, 1932–1945*, ed. Phan Trọng Thưởng, Nguyễn Cừ, and Nguyễn Hữu Sơn (Ho Chi Minh City: NXB Văn học, 2000), 1:5–14; Nguyễn Đình Lạp, "Muốn làm phóng sự," [To produce reportage], in *Tác phẩm* [Works], ed. Bạch Liên (Hanoi: NXB Văn hóa-Thông tin, 2003), 791–826; and Vũ Ngọc Phan, *Nhà văn hiện đại*, 3:557–631.

8. See Lukács, "Reportage or Portrayal?," 45–75.

9. George Orwell, "The Prevention of Literature," in *The Collected Essays, Journalism, and Letters of George Orwell*, ed. Sonia Orwell and Ian Angus (New York: Harcourt, Brace & World, 1968), 4:61.

10. In his remarks on *phóng sự*, Vũ Ngọc Phan gives a description that strikingly resembles the work of a participant observer: "to write *phóng sự* is to participate and to note" (*phóng sự là thăm dò lấy việc và ghi lấy việc*). Vũ Ngọc Phan, *Nhà văn hiện đại*, 3:557. This literary ethnography is historically parallel with Nguyen Phuong Ngoc's documentation of the origins of Vietnamese anthropology, particularly her focus on Vietnamese anthropologists associated with l'École française d'Extreme-Orient in the 1930s. See Nguyen Phuong Ngoc, *À l'origine de l'anthropologie au Vietnam: Recherche sur les auteurs de la première moitié du XXe siècle* (Aix-en-Provence: Presses Universitaires de Provence, 2012).

11. Sherry B. Ortner, "Resistance and the Problem of Ethnographic Refusal," *Comparative Studies in Society and History* 37.1 (1995): 173.

12. James Buzard, *Disorienting Fiction: The Autoethnographic Work of Nineteenth-Century British Novels* (Princeton, NJ: Princeton University Press, 2005), 71. Here, Buzard is building on Clifford Geertz's thinking on ethnography.

13. James Buzard, "On Auto-Ethnographic Authority," *Yale Journal of Criticism* 16.1 (Spring 2003): 71; original emphasis.

14. While culture was a vehicle for hegemonic rule in the hands of European imperialists and ethnographers, it was also a means of anticolonial thought in the hands of Vietnamese *phóng sự* writers. On this double-edged aspect of culture in the colonial encounter, see Nicholas B. Dirks, "Introduction: Colonialism and Culture," in *Colonialism and Culture*, ed. Nicholas B. Dirks (Ann Arbor: University of Michigan Press, 1992), 4.

15. Tam Ích praises Tam Lang's prose for its lasting effect, unlike contemporary luminaries such as Nhất Linh, Nguyễn Công Hoan, and Vũ Trọng Phụng. See Tam

Ích, "Nhân đọc: *Tôi kéo xe* của Tam Lang [Tam Lang's *I pull a rickshaw*," *Nhân Văn* [Humanity] 5 (May 1972): 37–43.

16. I have modified Lockhart's translation to emphasize the notion of a common, singular origin in the serialized text. Tam Lang, "I Pulled a Rickshaw," in *The Light of the Capital: Three Modern Vietnamese Classics*, trans. Greg Lockhart and Monique Lockhart (Kuala Lampur: Oxford University Press, 1996), 113.

17. Thượng Sỹ, "Thân thể và sự nghiệp Tam Lang" [The life and work Tam Lang], in *Cuộc đời viết văn, làm báo: Tam Lang, "Tôi kéo xe"* [A life of literature and journalism: Tam Lang, *I pull a rickshaw*], ed. Thế Phong (1996; repr., Hanoi: NXB Tổng hợp Đồng Nai, 2004), 6.

18. Benedict Anderson has suggested autoethnography's significance in anticolonial ethnology and folklore studies, and Charles Keyes has argued that modern Vietnamese and Thai literature can be used as if they were "indigenous ethnographies" or "participant observations." See Anderson, *Under Three Flags*, 1–25; and Charles Keyes, "Vietnamese and Thai Literature as Indigenous Ethnography," in *Southeast Asian Studies: Pacific Perspectives*, ed. Anthony Reid (Tempe, AZ: Program for Southeast Asian Studies Monograph Series, 2003), 193–232. Meanwhile, Pels and Salemink have called for the consideration of ethnographic practices beyond or, more accurately, before the institutionalization and professionalization of academic anthropology. Peter Pels and Oscar Salemink, "Introduction: Locating the Colonial Subjects of Anthropology," in *Colonial Subjects: Essays on the Practical History of Anthropology*, ed. Peter Pels and Oscar Salemink (Ann Arbor: University of Michigan Press, 2000), 1–52.

19. Some critics have defined *phóng sự* primarily as an instrument of social change, namely, by influencing readers as well as sociologists and lawmakers. See Nguyễn Đình Lạp, "Muốn làm phóng sự," 811.

20. Tam Lang, *Tôi kéo xe* (1932; repr., Los Alamitos, CA: NXB Xuân thu, 1988), 94–96.

21. In a 1969 postscript (reprinted in the 1988 edition), Tam Lang himself credits *Tôi kéo xe* for policy changes. See Bradley for a discussion of Tam Lang's reportage in the context of twentieth-century Vietnamese discourse on *văn minh* (civilization) as "transformative rearticulations of individual agency and the proper relations between self and society." Bradley, *Imagining Vietnam and America*, 66. See also David G. Marr, "Concepts of 'Individual' and 'Self' in Twentieth-Century Vietnam," *Modern Asian Studies* 34.4 (2000): 769–96, for another discussion of the individual self and Vietnamese society.

22. Vũ Ngọc Phan has noted that although the colonial government did not tolerate *phóng sự*, it was the most effective writing genre for social reform. See Vũ Ngọc Phan, *Nhà văn hiện đại*, 3:558.

23. Critics have gone so far as to say that the title, *Tôi kéo xe*, is misleading because the narrator had neither the strength nor the skills to pull a rickshaw himself. See Vũ Ngọc Phan, *Nhà văn hiện đại*, 3:560. In the text, Tam Lang's primary interview subject, Tư, observes that the author's body was neither fit nor conditioned for rickshaw pulling (38).

24. Tam Lang, *Tôi kéo xe*, 56.

25. Tam Lang, *Tôi kéo xe*, 35.

26. Tam Lang, *I Pulled a Rickshaw*, trans. Lockhart 83. I have modified parts of this translation. *Tôi kéo xe*, 51.

27. Tam Lang, *Tôi kéo xe*, 65.

28. Ibid., 69.

29. Ibid., 79–80.

30. Buzard, *Disorienting Fiction*, 16.

31. Vũ Trọng Phụng, "Cơm thầy cơm cô," 3:767.

32. Arjun Appadurai, "Introduction: Place and Voice in Anthropological Theory," *Cultural Anthropology* 3.1 (1988): 16.

33. Arjun Appadurai, "Putting Hierarchy in Its Place," *Cultural Anthropology* 3.1 (1988): 37.

34. Ibid., 36, 45.

35. Thạch Lam, "Hà Nội ban đêm" [Hanoi at night], *Phong hóa*, May 5, 1933, 2.

36. For a discussion of prostitution in colonial Vietnam, see Shaun Kingsley Malarney, "Introduction: Vũ Trọng Phụng and the Anxieties of 'Progress,'" in Vũ Trọng Phụng, *Lục Xì: Prostitution and Venereal Disease in Colonial Hanoi* (Honolulu: University of Hawai'i Press, 2011), 1–41. Isabelle Tracol-Huynh has explored French colonialism in Tonkin through prostitution, particularly through the relationship between the European male and the native woman. Elsewhere, she studies the "shadows" of the archives to examine the contradictions of French policies that policed sex workers (primarily through identification cards and medical examinations) but in a way that rendered them anonymous and faceless. See Isabelle Tracol-Huynh, "Between Stigmatisation and Regulation: Prostitution in Colonial Northern Vietnam," *Culture, Health & Sexuality* 12 (Aug. 1, 2010): S73–S87; Isabelle Tracol-Huynh, "The Shadow Theater of Prostitution in French Colonial Tonkin: Faceless Prostitutes under the Colonial Gaze," *Journal of Vietnamese Studies* 7.1 (Jan. 1, 2012): 10–51. For more recent works on contemporary Vietnamese commercial sex, see Kimberly Kay Hoang, *Dealing in Desire: Asian Ascendancy, Western Decline, and the Hidden Currencies of Global Sex Work* (Berkeley: University of California Press, 2015); Thu-hương Nguyễn-võ, *The Ironies of Freedom: Sex, Culture, and Neoliberal Governance in Vietnam* (Seattle: University of Washington Press, 2008).

37. Thạch Lam, "Hà Nội ban đêm," *Phong hóa*, Mar. 10, 1933, 2. *Hà Nội ban đêm* has been republished in the first volume of Phan Trọng Thưởng, Nguyễn Cừ, and Nguyễn Hữu Sơn's edited collection, *Phóng sự Việt Nam*. However, I am citing from the original *Phóng hóa* installments because the reprinted version in the *Phóng sự Việt Nam* collection does not include all serialized entries.

38. Thạch Lam, "Hà Nội ban đêm."

39. I am indebted to Jennifer Fay for pointing out this connection.

40. See Christopher Breu, *Hard-Boiled Masculinities* (Minneapolis: University of Minnesota Press, 2005).

41. See Frank Proschan, "'Syphilis, Opiomania, and Pederasty': Colonial Constructions of Vietnamese (and French) Social Disease," *Journal of the History of Sexuality* 11.4 (2002): 610–36.

42. Maryce Choisy, *A Month among the Girls,* trans. Lawrence G. Blochman (New York: Pyramid Books, 1960), 12–13.

43. Thạch Lam, "Hà Nội ban đêm," *Phong hóa*, Apr. 28, 1933, 4.

44. Ibid., 2.

45. See Malarney's translation, Vũ Trọng Phụng, *Lục xì*, 107.

46. This scenario is also significant in the context of Indonesia through the figure of the *nyai*, a term that refers to a kept woman or concubine in the homes of Dutch and European men. For the importance of *nyai* not only for modernity but also for Indonesian modernism and lingua franca, see GoGwilt, *The Passage of Literature*, 153–71; and James Siegel, *Fetish, Recognition, Revolution* (Princeton, NJ: Princeton University Press, 1997), 50–93.

47. Thạch Lam, "Hà Nội ban đêm," *Phong hóa*, July 28, 1933, 4.

48. Ibid.

49. See Proschan, "'Syphilis, Opiomania, and Pederasty,'" 620–21.

50. Proschan has suggested that such public health policies were not intended to protect Vietnamese sex workers but rather the male French colonials. Proschan, "'Syphilis, Opiomania, and Pederasty,'" 616 624.

51. The more common venereal diseases, gonorrhea and syphilis, were bacterial infections treatable with modern antibiotics; however these antibiotics were unavailable in the 1930s. The dispensaries administered ineffective medicines for treatment or preventive measures—such as the arsenic mercury and bismuth that Việt Sinh smelled when entering brothels. Consequently many admitted women were held indefinitely for months or even years. Malarney, "Introduction," xvii.

52. Malarney, "Introduction," 1–41.

53. Thạch Lam, "Hà Nội ban đêm," *Phong hóa*, July 7, 1933, 2.

54. Ibid., Mar. 10, 1933, 2.

55. Ibid., July 7, 1933, 2.

CHAPTER 2: PORNOGRAPHY AS REALISM, REALISM AS AESTHETIC MODERNITY

1. Vũ Trọng Phụng, *Làm đĩ*, in *Vũ Trọng Phụng: Toàn tập* [Vũ Trọng Phụng: Complete works] (1936; repr., Hanoi: NXB Hội nhà văn, 1999). Translated by Shaun Malarney as *Lục xì* (Honolulu: University of Hawai'i Press, 2011), 158n.

2. My thinking on realism here cuts against the grain of the poststructuralist and postmodernist tendency to dismiss realism as naive or "illusory in the sense of a rhetorical trick designed to mask the arbitrary character of the literary sign" (Christopher Prendergrast, *The Order of Mimesis* [Cambridge: Cambridge University Press, 1986], 2). Prendergrast provides an insightful assessment of literary mimesis and the "epistemic labyrinth" of scholarship, particularly from France, on the topic. While my reassessment of realism further develops Rancière's notion of aesthetic modernity, it is part of what Colleen Lye and Jed Esty have recently called the "new realist turn" in literary criticism. This recent turn focuses on realism's import beyond the well-rehearsed Euro-American purview—to peripheral realisms. Jed Esty and Colleen Lye, "Peripheral Realisms Now," *Modern Language Quarterly* 73.3 (Sept. 2012): 278.

3. For discussion of Phụng's tumultuous literary and intellectual legacy, as well as comprehensive primary and secondary sources on Phụng and his work, see Zinoman, *Vietnamese Colonial Republican*. Shortly after Phụng's death, a

number of colleagues associated with the Tân Dân Publishing House assessed his works; see Ngọc Thiện Nguyễn and Huy Nguyên Lữ, eds., *Tao Đàn 1939* [Literary coterie 1939] (Hanoi: Văn học, 1999), 2:1347–1435. Collections of key works that contributed to the debate on Phụng's literary works include Hữu Tá Trần, *Vũ Trọng Phụng, hôm qua và hôm nay* ([Ho Chi Minh City]: Nhà xuất bản Thành phố Hồ Chí Minh, 1992); Hoành Khung Nguyễn and Lại Nguyên Ân, eds., *Vũ Trọng Phụng, con người và tác phẩm: hồi ức, chân dung, tiểu luận* [Vũ Trọng Phụng, an author and his works: Memoirs, portraits, and essays] (Hanoi: Hội nhà văn, 1994); Lại Nguyên Ân, ed., *Vũ Trọng Phụng, tài năng và sự thật* [Vũ Trọng Phụng, talent and truth] (Hanoi: Nhà xuất bản Văn học, 1997); Ngọc Thiện Nguyễn, ed., *Vũ Trọng Phụng, về tác gia và tác Phẩm* [Vũ Trọng Phụng, on the author and his work] (Hanoi: Nhà xuất bản Giáo dục, 2007).

4. Zinoman, *Vietnamese Colonial Republican*, 86–87.

5. Ibid., 4–5.

6. Trương Tửu, "Địa vị Vũ Trọng Phụng trong văn học Việt Nam cận đại" [Vũ Trọng Phụng's place in modern Vietnamese literature], in Nguyễn and Lữ, *Tao Đàn 1939*, 3.

7. Cited in Vũ Trọng Phụng, *Household Servants*, 154.

8. Nguyễn Văn Vĩnh, an avid translator of French literature, including realism, had observed in 1913 that Vietnamese writers, so indebted to Chinese literature, rarely referenced their own native geography: "If our people write poetry they chant about the landscape of Mount T'ai and the Yellow River, the skies that are high and the seas that are broad. As for the Tân Viên mountains (on the border of Sơn Tây province in northern Vietnam) and the Red River, which are obvious and right in front of their noses, these are landscapes to which they never respond." Cited in Woodside, *Vietnam and the Chinese Model*, 208.

9. Rancière, *Politics of Literature*, 7.

10. Ibid., 4.

11. Đặng Thai Mai, *Văn học khái luận*, 1:88–89.

12. See Anderson, *Imagined Communities*. Anderson extends his discussion of the relationship between print capitalism and nationalism, particularly in terms of seriality and comparison, in *Spectres of Comparison: Nationalism, Southeast Asia, and the World* (London: Verso, 1998).

13. Rancière, *Politics of Literature*, 37.

14. Phan Khôi published this 1936 essay, the same year as the serial publication of *Làm đĩ*, in *Hà Nội báo* [Hanoi newspaper]. See Phan Khôi, "Văn học tiểu thuyết là cái quái gì?" [What is this literary novel?], in *Tác phẩm đăng báo 1936*, ed. Lại Nguyên Ân (Hanoi: NXB Trí thức, 2014), 41–43.

15. Ibid., 41–42.

16. David Der-wei Wang, *Fictional Realism* (New York: Columbia University Press, 1992), 13.

17. Hoài Thanh, "Vấn đề học thuật nước ta" [On the education of our nation], *Sông Hương* [Perfume River] 1 (Aug. 1, 1936), 1.

18. Phan Khôi, "Học với sách và học với chung quanh ta" [To learn with books and to learn with our surroundings], *Sông Hương* 2 (Aug. 8, 1936), 1.

19. Vũ Ngọc Phan, "Quan niệm về lịch sử" [An approach to history], *Sông Hương* 1 (Aug. 1, 1936), 2. Also see Vũ Ngọc Phan, "Về sử học, muốn gần sự thật, cần phải theo phương pháp" [On history, to get at the truth is to have method], *Sông Hương* 2 (Aug. 8, 1936), 2.

20. Phụng, *Household Servants*, 3:755; *Lục xì*, 3:805.

21. Phạm Thế Ngũ goes so far as to define *phóng sự* in contradistinction to the novel: "*phóng sự* writing differs from the novel because the novel requires the form of narrative, authorial inflections, and literary aesthetics to create a work with hues of art, while *phóng sự* is merely a photograph that captures the truth in an unbiased manner, mundane and objective images." See Phạm Thế Ngũ, *Việt Nam văn học sử giản ước tân biên* [History of Vietnamese literature: A new survey], 3 vols (1961; repr., Đong Thap: NXB Đồng Tháp, 1997), 3:521. For a discussion of reportage as a genre distinct from other forms of literature, specifically in the Chinese context, see Laughlin, *Chinese Reportage*, 19–28; and Wagner, *Inside a Service Trade*, 76–77, 260–61.

22. *Làm đĩ* was first published serially, beginning in 1936, in the journal *Sông Hương*. It appeared in book form in 1939.

23. See Zinoman, *Vietnamese Colonial Republican*, 131–55. For the author's response, see Vũ Trọng Phụng, "Để đáp lời báo *Ngày nay*: Dâm hay là không dâm" [To answer the journal *Ngày nay*: Obscene or not obscene], in *Vũ Trọng Phụng, tài năng và sự thật* [Vũ Trọng Phụng, talent and truth], ed. Lại Nguyên Ân (Hanoi: NXB Văn học, 1997), 211–20.

24. Lan Khai, *Vũ Trọng Phụng: Một tài liệu cho văn sử Việt Nam* [Vũ Trọng Phụng: A source for Vietnamese literature] (Hanoi: Minh phương, 1941), 17.

25. Vũ Trọng Phụng, "Lời giao hẹn với độc giả trước khi đọc truyện" [A preface to the reader], *Sông Hương* 2 (Aug. 8, 1936), 4.

26. Ann Stoler, "Making of Empire Respectable: The Politics of Race and Sexual Morality in 20th-Century Colonial Cultures," *American Ethnologist* 1.4 (Nov. 1989): 635.

27. Vũ Trọng Phụng, "Lời giao hẹn với độc giả trước khi đọc truyện," 4.

28. Haiyan Lee, *Revolution of the Heart* (Stanford, CA: Stanford University Press, 2007), 113.

29. Vũ Trọng Phụng, "Lời giao hẹn với độc giả trước khi đọc truyện," 4.

30. This was precisely his critique against the Self-Strength Literary Group. See Vũ Trọng Phụng, "Để đáp lời báo *Ngày nay*: Dâm hay là không dâm," in *Vũ Trọng Phụng, tài năng và sự thật* [Vũ Trọng Phụng, talent and truth], ed. Lại Nguyên Ân (Hanoi: NXB Văn học, 1997), 211–20.

31. Vũ Trọng Phụng, *Làm đĩ*, in *Vũ Trọng Phụng: Toàn tập*, 3:249.

32. I maintain that the conflicting pursuits of leisure and investigation produce a gray area that disguises the men's simultaneous desires and anxiety. For me, this is a complex duality of intellectual, social investigation coupled with marginalized masculinity, a kind of guiltless spoliation. Vũ Trọng Phụng's critics, however, have viewed his methods of participant observation as an alibi for pleasure-seeking excursions to brothels—to which he responds: "For a journalist who wants to do a reportage on prostitution, it is necessary to search for prostitutes in remote places. But our ethics do not allow for such activities, even though they are duties that our profession

forces upon us. For that reason as well, the task of 'investigative interviewing' is regarded as a pretext for carousing, and the relating of those matters in a newspaper has been derided by some as pandering to the corrupt, perverted, obscene (*Lục xì*, Malarney trans., 107).

33. Vũ Trọng Phụng, *Làm đĩ*, 3:251.

34. Ibid., 3:250.

35. Ibid., 3:248.

36. Ibid., 3:411.

37. Ibid., 3:410.

38. Ibid., 3:415. In his brief monograph on Phụng, Lan Khai pushes this identity further, categorizing the author as "nhà phóng sự kiêm tiểu thuyết" (a reportage writer doubling as a novelist). See Lan Khai, *Vũ Trọng Phụng*, 5.

39. Vũ Trọng Phụng, *Làm đĩ*, 3:259.

40. The fictionalization of real-life authors is further apparent in a peculiar mention of Mán Xá, another name for the author Lan Khai, a friend of Vũ Trọng Phụng's. Although the name was known within literary circles as a reference to Lan Khai, it still comes across as fictional to reading audiences.

41. Vũ Trọng Phụng, *Làm đĩ*, 3:268–69.

42. Ibid., 3:277.

43. Ibid., 3:274.

44. Ibid., 3:287.

45. Ibid., 3:319.

46. Ibid., 3:384.

47. Ibid., 3:388.

48. Ibid., 3:394.

49. Rebecca Karl, "Journalism, Social Value, and a Philosophy of the Everyday in 1920s China," *positions: East Asia Culture and Critique* 16.3 (2008): 542.

50. Vũ Trọng Phụng, *Dumb Luck*, trans. Peter Zinoman and Nguyễn Nguyệt Câm (Ann Arbor: University of Michigan Press, 2002), 60.

51. Ibid., 114.

52. Ibid., 100.

53. Ibid., 105.

54. Ibid., 106.

55. Ibid., 107.

56. Ibid.

57. Ibid., 40.

58. Ibid., 55.

CHAPTER 3: THE SOCIOLOGICAL NOVEL AND ANTICOLONIALISM

1. Nhất Linh, *Đoạn tuyệt* [Breaking away] (1935; repr., Saigon: Tự Do, 1972), 190.

2. See Vũ Trọng Phụng, "Để đáp lời báo *Ngày nay*: Dâm hay là không dâm," 211–20.

3. Lee, *Revolution of the Heart*, 7.

4. Wolf Lepenies, *Between Literature and Science: The Rise of Sociology* (Cambridge: Cambridge University Press, 1988), 7.

5. I have in mind here Durkheim's definition of social facts: "any way of acting, whether fixed or not, capable of exerting over the individual an external
constraint . . . which is general over the whole of a given society whilst having
an existence of its own, independent of its individual manifestations." Independent of an individual's will, social facts are produced by a collective society's
"beliefs, tendencies and practices," manifested and imposed on the individual through various forms, including cultural and legal rules, moral maxims,
social convention, and popular expressions. See Émile Durkheim, *The Rules of
Sociological Method*, ed. Steven Lukes, trans. W. D. Halls (London: Macmillan,
1982), 59.

6. See Greg Lockhart, introduction to "Nhất Linh's *Going to France*," *East Asian
History* 8 (1994): 78–81; Phạm Thế Ngữ, *Việt Nam văn học sử* [History of Vietnamese literature], 3:422–44; Vũ Gia, *Nhất Linh trong tiến trình hiện đại hóa văn
học* [Nhất Linh and the modernization of literature] (Hanoi: NXB Văn hóa, 1995).
In 1939 Nhất Linh became heavily involved in politics. With Self-Strength members Hoàng Đạo and Khái Hưng, he founded the Đảng Hưng Việt (Hưng Việt
Party), which later became the Đảng Đại Việt (Đại Việt Party). Both would merge
in 1945 with the Việt Nam Quốc dân Đảng (VNQDD; Vietnamese Nationalist
Party), which had been suppressed by French colonial officials in 1930. In 1945 he
returned to Hanoi and served as foreign minister in the coalition government of
the Democratic Republic of Vietnam. He fled Vietnam again in 1946, for fear that
the Việt Minh were targeting VNQDD members. After a five-year stint in Hong
Kong, he settled in Da Lat and Saigon, where he revived his literary career and
republished works by the Self-Strength group. The Ngô Đình Diệm regime accused
the writer of corroborating in the 1960 attempted government coup. He was not
arrested until 1963, and before his sentencing he ingested cyanide and committed
suicide.

7. Other key members included the novelists Khái Hưng and Thạch Lam;
prominent lyricists of the Thơ mới (New poetry) movement, Xuân Diệu, Huy
Cận, and Thế Lữ; the satirist Tú Mỡ; and the cultural and political commentator Hoàng Đạo.

8. Hoàng Đạo, *Mười điều tm niệm* [Ten points] (1939; repr., Los Alamitos, CA:
Xuân Thu Publishing, 1989), 17–22.

9. Cited and translated in Hùynh Sanh Thông, "Main Trends of Vietnamese Literature between the Two World Wars," 113–14.

10. Thanh Lãng, *Phê bình văn học thế hệ 1932* [A literary critique of the 1932 gen-
eration] (Saigon: Phong trào văn hóa, 1972), 1:16–27.

11. Tứ Ly. "Bên đường dừng bước" [On the side of the road], *Phong hóa* [Cus-
toms], Mar. 2, 1934.

12. Nhất Linh, "Thanh niên và công việc xã hội," [Youth and the work of society].
Ngày nay [Today], June 19, 1938: 23.

13. Nguyễn Hoành Khung has observed: "From the August Revolution until now
(1989), the Marxist literary discourse and the public masses are most unified in their
perception of romanticist literature as passive and negative." Nguyễn Hoành Khung,
"Lời giới thiệu" [Introduction], in *Văn xuôi lãng mạn Việt Nam 1930–1945* [Viet-
namese romanticist prose, 1930–1945], ed. Nguyễn Hoành Khung and Phong Hà
(Hanoi: NXB Khoa học xã hội, 1989), 1:11. Also see Trương Tửu, "Văn học Việt

Nam hiện đại"; Trương Tửu, "Văn-chương lãng mạn ở xứ ta" [Our romanticist literature]; Trường Chinh, *Chủ nghĩa Mác và văn hóa Việt Nam* [Marxism and Vietnamese culture] (Hanoi: NXB Sự thật, 1974); Phan Cự Đệ, *Tiểu thuyết Việt Nam hiện đại* [The modern Vietnamese novel], 2 vols. (Hanoi: NXB Đại học và trung học chuyên nghiệp, 1975).

14. Trương Tửu, "Khi ông Nhất Linh muốn làm nhà xã hội học" [When Nhất Linh wanted to be a sociologist], in *Tiểu thuyết Thứ Năm: Tác giả và tác phẩm* [Authors and works of *Thursday Novel*], ed. Anh Chi (1938; repr., Hanoi: NXB Văn học, 2002), 2:691–92.

15. For a discussion on this aspect of Vietnamese intellectuals' roles during the 1920s, see Woodside, *Community and Revolution in Modern Vietnam*, 70–71.

16. For instance, there is the Vietnamese notion of *tứ đức* (four virtues). Although the English translation of this term suggests an ungendered denotation, it applies only to women. The four virtues are *công, dung, ngôn, hạnh* (labor, tolerance, words and deeds, geniality). Besides providing labor in the domestic sphere, a complete or ideal woman is supposed to be cheery, tolerant, and humble in her mannerisms, disposition, words, and deeds—never acting, expressing herself, or even holding herself in a manner that is emotional or rash. Such social expectations exist independently of an individual's will, yet are instilled with a coercive power that exerts control over the individual.

17. I am borrowing from Robert Campany's rethinking of "religion" in terms of repertoire. See Robert Ford Campany, "On the Very Idea of Religions (in the Modern West and in Early Medieval China)," *History of Religions* 42.4 (May 2003): 287–319.

18. In a series of essays, the Self-Strengthening group's political essayist Hoàng Đạo argued for the mutualism between French colonialism and Confucian social structures. See Hoàng Đạo, *Mười điều tâm niệm*.

19. See Nguyễn Hoành Khung, "Lời giới thiệu."

20. Anthony Giddens, *The Consequences of Modernity* (Stanford, CA: Stanford University Press, 1990), 39.

21. Ibid., 16; original emphasis.

22. Gyan Prakash, "Writing Post-Orientalist Histories of the Third World: Perspectives from Indian Historiography," *Comparative Studies in Society and History* 32.2 (1999): 390.

23. Dipesh Chakrabarty, *Provincializing Europe: Postcolonial Thought and Historical Difference* (Princeton, NJ: Princeton University Press, 2000).

24. Pheng Cheah, *Spectral Nationality*, 268–69.

25. Gayatri Chakravorty Spivak, *A Critique of Postcolonial Reason: Toward a History of the Vanishing Present* (Cambridge, MA: Harvard University Press, 1999), 272.

26. Ibid., 274.

27. Steven Seidman, "Empire and Knowledge: More Troubles, New Opportunities for Sociology," *Contemporary Sociology* 25.3 (May 1996): 314.

28. Manuela Boatcă and Sergio Costa, "Postcolonial Sociology: A Research Agenda," in *Decolonizing European Sociology*, ed. Encarnación Gutierrez Rodriguez, Manuela Boatcă, and Sérgio Costa (Aldershot: Ashgate, 2010), 13–31.

29. Nhất Linh, *Đoạn tuyệt*, 117.

30. Ibid., 177.

31. Ibid., 69.

32. Ibid., 70.

33. For a discussion of the critical significance of train travel and technology, see Wolfgang Schivelbusch, *Railway Journey: The Industrialization of Time and Space in the 19th Century* (Berkeley: University of California Press, 1986), 16–44.

34. Phan Cự Đệ, *Tự Lực văn đoàn: con người và văn chương* [The Self-Strength Literary Group: The authors and the literature] (Hanoi: Văn Học, 1990), 23; original emphasis.

35. This accusation against these pseudorevolutionary, romanticist characters is levied at their authorial creators as well. Phan Cự Đệ continues, "These primary characters have been idealized by romanticist literature, to the point where they are merely characteristics of the authors." See Phan Cự Đệ, *Tự Lực văn đoàn*, 24.

36. Nhất Linh, *Đoạn tuyệt*, 100.

37. Ibid., 101.

38. Ibid., 117.

39. Ibid., 162.

40. The novel's focus on and criticism of rituals directly challenge Phạm Quỳnh's promotion of Confucian tradition through his journalistic and photographic descriptions of rituals. His writings and images of ritual were published in *Nam Phong*. For a discussion of Phạm Quỳnh's publications on traditional Vietnamese rituals, see Marr, *Vietnamese Tradition on Trial*, 111. For Phạm Quỳnh's connections to the French colonial government, see Nguyễn Văn Hoàn, "Chung Quanh Cuộc Tranh Luận Về "Phạm Quỳnh-Ngô Đức Kế và Truyện Kiều" ở Miền Nam" [Surrounding the "Phạm Quỳnh-Ngô Đức Kế and Truyện Kiều" debate in Vietnam], *Tạp chí văn học* 7 (1964): 59–61.

41. Nhất Linh, *Đoạn tuyệt*, 64–65.

42. Ibid., 80.

43. Loan has little faith in the sincerity of the relationships ritualistically forged (again, we have the image of strings): "In the familial tradition, there are no natural strings of affection that bring together one person with another, so they take the strings of insincere relationship and tie each other up." Ibid., 68.

44. Ibid., 144.

45. Ibid., 165.

46. These specific claims are made, respectively, by Bạch Năng Thi, "Nhất Linh—tác giả tiêu biểu" [Nhất Linh—A representative author], in *Tự Lực văn đoàn: trong tiến trình văn học dân tộc* [Tự Lực văn đoàn: Within the progress of national literature], ed. Mai Hương (Hanoi: Nhà xuất bản Văn hóa—Thông tin, 2000), 211–32; Trường Chinh, "Nhất Linh," in *Tự Lực văn đoàn: trong tiến trình văn học dân tộc*, ed. Mai Hương (Hanoi: Nhà xuất bản Văn hóa—Thông tin, 2000), 236–37; Bùi Xuân Bảo, *Le Roman vietnamien contemporain: Tendances et évolution du roman vietnamien contemporain, 1925–1945* [The contemporary Vietnamese novel: Tendencies and evolution of the contemporary Vietnamese novel, 1925–1945] (Saigon: Imprimerie Long Vân, 1972), 171–75; and Trương Chính, *Dưới mắt tôi* [Beneath my eyes] (Hanoi, 1939), 17–18.

47. The initial accusation was written in a sarcastic manner and published in a column that poked fun at a number of authors, including Phạm Quỳnh, recounting the high and low moments of their writing careers. The comments on Nguyễn Công Hoan read: "Nguyễn Công Hoan has done extensive research to write *Golden branches, leaves*

of jade just like *In the Midst of Spring*, and *Miss Minh, a Schoolteacher* exactly like *Breaking Away*." The implications of these remarks cannot be underestimated. The accusations exploded into a heated debate that permanently split the literary field into those who belonged to the Self-Strengthening group and those who did not. See "Xuân thủ đàm ân," *Phong hóa*, Jan. 31, 1936, 3. For a discussion of the debate and the subsequent division of literary camps, see Thanh Lãng, *Phê bình văn học thế hệ 1932*, 2:202–24.

48. Nguyễn Công Hoan, "Từ *Đoạn tuyệt* đến *Cô giáo Minh*," in *13 năm tranh luận văn học* [Thirteen years of literary debates], ed. Thanh Lãng (1936; repr., Ho Chi Minh City: Nhà xuất bản Văn học, 1995), 1:74–75.

49. Ibid., 1:75.

50. Nguyễn Công Hoan, *Cô giáo Minh* [Miss Minh, schoolteacher] (1936; repr., Ho Chi Minh City: Nhà xuất bản văn nghệ, 1998), 195.

51. In their Marxist analysis of women's subjugated position within Vietnamese patriarchy, for example, Cựu Kim Sơn and Văn Huệ emphasized the significance of interrelated discourses. While arguing for women's liberation through a reconfiguration of the social relations between classes, they focused on the importance of women's writing in periodicals like *Phụ nữ tân văn*, *Phụ nữ thời đàm*, and *Đàn bà mới*, as well as literary representations of women—specifically Nhất Linh's *Đoạn tuyệt*. Discourses also had broader implications, taking advantage of "Indochina's fascination with books in which characters demand the right to organize unions, demand the improvement of working conditions for the masses." See Cựu Kim Sơn and Văn Huệ, *Đời chị em* [The life of women] (Hanoi: Dân Chúng, 1938), 1–2, 16, 24.

52. Hùynh Sanh Thông, "Main Trends of Vietnamese Literature between the Two World Wars," 117, 120–21.

53. Giddens, *The Consequences of Modernity*, 176.

54. Hoàng Đạo, *Bùn lầy nước đọng* [Muddied, stagnant water] (1938; repr., Saigon: Tự do, 1959), 116.

CHAPTER 4: I SPEAK IN THE THIRD PERSON: WOMEN AND LANGUAGE IN COLONIAL VIETNAM

1. Khái Hưng, *Nửa chừng xuân* [In the midst of spring] (Saigon: Văn nghệ, 1969), 8.

2. Ibid., 10.

3. For a history of Western ideas of individualism in Vietnam, beginning with their introduction by European Catholic missionaries in the seventeenth century to the 1930s, see Marr, "Concepts of 'Individual' and 'Self,'" 774–78.

4. Marr, *Vietnamese Tradition on Trial*, 190–251; McHale, *Print and Power*.

5. Consider Vũ Ngọc Phan's 1941 *Nhà văn hiện đại* [Modern writers], a survey of literary editors, essayists, translators, poets, and novelists from the first three decades of the twentieth century. Only two of the sixty-seven writers profiled by Vũ Ngọc Phan were women. See Vũ Ngọc Phan, *Nhà văn hiện đại*.

6. Hùynh Sanh Thông, "Main Trends of Vietnamese Literature between the Two World Wars," 105–7; Marr, *Vietnamese Tradition on Trial*, 196, 203. For readings of Mai as an appropriated symbol by Khái Hưng's moral vision, see Wynn Wilcox, "Women, Westernization and the Origins of Modern Vietnamese Theatre," *Journal of Southeast Asian Studies* 37.2 (2006): 205–24; Neil Jamieson, *Understanding Vietnam* (Berkeley: University of California Press, 1995), 118.

7. Greg Lockhart, introduction to *The Light of the Capital: Three Modern Vietnamese Classics*, trans. Greg Lockart and Monique Lockhart (Oxford: Oxford University Press, 1996), 6.

8. Ibid., 7.

9. Ibid., 13.

10. Marr, "Concepts of 'Individual' and 'Self,'" 788–90.

11. Ibid., 786.

12. Ibid., 788–89.

13. Ibid., 788.

14. Critics have pinpointed the conflict between the modern individual and the
traditional family as the central issue of *Nửa chừng xuân*. Trương Chính emphasizes
the novel's depiction of a struggle between an individual and the larger family, while
Neil Jamieson underscores the conflict between "moral individualism" and "tradition." See Trương Chính, *Dưới mắt tôi* [Beneath my eyes], 43–47; and Jamieson,
Understanding Vietnam, 118.

15. Émile Benveniste, *Problems in General Linguistics*, trans. Mary Elizabeth
Meek (Coral Gables, FL: University of Miami Press, 1971), 218; original emphasis.

16. Lydia Liu, *Translingual Practice: Literature, National Culture, and Translated
Modernity—China 1900–1937* (Stanford, CA: Stanford University Press, 1995), 152.

17. Ibid., 150–55.

18. Ibid., 152.

19. Ibid., 154–55; original emphasis.

20. Understood as a practical activity in a social context, language is the medium
that relates a community of speakers to the object world. Meanings of words are contingent on and contribute to the "forms of life," the situational contexts in which language is used. See Ludwig Wittgenstein, *Philosophical Investigations*, trans. G. E. M.
Anscombe (Oxford: Blackwell, 2001), no. 23 and no. 31.

21. Phan Khôi has even hypothesized that the Vietnamese language's person-
reference system was one of *trung lập* (neutrality) and *phổ thông* (commonality)—
until Confucius's time when common nouns that signified social rank and
kinship relations were used as if they were pronouns for first-, second-, and
third-person references. "Kiểm thảo về đại danh từ" [To critique pronouns], in
Việt ngữ nghiên cứu [Vietnamese linguistics] (Danang: NXB Đà Nẵng, 1997),
129–40.

22. For a discussion of the relationship between discursive practices, particularly person-referring forms, and Vietnamese class-structured opposition to French
colonialism, see Hy Văn Lương, "Discursive Practices and Power Structure: Person-
Referring Forms and Sociopolitical Struggle in Colonial Vietnam," *American Ethnologist* 15 (1988): 239–53.

23. Hy Văn Lương, *Discursive Practices and Linguistic Meanings: The Vietnamese
System of Person Reference* (Amsterdam: John Benjamins, 1990), 70.

24. Ibid., 129–30.

25. Marr, "Concepts of 'Individual' and 'Self,'" 775–81.

26. Hy Văn Lương, *Discursive Practices and Linguistic Meanings*, 126.

27. Ibid., 131.

28. Pierre Bourdieu, *Language and Symbolic Power*, trans. Gino Raymond and
Matthew Adamson (Cambridge, MA: Harvard University Press, 1991), 54.

29. Akio Tanabe and Yumiko Tokita-Tanabe, "Introduction: Gender and Modernity in Asia and the Pacific," in *Gender and Modernity*, 8.

30. Thanh Lãng writes, "As a woman, Mai is noble, sincere towards people, loyal to her parents, and selflessly dedicated to her younger brother." Similarly, Neil Jamieson concludes that in Mai there is the "capacity of the individual human spirit for courage, self-sacrifice and perseverance in the face of adversity." Phạm Thế Ngũ describes her relationship with Lộc as an "ái tình cao thượng" (noble love). Meanwhile, Vũ Ngọc Phan not only calls it a "bạn tình lý tưởng" (ideal friendship) but also comments on how it is unrealistic, thus never realizable. For Trương Chính, Khái Hưng's portrayal of Mai is too idealistic and ambiguous to resolve her struggles against traditional, familial values. See Thanh Lãng, *Bảng lược đồ văn học Việt Nam* [A concise history of Vietnamese literature], 2 vols. (Saigon: NXB Trình bầy, 1967), 2:723; Jamieson, *Understanding Vietnam*, 118; Phạm Thế Ngũ, *Việt Nam văn học sử: Giản ước tân biên* [History of Vietnamese literature: A new survey], 3:463; Vũ Ngọc Phan, *Nhà văn hiện đại* [Modern authors], 3:829; and Trương Chính, *Dưới mắt tôi* [Beneath my eyes], 47–50.

31. Khái Hưng, *Nửa chừng xuân*, 115.

32. Ibid., 115–16.

33. Hy Văn Lương, *Discursive Practices and Linguistic Meanings*.

34. Khái Hưng, *Nửa chừng xuân*, 73–74.

35. The onomatopoetic name Ái, then, proves exceptional, given that in the Vietnamese language proper names typically have significant pragmatic implications. Take the protagonist's full name as an example: Dương Thị Mai. With the middle name's nondescript meaning of "person," the name "Thị" is always used as a middle name for females. Conversely, Văn is the most popular middle name for males, and not coincidentally it is also the word for literature. Hy Văn Lương writes: "All these middle and proper names imply an expectation of the bearers' behavioral conformity to the rules of the male-oriented model. . . . They also reinforce the male-dominated pragmatic implications and conception of male and female behavior—a conception which is inextricably linked to the male/female distinction itself." The assumed relationship between male distinction, education, and literature, as we have seen, is a point that Mai contests in the novel. Hy Văn Lương, *Discursive Practices and Linguistic Meanings*, 92–93.

36. Khái Hưng, *Nửa chừng xuân*, 255–56.

37. Ibid., 252.

38. Ibid.

39. Ibid.

40. Ibid., 253.

41. Ibid., 257.

42. Ibid., 268.

43. Ibid., 269.

44. Hy Văn Lương, *Discursive Practices and Linguistic Meanings*, 70.

45. As Hue-Tam Ho Tai has observed, though Khái Hưng and his peers in the Self-Strength group were progressive writers concerned about women and their rights, their representations situated women in "a suffocating web of familial relationships . . . their female protagonists were denied the right to be individual women acting in a context larger than the family system." The domestic space, in this case, is

analogous to colloquial language, and political activity to the agency of writing. Hue-Tam Ho Tai, *Radicalism and the Origins of the Vietnamese Revolution*, 253.

CHAPTER 5: QUEER INTERNATIONALISM AND MODERN VIETNAMESE AESTHETICS

1. Pierre Do-Dinh, "Pierre Do-dinh à André Gide. 4 August 1928. Letter I of Correspondance inédite avec André Gide," in *Question colonial et écriture: Actes du colloque organisé par le RIASEM à Nice,* ed. Guy Degas (Poitiers: Torii, 1994), 93.

2. Pierre Do-Dinh, "Les Conditions veritable d'un accord," in *L'Homme de couleur,* ed. S. E. le Cardinal Verdier (Paris: Librarie Plon, 1939), 41.

3. For a survey of Gide's presence in modern Vietnamese literature, see Lộc Phương Thủy, "André Gide ở Việt Nam: Một vài nhận xét bước đầu" [André Gide in Vietnam: Some initial observations], in *André Gide: Đời văn và tác phẩm* [André Gide: Life and works], ed. Lộc Phương Thủy (Hanoi: Khao học xã hội, 2002), 77–108.

4. This is not to say that Gide's same-sex sensibilities did not inform his modernist techniques, such as stylistic indirection and fragmentation, but that Vietnamese writers were invested, primarily, in Gide's expressed literary politics and, secondarily, his literary practice.

5. Vietnam's art-versus-life debate, for instance, runs parallel with Bloch and Lukács's heated discussion of expressionism. Both of these exchanges had the 1935 International Writers' Congress for the Defense of Culture as their backdrop. In both cases, it is realism, as a "coherent, infinitely mediated totality," that is set against the subjectivity of idealism. Ernst Bloch, "Discussing Expressionism," trans. Rodney Livingstone, in *Aesthetics and Politics*, ed. Ronald Taylor (London: Verso, 2002), 22. There are, of course, multiple deviations. Whereas the German case was a dispute between realism and modernism, the Vietnamese debate was a division between realism and romanticism. As I am attempting to demonstrate, one of the most distinctive differences in the Vietnamese exchange was the influence of Gide's sexual politics. For a discussion of the German case, see Bloch, "Discussing Expressionism"; and Georg Lukács, "Realism in the Balance," trans. Rodney Livingstone, in *Aesthetics and Politics*, ed. Ronald Taylor (London: Verso, 2002), 29–59.

6. Timothy Brennan offers a suggestive intellectual history of how the Comintern's dissemination of Marxist ideas sought to level out the differences between Europe and its colonies during the interwar period, effectively altering the cultural politics and intellectual activism internationally. See Timothy Brennan, "Postcolonial Studies between the European Wars," in *Marxism, Modernity and Postcolonial Studies,* ed. Crystal Bartolovich and Neil Lazarus (Cambridge: Cambridge University Press, 2002), 185–203.

7. Hue-Tam Ho Tai, "Literature for the People: From Soviet Policies to Vietnamese Polemics," in *Borrowings and Adaptations in Vietnamese Culture,* ed. Truong Buu Lam (Honolulu: Center for Asian and Pacific Studies, 1987), 64.

8. Pheng Cheah has discussed the nuances and differences between Goethe's, Kant's, and Marx's conceptualization of a "world literature." According to Cheah, Goethe perceives world literature as a process of translation and literary exchanges that moves beyond national borders; Kant's *Third Critique* argues for the constitution of sociability through the communication, universally, of one's inmost self; and

Marx understood world literature as an "epiphenomenon" of the global forces of capitalist production. What the three thinkers, however, hold in common—the belief in world literature's transcendence of local conditions—differs from Gide's international model premised on particularity. Cheah writes, "Like Kant and Goethe, Marx uses the word *world* to describe the transcendence of particular local and national barriers and limitations." Pheng Cheah, What Is a World? On World Literature as a World-Making Activity," *Daedalus* 137.3 (2008): 32. Elsewhere, he insightfully argues that a "concrete universal is constitutively open to being affected by *other particulars* and, hence, by alterity and particularity in general. This radical openness to alterity and particularity is a type of finitude that cannot be transcended." Pheng Cheah, "Universal Areas: Asian Studies in a World of Motion," in *The Postcolonial and the Global*, ed. Ravathi Khishnaswarmy and John C. Hawley (Minneapolis: University of Minnesota Press, 2008), 64; original emphasis.

9. Fanon, *The Wretched of the Earth*, 180.

10. Pheng Cheah, "Universal Areas," 10–11.

11. With the tide of fascism rising in Germany and Italy, 230 delegates from 38 countries gathered in Paris to reevaluate the purposes of cultural aesthetics and literature. Foreshadowing the formation of the Popular Front (which was officially proclaimed three weeks after the International Writers' Congress), the organizers of the congress invited writers of various leftist perspectives—Communists and non-Communist leftists, radicals and moderates—from E. M. Forster to Bertolt Brecht to Louis Aragon. For English versions of Gide's speech, see Gide, "The Individual." For accounts of the conference, see Christina Stead, "The Writers Take Sides," *Left Review* 1.11 (1935): 453–62; Patricia Hilden and Timothy Reiss, "Discourse, Politics, and the Temptations of Enlightenment: Paris 1935," *Annals of Scholarship* 8.1 (1991): 61–78; Roger Shattuck, *The Innocent Eye* (New York: Farrar, Straus & Giroux, 1984), 3–30; and Malcolm Cowley, *The Dreams of the Golden Mountains* (New York: Penguin Books, 1992), 280–93.

12. André Gide, "Allocution d'ouverture," in *Littérature engagée*, ed. Yvonne Davet (Paris: Gallimard, 1950), 84.

13. André Gide, "Défense de la culture," in Davet, *Littérature engagée*, 86.

14. Ibid., 85.

15. Ibid., 86; original emphasis.

16. Thiếu Sơn, "Hai quan niệm về văn học" [Two literary perspectives], in *13 năm tran luận văn học* [13 years of literary debates], ed. Thanh Lãng (1935; repr., Ho Chi Minh City: Hội nghiên cứu và giảng dạy văn học, 1995), 1:109.

17. Thiếu Sơn, "Nghệ thuật với đời người" [Art and human life], in Thanh Lãng, *13 năm tran luận văn học*, 1: 114.

18. Hải Triều, "Nghệ thuật vị nghệ thuật hay nghệ thuật vị nhân sinh" [Art for art's sake or art for life's sake], in *Toàn tập* [Collected works] (Hanoi: Văn học, 1996), 1:261. Hải Triều's insistence on realism anticipates Lukács's dismissal of avant-garde and modernist movements in his 1938 debate with Bloch on expressionism. Lukács specifically attacked expressionism's path toward fascism, its irrational mythology and subjectivity, "abstract pacifism," "bourgeois qualities," and "escapist quality." Lukács, "Realism in the Balance," 19. With Hải Triều's words as precedent, the attacks in Vietnam against "subjective" aesthetics persisted through the revolution against French colonialism, the two Indochinese Wars, and up to the 1986 perestroika, when the government opened

the country to foreign capital investment. This literary history resulted from state-sponsored Marxist criticism and its attempts to legitimate a cultural history that justified Communist insurgency while condemning bourgeois sensibilities.

19. Đặng Thai Mai also invokes in a similar manner Gide's politics and aesthetics as a argument for socialist realism. See Đặng Thai Mai, *Văn học khái luận* [Outline of literature], in *Toàn tập Đặng Thai Mai* [Collected works of Đặng Thai Mai], 1:125–73.

20. Thiếu Sơn, "Hai quan niệm về văn học," 108.

21. Thiếu Sơn, "Văn học bình dân" [Popular literature], *13 năm tran luận văn học*, 1:114.

22. Cited in Hoài Thanh, "Văn chương là văn chương" [Literature is literature], in *Bình luận văn chương* [Comments on literature], ed. Nguyễn Ngọc Thiện and Từ Sơn (Hanoi: Giáo dục, 1998), 33.

23. Hoài Thanh, "Một bài diễn văn tối quan trọng về văn hóa" [A crucial expression on literature], in *Văn chương và hành động* [Literature and action] (Hanoi: Hội nhà văn, 1999), 84.

24. Hoài Thanh, "Văn chương là văn chương," 25.

25. Hải Triều, "*Kép Tư Bền*, Một tác phẩm thuộc về cái triều lưu 'nghệ thuật vị dân sinh' ở nước ta" [*Tư Bền the Actor*, a literary work for 'Art for Life's Sake' in our country], in *Toàn tập* [Collected works] (Hanoi: Văn học, 1996), 1:268–69, 273.

26. Hải Triều, "Nghệ thuật và sự sinh hoạt xã hội" [Art and social life], in *Toàn tập* [Collected works], 1:288.

27. Ibid., 1:305.

28. Ibid., 1:304.

29. Hải Triều, "*Kép Tư Bền*, 1:272–73.

30. Hải Triều, "*Lầm Than*: Một tác phẩm đầu tiên của nên văn tả thực xã hội ở nước ta" [*Misery*: An initial work of socialist realism in our country], in *Về văn học nghệ thuật* [On literary arts] (Hanoi: Văn Học, 1969), 59.

31. For example, a prostitute tricks a rickshaw puller into helping her solicit customers by delaying payment in "Ngựa người, người ngựa" (Human horse, horse human). In "Thằng ăn cắp" (Thief), a beggar steals from a food vendor and is beaten by a street mob. A fatherless child remembers his father as his mother sleeps with another man in "Nỗi vui sướng của thằng bé khốn nạn" (The comforts of a wretched child).

32. Literary realism in Vietnam burgeoned during the rise of the Popular Front in France and its loosened censorship policies. However, this does not completely explain the rapid emergence of Vietnamese realism. The significance of Vietnamese realism, I argue, originates from a democratic approach to subject matter that is in itself revolutionary but often presupposed.

33. Cited in Hải Triều, "Nghệ thuật và sự sinh hoạt xã hội" [Art and social activism], 1:292–93n. For the original letter, see Gustave Flaubert, "À George Sand," Mar. 10, 1876, in *Correspondance*, ed. Jean Bruneau (Paris: Gallimard, 1973), 5:25–27.

34. See Flaubert to Sand, Dec. 31, 1875, in Bruneau, *Correspondance*, 5: 999–1001.

35. Sand to Flaubert, Jan. 15, 1876, in *Gustave Flaubert–George Sand Correspondance*, ed. Alphonse Jacobs (Paris: Flammarion, 1981), 519.

36. In a discussion of Flaubert's aesthetics, Rancière elucidates the "law of democracy, the law of universal equivalence" that underpins Hải Triều's and Thiếu Sơn's

references to Flaubert. Rancière writes about Flaubert's aesthetics: "There is no border separating poetic matters from prosaic matters, no border between what belongs to the poetical realm of noble action and what belongs to the territory of prosaic life. This statement is not a personal conviction. It is the principle that constitutes literature as such. Flaubert underlines it as the principle of pure Art; pure Art has it that Art owes no dignity to its subject matters." Jacques Rancière, "Why Emma Bovary Had to Be Killed," *Critical Inquiry* 34.2 (2008): 237.

37. Flaubert wrote to Louise Colet, "What seems beautiful to me, what I should like to write, is a book about nothing, a book dependent on nothing external, which would be held together by the internal strength of its style." Flaubert, "À Louise Colet," Jan. 16, 1852, in Bruneau, *Correspondance*, 2:31.

38. Hoài Thanh, "Văn chương là văn chương," 25.

39. Cited in Thiếu Sơn, "Nghệ thuật và đời người," 112.

40. As Flaubert stated, "In my ideals of art, I believe that an author should not reveal any of this [convictions, anger, indignations], that an artist not appear in his work more than God in nature." See Flaubert to Sand, Dec. 31, 1875, in Bruneau, *Correspondance*, 4:999–1001.

41. Thiếu Sơn, "Nghệ thuật và đời người," 112.

42. Hoài Thanh, "Một bài diễn văn tối quan trọng về văn hóa," 89.

43. Ibid., 91.

44. Lưu Trọng Lư, "Con đường riêng của trí thức" [An intellectual's own path], in *André Gide: Đời văn và tác phẩm* [André Gide: Life and works], ed. Lộc Phương Thủy (Hanoi: Khao học xã hội, 2002), 432–33.

45. Lưu Trọng Lư, "Con đường riêng của trí thức," 435.

46. Michael Lucey, *Gide's Bent: Sexuality, Politics, Writing* (New York: Oxford University Press, 1995), 216.

47. Nguyễn Công Hoan, "Nhân tình tôi," in *Toàn tập* [Collected works], ed. Lê Minh (Hanoi: Văn Học, 2003), 1:119.

48. Ibid., 121.

49. The fact that the short story is one of the primary literary genres at the crux of Vietnam's art-versus-life debate indicates print culture's significance in the formation of social relations and communities that previously had not existed. The short story's compact form and accessible prose made it the preferred literary genre for editors, authors, and readers of a burgeoning literary field that had been restructured and reoriented by print capitalism. Modern Vietnamese novels, most of which were published during the 1930s, first appeared serially as short fiction in magazines and journals. The specific case of *Kép Tư Bền* attests to the success of short fiction printed in journals and magazines. Before printing stories in book form under the title *Kép Tư Bền*, the publishing house *Tân Dân* ran the stories individually in its journals *Tiểu thuyết thứ bảy* (Saturday novel) and *Phổ thông bàn nguyệt san* (Monthly bulletin).

CONCLUSION

1. As W. E. B. Du Bois has said of the "twoness" of the American Negro's double consciousness, it "lets him see himself through the revelation of the other world. It is a peculiar sensation, this double consciousness, this sense of always looking at one's self through the eyes of others, of measuring one's soul by the tape of a world that

looks on in amused contempt and pity." William Edward Burghardt Du Bois, *The Souls of Black Folk: Authoritative Text, Contexts, Criticism*, ed. Henry Louis Gates and Terri Hume Oliver (New York: W. W. Norton, 1999), 10–11.

2. Pheng Cheah, "Grounds of Comparison," 11.

3. Anderson, *Spectres of Comparison*, 5.

4. Pheng Cheah, *Spectral Nationality*, 273.

5. Harry Harootunian has identified the everyday as the critical site of modernity: "Thus modernity, especially everyday existence and experience, becomes the site where the past is always situated in the present and where differing forms of historical consciousness constantly commingle and interact." See Harootunian, *History's Disquiet* (New York: Columbia University Press, 2002), 105.

6. Rancière, *The Politics of Aesthetics*, 32.

7. Harootunian, *History's Disquiet*, 51.

8. Frederick Cooper, *Colonialism in Question: Theory, Knowledge, History* (Berkeley: University of California Press, 2005), 10, 116, 133.

9. Liesl Olson, *Modernism and the Ordinary* (Oxford: Oxford University Press, 2009).

10. Saikat Majumdar, *Prose of the World: Modernism and the Banality of Empire* (New York: Columbia University Press, 2013), 36.

11. Ibid., 36.

12. See Harootunian, *History's Disquiet*.

13. Fanon, *The Wretched of the Earth*, 5.

Allan, Michael. "Reading with One Eye, Speaking with One Tongue: On the Problem of Address in World Literature." *Comparative Literature Studies* 44 (2007): 1–19.

Aira, César. *How I Became a Nun*. Trans. Chris Andrews. New York: New Directions Books, 1993.

Andaya, Barbara Watson. *Flaming Womb: Repositioning Women in Early Modern Southeast Asia*. Honolulu: University of Hawai'i Press, 2006.

Anderson, Benedict. *Imagined Communities: Reflections on the Origin and Spread of Nationalism*. London: Verso, 1991.

———. *Spectres of Comparison: Nationalism, Southeast Asia, and the World*. London: Verso, 1998.

———. *Under Three Flags: Anarchism and the Anti-Colonial Imagination*. London: Verso, 2005.

Appadurai, Arjun. "Introduction: Place and Voice in Anthropological Theory." *Cultural Anthropology* 3.1 (1988): 16–20.

———. "Putting Hierarchy in Its Place." *Cultural Anthropology* 3.1 (1988): 36–49.

Bạch Năng Thi. "Nhất Linh—tác giả tiêu biểu" [Nhất Linh—A representative author]. In *Tự Lực văn đoàn: trong tiến trình văn học dân tộc* [Self-Strengthening Literary Group: Within the progress of national literature]. Ed. Mai Hương. Hanoi: Nhà xuất bản Văn hóa—Thông tin, 2000.

Barlow, Tani, ed. *Formations of Colonial Modernity in East Asia*. Durham, NC: Duke University Press, 1997.

Benveniste, Émile. *Problems in General Linguistics*. Trans. Mary Elizabeth Meek. Coral Gables, FL: University of Miami Press, 1971.

Bergner, Gwen. "Who Is That Masked Woman? or the Role of Gender in Fanon's *Black Skin, White Masks*." *PMLA* 110.1 (1995): 75–88.

Bergson, Henri. *Matter and Memory*. Trans. N. M. Paul and W. S. Palmer. New York: Zone Books, 1988.

Berman, Jessica. *Modernist Commitments: Ethics, Politics, and Transnational Modernism*. New York: Columbia University Press, 2011.

Bezancon, Pascale. *Une colonisation educatrice? L'Experience Indochinoise (1860–1945)*. Paris: L'Harmattan, 2002.

Bloch, Ernst. "Discussing Expressionism." Trans. Rodney Livingstone. In *Aesthetics and Politics*. Ed. Ronald Taylor. 1938. London: Verso, 2002. 16–27.

Boatcă, Manuela, and Sergio Costa. "Postcolonial Sociology: A Research Agenda." In *Decolonizing European Sociology*. Ed. Encarnación Gutierrez Rodriguez, Manuela Boatcă, and Sérgio Costa. Aldershot: Ashgate, 2010.

Bourdieu, Pierre. *Language and Symbolic Power*. Trans. Gino Raymond and Matthew Adamson Cambridge, MA: Harvard University Press, 1991.

Bradley, Mark Philip. *Imagining Vietnam and America: The Making of Postcolonial Vietnam, 1919–1950*. Chapel Hill: University of North Carolina Press, 2000.

Brennan, Timothy. "Postcolonial Studies between the European Wars." In *Marxism, Modernity and Postcolonial Studies*. Ed. Crystal Bartolovich and Neil Lazarus. Cambridge: Cambridge University Press, 2002. 185–203.

Breu, Christopher. *Hard-Boiled Masculinities*. Minneapolis: University of Minnesota Press, 2005.

Brocheux, Pierre, and Daniel Hémery. *Indochina: An Ambiguous Colonization, 1858–1954*. Trans. Ly Lan Dill-Klein. Berkeley: University of California Press, 2011.

Bùi Xuân Bào. *Le Roman vietnamien contemporain: Tendances et évolution du roman vietnamien contemporain, 1925–1945* [The contemporary Vietnamese novel: Tendencies and evolution of the contemporary Vietnamese novel, 1925–1945]. Saigon: Imprimerie Long Vân, 1972.

Burton, Antoinette. "Introduction: The Unfinished Business of Colonial Modernities." In *Gender, Sexuality, and Colonial Modernities*. Ed. Antoinette Burton. London: Routledge, 1999. 1–16.

Buzard, James. *Disorienting Fiction: The Autoethnographic Work of Nineteenth-Century British Novels*. Princeton, NJ: Princeton University Press, 2005.

———. "On Auto-Ethnographic Authority." *Yale Journal of Criticism* 16.1 (Spring 2003): 61–91.

Cabral, Amilcar. "National Liberation and Culture." In *Return to the Source: Selected Speeches of Amilcar Cabral*. Ed. Africa Information Service. 1970. Repr., New York: Monthly Review Press, 1973.

Campany, Robert Ford. "On the Very Idea of Religions (in the Modern West and in Early Medieval China)." *History of Religions* 42.4 (2003): 287–319.

Carey, John. Introduction to *The Faber Book of Reportage*. Ed. John Carey. London: Faber and Faber, 1987. xxix–xxxviii.

Chakrabarty, Dipesh. "The Difference-Deferral of a Colonial Modernity: Public Debates on Domesticity in British India." In *Subaltern Studies VIII*. Ed. David Arnold and David Hardiman. Delhi: Oxford University Press, 1994.

———. *Provincializing Europe: Postcolonial Thought and Historical Difference*. Princeton, NJ: Princeton University Press, 2000.

Chatterjee, Partha. *The Nation and Its Fragments: Colonial and Postcolonial Histories.* Princeton, NJ: Princeton University Press, 1993.

Cheah, Pheng. "Grounds of Comparison." In *Grounds of Comparison: Around the Work of Benedict Anderson.* Ed. Pheng Cheah and Jonathan Culler. New York: Routledge, 2013.

———. *Spectral Nationality: Passages of Freedom from Kant to Postcolonial Literatures of Liberation.* New York: Columbia University Press, 2012.

———. "Universal Areas: Asian Studies in a World of Motion." In *The Postcolonial and the Global.* Ed. Ravathi Khishnaswarmy and John C. Hawley. Minneapolis: University of Minnesota Press, 2008. 54–68.

———. "What Is a World? On World Literature as a World-Making Activity." *Daedalus* 137.3 (2008): 26–38.

Choisy, Maryce. Preface to *A Month among the Girls.* Trans. Lawrence G. Blochman. New York: Pyramid Books, 1960.

Chow, Rey. *Entanglements, or Transmedial Thinking about Capture.* Durham, NC: Duke University Press, 2012.

Cowley, Malcolm. *The Dreams of the Golden Mountains.* New York: Penguin Books, 1992. 280–93.

Cựu Kim Sơn and Văn Huệ. *Đời chị em* [The life of women]. Hanoi: Dân Chúng, 1938.

Đặng Thai Mai. *Vai trò lãng đạo của Đảng trên mặt trận văn học ba mươi năm nay* [The Party's lead in the cultural front in the past thirty years]. In *Toàn tập Đặng Thai Mai* [Collected works of Đặng Thai Mai]. 1960. Repr. Hanoi: NXB Văn học, 1997.

———. *Văn học khái luận* [Outline of literature]. In *Toàn tập Đặng Thai Mai* [Collected works of Đặng Thai Mai]. 4 vols. 1944. Repr., Hanoi: NXB Văn học, 1997.

DeFrancis, John. *Colonialism and Language Policy in Viet Nam.* The Hague: Mouton, 1977.

Dirks, Nicholas B. "Introduction: Colonialism and Culture." In *Colonialism and Culture.* Ed. Nicholas B. Dirks. Ann Arbor: University of Michigan Press, 1992. 1–25.

Do-Dinh, Pierre. "Les conditions veritable d'un accord." *L'Homme de couleur.* Ed. S. E. le Cardinal Verdier. Paris: Librarie Plon, 1939. 34–48.

———. "Pierre Do-dinh à André Gide. 4 August 1928. Letter I of "Correspondance inédite avec André Gide." In *Question colonial et écriture: Actes du colloque organisé par le RIASEM à Nice.* Ed. Guy Degas. Poitiers: Torii, 1994. 93–94.

Doyle, Laura, and Laura Winkiel, eds. *Geomodernisms: Race, Modernism, Modernity.* Bloomington: Indiana University Press, 2005.

Dube, Saurabh. "Colonialism, Modernity, Colonial Modernities." *Nepanthala: Views from the South* 3.2 (2002): 197–219.

Du Bois, William Edward Burghardt. *The Souls of Black Folk: Authoritative Text, Contexts, Criticism*. Ed. Henry Louis Gates and Terri Hume Oliver. New York: W. W. Norton, 1999.

Durkheim, Émile. *The Rules of Sociological Method*. Ed. Steven Lukes. Trans. W. D. Halls. London: Macmillan, 1982.

Esty, Jed and Colleen Lye. "Peripheral Realisms Now." *Modern Language Quarterly* 73.3 (2012): 269–88.

Fanon, Frantz. *The Wretched of the Earth*. Trans. Richard Philcox. 1963. New York: Grove Press, 2004.

Felski, Rita. *The Gender of Modernity*. Cambridge, MA: Harvard University Press, 1995.

Flaubert, Gustave. "À Louise Colet." January 16, 1852. In *Correspondance*. Vol. 2. Ed. Jean Bruneau. Paris: Gallimard, 1973. 31.

———. "À George Sand." December 31, 1875. In *Correspondance*. Vol. 4. Ed. Jean Bruneau. Paris: Gallimard, 1973. 999–1001.

———. "À George Sand." March 10, 1876. In *Correspondance*. Vol. 5. Ed. Jean Bruneau. Paris: Gallimard, 1973. 25–27.

Friedman, Susan Stanford. *Mappings: Feminism and the Cultural Geographies of Encounter*. Princeton, NJ: Princeton University Press, 1998.

de Gantès, Gilles. "Protectorate, Association, Reformism: The Roots of the Republican Policy Pursued by the Popular Front in Indochina." In *French Colonial Empire and the Popular Front*. Ed. Tony Chafer and Amanda Sackur. New York: St. Martin's Press, 1999. 103–30.

Giddens, Anthony. *The Consequences of Modernity*. Stanford, CA: Stanford University Press, 1990.

Gide, André. "Allocution d'ouverture." In *Littérature engagée*. Ed. Yvonne Davet. Paris: Gallimard, 1950. 83–84.

———. "Défense de la culture." In *Littérature engagée*. Ed. Yvonne Davet. Paris: Gallimard, 1950. 85–96.

———. "The Individual." *Left Review* 1.11 (1935): 447–52.

Gikandi, Simon. *Writing in Limbo: Modernism and Caribbean Literature*. Ithaca, NY: Cornell University Press, 1992.

GoGwilt, Chris. *The Passage of Literature: Genealogies of Modernism in Conrad, Rhys, & Pramoedya*. New York: Oxford University Press, 2011.

Goscha, Christopher E. *Vietnam or Indochina? Contesting Concepts of Space in Vietnamese Nationalism, 1887–1954*. Copenhagen: NIAS Books, 1995.

Hải Triều. "*Kép Tư Bền*, Một tác phẩm thuộc về cái triều lưu 'nghệ thuật vị dân sinh' ở nước ta" [*Tư Bền the actor*, a literary work for 'Art for Life's Sake' in our country]. 1935. In *Toàn tập* [Collected works]. 2 vols. Hanoi: Văn học, 1996. 1:268–74.

———. "*Lầm Than*: Một tác phẩm đầu tiên của nền văn tả thực xã hội ở nước ta"

[*Misery*: An initial work of socialist realism in our country]. 1938. In *Về văn học nghệ thuật* [On literary arts]. Hanoi: Văn Học, 1969. 57–61.

———. "Nghệ thuật vị nghệ thuật hay nghệ thuật vị nhân sinh" [Art for art's sake or art for life's sake]. In *Toàn tập* [Collected works]. 1935. 2 vols. Hanoi: Văn học, 1996. 1:252–67.

———. "Nghệ thuật và sự sinh hoạt xã hội" [Art and social life]. In *Toàn tập* [Collected works]. 1935. 2 vols. Hanoi: Văn học, 1996. 1:287–306.

———. "Ông Phan Khôi là một học giả duy tâm" [Phan Khôi is a materialist]. In *Toàn tập* [Collected works]. 2 vols. Hanoi: NXB Văn học, 1996. 1:241–51.

———. "Sự tiến hóa của văn học và sự tiến hóa của nhân sinh" (The evolution of literature and human life). In *Toàn tập* [Collected works]. 2 vols. Hanoi: NXB Văn học, 1996. 1:129–40.

Harootunian, Harry. *History's Disquiet*. New York: Columbia University Press, 2002.

———. *Overcome by Modernity: History, Culture, and Community in Interwar Japan*. Durham, NC: Duke University Press, 2000.

Hilden, Patricia, and Timothy Reiss. "Discourse, Politics, and the Temptations of Enlightenment: Paris 1935." *Annals of Scholarship* 8.1 (1991): 61–78.

Hoài Thanh. "Một bài diễn văn tối quan trọng về văn hóa" [A crucial expression on literature]. In *Văn chương và hành động* [Literature and action]. 1935. Hanoi: Hội nhà văn, 1999. 65–97.

———. "Văn chương là văn chương" [Literature is literature]. In *Bình luận văn chương* [Comments on literature]. Ed. Nguyễn Ngọc Thiện and Từ Sơn. 1935. Hanoi: Giáo dục, 1998. 23–35.

———. "Vấn đề học thuật nước ta" [On the education of our nation]. *Sông Hương* 1 (1 August 1936).

Hoài Thanh and Hoài Chân. *Thi nhân Việt Nam* [Vietnamese poets]. 1941. Repr., Hanoi: NXB Văn học, 1998.

Hoàng Đạo. *Bùn lầy nước đọng* [Muddied, stagnant water]. 1938. Repr., Saigon: Tự do, 1959.

———. *Mười điều tâm niệm* [Ten points]. 1939. Repr., Los Alamitos, CA: Xuân Thu Publishing, 1989.

Hoang, Kimberley Kay. *Dealing in Desire: Asian Ascendancy, Western Decline, and the Hidden Currencies of Global Sex Work*. Berkeley: University of California Press, 2015.

Hoàng Xuân Việt. *Tìm hiểu lịch sử chữ quốc ngữ* [Exploring the history of *quốc ngữ*]. Ho Chi Minh City: NXB Văn hóa thông tin, 2007.

Horkheimer, Max, and Theodor W. Adorno. *Dialectic of Enlightenment: Philosophical Fragments*. Trans. Edmund Jephcott. Stanford, CA: Stanford University Press, 2002.

Hue-Tam Ho Tai. "Literature for the People: From Soviet Policies to Vietnamese

Polemics." *Borrowings and Adaptations in Vietnamese Culture*. Ed. Truong Buu Lam. Honolulu: Center for Asian and Pacific Studies, 1987.

———. *Radicalism and the Origins of the Vietnamese Revolution*. Cambridge, MA: Harvard University Press, 1992.

Huỳnh Sanh Thông. "Main Trends of Vietnamese Literature between the Two World Wars." *Vietnam Forum* 3 (1984): 99–125.

Huỳnh Văn Tòng. *Báo chí Việt Nam: Từ khởi thủy đến 1945* [Vietnamese newspapers: From origins to 1945]. Ho Chi Minh City: NXB Thành phố Hồ Chí Minh, 2000.

Ikeya, Chie. *Refiguring Women, Colonialism, and Modernity in Burma*. Honolulu: University of Hawai'i Press, 2011.

Jamieson, Neil. *Understanding Vietnam*. Berkeley: University of California Press, 1995.

Karl, Rebecca. "Journalism, Social Value, and a Philosophy of the Everyday in 1920s China." *positions: East Asia Culture and Critique* 16.3 (2008): 539–66.

Kaviraj, Sudipta. "The Filth and the Public Sphere: Concepts and Practices about Space in Calcutta." *Public Culture* 10.1 (1997): 83–113.

Kelly, Gail Paradise. *French Colonial Education: Essays on Vietnam and West Africa*. Ed. David H. Kelly. New York: AMS Press, 2000.

Keyes, Charles. "Vietnamese and Thai Literature as Indigenous Ethnography." In *Southeast Asian Studies: Pacific Perspectives*. Ed. Anthony Reid. Tempe: Program for Southeast Asian Studies Monograph Series, 2003. 191–232.

Khái Hưng. *Nửa chừng xuân* [In the midst of spring]. Saigon: Văn nghệ, 1969.

Kim Ngoc Bao Ninh. *A World Transformed: The Politics of Culture in Revolutionary Vietnam, 1945–1965*. Ann Arbor: University of Michigan Press, 2002.

Kronfeld, Chana. *On the Margins of Modernism: Decentering Literary Dynamics*. Berkeley: University of California Press, 1996.

Lại Nguyên Ân, ed. *Vũ Trọng Phụng, tài năng và sự thật* [Vũ Trọng Phụng, talent and truth]. Hanoi: Nhà xuất bản Văn học, 1997.

Lan Khai. *Vũ Trọng Phụng: Một tài liệu cho văn sử Việt Nam* [Vũ Trọng Phụng: A source for Vietnamese literature]. Hanoi: Minh phương, 1941.

Larcher, Agathe. "La voie étroite de réformes colonials et la 'collaboration Franco-Annamite' (1917-1928)" [The single road to colonial reform and the Franco-Annamite collaboration (1917-1928]. *Revue française d'histoire d'outre-mer* 82.309 (1995): 387–420.

Laughlin, Charles. *Chinese Reportage: The Aesthetics of Historical Experience*. Durham, NC: Duke University Press, 2002.

Lazarus, Neil. *Nationalism and Cultural Practice in the Postcolonial World*. Cambridge: Cambridge University Press, 1999.

Lee, Haiyan. *Revolution of the Heart*. Stanford, CA: Stanford University Press, 2007.

Lepenies, Wolf. *Between Literature and Science: The Rise of Sociology.* Cambridge: Cambridge University Press, 1988.

Liu, Lydia. *Translingual Practice: Literature, National Culture, and Translated Modernity—China, 1900-1937.* Stanford, CA: Stanford University Press, 1995.

Lloyd, David. "Nationalisms against the State." In *Gender and Colonialism.* Ed. Timothy P. Foley. Galway: Galway University Press, 1995. 256–81.

Lộc Phương Thủy. "André Gide ở Việt Nam: Một vài nhận xết bước đầu" [André Gide in Vietnam: Some initial observations]. In *André Gide: Đời văn và tác phẩm* [André Gide: Life and works]. Ed. Lộc Phương Thủy. Hanoi: Khao học xã hội, 2002. 77–108.

Lockhart, Greg. Introduction to *The Light of the Capital: Three Modern Vietnamese Classics.* Trans. Greg Lockart and Monique Lockhart. Oxford: Oxford University Press, 1996. 1–49.

———. Introduction to "Nhất Linh's *Going to France." East Asian History* 8 (1994): 78–81.

Lucey, Michael. *Gide's Bent.* New York: Oxford University Press, 1995.

Lukács, Georg. "Realism in the Balance." Trans. Rodney Livingstone. In *Aesthetics and Politics.* Ed. Ronald Taylor. 1938. London: Verso, 2002. 29–59.

———. "Reportage or Portrayal?" In *Essays on Realism.* Trans. David Fernbach. London: Lawrence and Wishart, 1980. 45–75.

Lương, Hy Văn. *Discursive Practices and Linguistic Meanings: The Vietnamese System of Person Reference.* Amsterdam: John Benjamins, 1990.

———. "Discursive Practices and Power Structure: Person-Referring Forms and Sociopolitical Struggle in Colonial Vietnam." *American Ethnologist* 15 (1988): 239–53.

Lưu Trọng Lư. "Con đường riêng của trí thức" [An intellectual's own path]. In *André Gide: Đời văn và tác phẩm* [André Gide: Life and works]. Ed. Lộc Phương Thủy. 1939. Hanoi: Khao học xã hội, 2002. 429–40.

Majumdar, Saikat. *Prose of the World: Modernism and the Banality of Empire.* New York: Columbia University Press, 2013.

Malarney, Shaun Kingsley. "Introduction: Vũ Trọng Phụng and the Anxieties of 'Progress.'" In *Lục Xì: Prostitution and Venereal Disease in Colonial Hanoi.* By Vũ Trọng Phụng. Honolulu: University Hawai'i Press, 2011. 1–41.

Mao, Douglas and Rebecca L. Walkowitz. "The New Modernist Studies." *PMLA* 123.3 (2008): 737–48.

Marr, David. "Concepts of 'Individual' and 'Self' in Twentieth-Century Vietnam." *Modern Asian Studies* 34 (2000): 769–96.

———. *Vietnamese Anti-Colonialism, 1882-1925.* Berkeley: University of California Press, 1980.

———. *Vietnamese Tradition on Trial, 1920–1945.* Berkeley: University of California Press, 1981.

Marx, Karl. "The *Grundrisse*." In *The Marx-Engels Reader.* 2nd rev. and enl. ed. New York: W. W. Norton, 1978. 221–93.

Matz, Jesse. *Literary Impressionism and Modernist Aesthetics.* Cambridge: Cambridge University Press, 2001.

McAlister, John T., and Paul Mus. *The Vietnamese and Their Revolution.* New York: Harper and Row, 1970.

McClintock, Anne. "'No Longer in a Future Heaven': Gender, Race, and Nationalism." In *Becoming National: A Reader.* Ed. Geoff Eley and Ronald Suny. Oxford: Oxford University Press, 1996. 89–112.

McHale, Shawn. "Mapping a Vietnamese Confucian Past and Its Transition to Modernity." In *Rethinking Confucianism: Past and Present in China, Japan, and Vietnam.* Ed. Benjamin A. Elman, John B. Duncan, and Herman Ooms. Los Angeles, CA: UCLA Asian Pacific Monograph Series, 2001. 173–94.

———. *Print and Power: Confucianism, Communism, and Buddhism in the Making of Modern Vietnam.* Honolulu: University of Hawai'i Press, 2003.

———. "Printing and Power: Vietnamese Debates over Women's Place in Society, 1918–1934." In *Essays into Vietnamese Pasts.* Ed. K. W. Taylor and John K. Whitmore. Ithaca, NY: Cornell Southeast Asia Program, 1995. 173–94.

The Modern Girl around the World Research Group et al., eds. *The Modern Girl around the World: Consumption, Modernity, and Globalization.* Durham, NC: Duke University Press, 2008.

Nandy, Ashis. *The Intimate Enemy: Loss and Recovery of Self under Colonialism.* Delhi: Oxford University Press, 1983.

Nguyễn-võ, Thu-hương. *The Ironies of Freedom: Sex, Culture, and Neoliberal Governance in Vietnam.* Seattle: University of Washington Press, 2008.

Nguyễn Công Hoan. *Cô giáo Minh* [Miss Minh, a schoolteacher]. 1936. Repr., Ho Chi Minh City: Nhà xuất bản văn nghệ, 1998.

———. "Nhân Tình Tôi" [My love] In *Toàn tập* [Collected works]. Ed. Lê Minh. 1929. 4 vols. Hanoi: Văn Học, 2003. 1:107–21.

———. "Từ Đoạn tuyệt đến Cô giáo Minh" [From *Breaking Away to Miss Minh, a schoolteacher*]. In *13 Năm tranh luận văn học* [Thirteen years of literary debates]. Ed. Thanh Lãng. 1936. Repr., Ho Chi Minh City: Nhà xuất bản văn học, 1995). 1:74–75.

Nguyễn Đình Lạp. "Muốn làm phóng sự" [To produce reportage]. In *Tác phẩm* [Works]. Ed. Bạch Liên. Hanoi: NXB Văn hóa-thông tin, 2003. 791–826.

Nguyễn Hoành Khung, "Lời giới thiệu" [Introduction]. In *Văn xuôi lãng mạn Việt Nam 1930–1945* [Vietnamese romanticist prose, 1930–1945]. Ed. Nguyễn Hoành Khung and Phong Hà. 8 vols. Hanoi: NXB Khoa học xã Hội, 1989. 1:7–46.

Nguyễn Hoành Khung and Lại Nguyên Ân, eds. *Vũ Trọng Phụng, con người và tác phẩm: hồi ức, chân dung, tiểu luận* [Vũ Trọng Phụng, an author and his works: Memoirs, portraits, and essays]. Hanoi: Hội Nhà văn, 1994.

Nguyễn Huệ Chi. "Đổi mới nhân thức lịch sử trong nghiên cứu khoa học xã hội nói chung, nghiên cứu văn học nói riêng" [To renovate the truth in social scientific research in general, literary criticism in particular]. *Tạp chí Văn học* [Journal of literature] 6 (1990): 1–9.

Nguyen Ngoc Tuan. *Socialist Realism in Vietnamese Literature*. n.p.: Vdm Verlag Dr Muller, 2008.

———. *Văn học Việt Nam dưới chế độ Cộng sản* [Vietnamese literature under the communist regime]. Stanton, CA: NXB Văn Nghệ, 1996.

Nguyễn Ngọc Thiện, ed. *Vũ Trọng Phụng, về tác giả và tác phẩm* [Vũ Trọng Phụng, on the author and his work]. Hanoi: Nhà xuất bản Giáo dục, 2007.

Nguyễn Ngọc Thiện and Lữ Huy Nguyên, eds. *Tao Đàn 1939* [Literary coterie, 1939]. 2 vols. Hanoi: Văn học, 1999.

Nguyen Phuong Ngoc. *À l'origine de l'anthropologie au Vietnam: Recherche sur les auteurs de la première moitié du XXe siècle*. Aix-en-Provence: Presses Universitaires de Provence, 2012.

Nguyễn Văn Hoàn."Chung Quanh Cuộc Tranh Luận Về "Phạm Quỳnh-Ngô Đức Kế và Truyện Kiều" ở Miền Nam" [Surrounding the "Phạm Quỳnh-Ngô Đức Kế and Truyện Kiều" debate in South Vietnam]. *Tạp chí văn học* 7 (1964): 59–61.

Nhất Linh. *Đoạn tuyệt* [Breaking away]. 1935. Repr., Saigon: Tự Do, 1972.

———. "Thanh niên và công việc xã hội" [Youth and the work of society]. *Ngày nay* [Today], June 19, 1938.

Như Hiên and Nguyễn Ngọc Hiền, eds. *Nữ sĩ Việt Nam: Tiểu sử và giai thoại* [Vietnam's female authors: Biographies and recollection]. Ho Chi Minh City: NXB Văn học, 2006.

Olson, Liesl. *Modernism and the Ordinary*. Oxford: Oxford University Press, 2009.

Ortner, Sherry B. "Resistance and the Problem of Ethnographic Refusal." *Comparative Studies in Society and History* 37.1 (1995): 173–93.

Orwell, George. "The Prevention of Literature." In *The Collected Essays, Journalism, and Letters of George Orwell*. Ed. Sonia Orwell and Ian Angus. 4 vols. New York: Harcourt, Brace & World, 1968. 4:59–72.

Osborne, Milton. *The French Presence in Cochinchina and Cambodia: Rule and Response*. Ithaca, NY: Cornell University Press, 1969.

Parry, Amie Elizabeth. *Interventions into Modernist Culture*. Durham, NC: Duke University Press, 2007.

Pels, Peter, and Oscar Salemink. "Introduction: Locating the Colonial Subjects of Anthropology." In *Colonial Subjects: Essays on the Practical History of Anthropology*. Ed. Peter Pels and Oscar Salemink. Ann Arbor: University of Michigan Press, 2000. 1–52.

Peycam, Philippe. *The Birth of Vietnamese Political Journalism: Saigon, 1916–1930*. New York: Columbia University Press, 2012.

Phạm Thế Ngũ. *Việt Nam văn học sử: Giản ước tân biên* [History of Vietnamese literature: A new survey]. 3 vols. Dong thap: NXB Đồng tháp, 1996.

Phan Châu Trinh. "Thư gửi toàn quyền Đông Dương" [Letter to the governor-general of Indochina). In *Toàn tập* [Complete works]. 3 vols. Da Nang: NXB Đà nẳng, 2005. 2:51–65.

Phan Cự Đệ. *Tiểu thuyết Việt Nạm hiện đại* [The modern Vietnamese novel]. 2 vols. Hanoi: NXB Đại học và trung học chuyên nghiệp, 1975.

———. *Tự Lực văn đòan: con người và văn chương* [The Self-Strengthening Literary Group: The authors and the literature]. Hanoi: Văn Học, 1990.

Phan Khôi. "Học với sách và học với chung quanh ta" [To learn with books and to learn with our surroundings]. *Sông Hương* 2 (8 August 1936).

———."Kiểm thảo về đại danh từ" [To critique pronouns]. In *Việt ngữ nghiên cứu* [Vietnamese linguistics]. Danang: NXB Nẳng, 1997. 129–40.

———."Văn học tiểu thuyết là cái quái gì?" [What is this literary novel?]. In *Tác phẩm đăng báo 1936* [Newspaper articles published in 1936]. Ed. Lại Nguyên Ân. Hanoi: NXB Trí thức, 2014. 41–43.

Phan Trọng Thưởng. Introduction to *Phóng sự Việt Nam, 1932–1945* [Vietnamese reportage, 1932–1945]. Ed. Phan Trọng Thưởng, Nguyễn Cừ, and Nguyễn Hữu Sơn. 3 vols. Ho Chi Minh City: NXB Văn học, 2000. 1:5–14.

Poisson, Emmanuel. *Mandarins et subalterns au nord du Viet Nam: Une bureaucratie à l'éprueve (1820–1918)*. Paris: Maisonneuve & Larose, 2004.

Prakash, Gyan. "Writing Post-Orientalist Histories of the Third World: Perspectives from Indian Historiography." *Comparative Studies in Society and History* 32.2 (1999): 383–408.

Prendergrast, Christopher. *The Order of Mimesis*. Cambridge: Cambridge University Press, 1986.

Proschan, Frank. "'Syphilis, Opiomania, and Pederasty': Colonial Constructions of Vietnamese (and French) Social Disease." *Journal of the History of Sexuality* 11.4 (2002): 610–36.

Rancière, Jacques. *The Politics of Aesthetics*. Trans. Gabriel Rockhill. New York: Continuum, 2004.

———. *Politics of Literature*. Trans. Julie Rose. Cambridge: Polity, 2011.

———. "Why Emma Bovary Had to Be Killed." *Critical Inquiry* 34.2 (2008): 233–48.

Rofel, Lisa. *Other Modernities: Gendered Yearnings in China after Socialism*. Berkeley: University of California Press, 1999.

Sand, George. Letter to Gustave Flaubert, January 15, 1876. In *Gustave Flaubert-George Sand Correspondance*. Ed. Alphonse Jacobs. Paris: Flammarion, 1981. 519.

Sarkar, Tanika. "The Hindu Wife and the Hindu Nation: Domesticity and Nationalism in Nineteenth-Century Bengal." *Studies in History* 8.2 (1992): 213–35.

Sarraut, Albert. "Discours prononcé le 17 avril 1919 au Van-Mieu" [Address delivered April 17, 1919 at Van Mieu]. Annex in Agathe Larcher, "Réalisme et idéalisme en politique coloniale: Albert Sarraut et l'Indochine, 1911-1914" [Realism and idealism in colonial politics: Albert Sarraut et Indochina, 1911-1914]. MA thesis, Université Paris VII, 1992.

Schivelbusch, Wolfgang. *Railway Journey: The Industrialization of Time and Space in the 19th Century*. Berkeley: University of California Press, 1986.

Scott, David. *Refashioning Futures: Criticism after Postcoloniality*. Princeton, NJ: Princeton University Press, 1999.

Seidman, Steven. "Empire and Knowledge: More Troubles, New Opportunities for Sociology." *Contemporary Sociology* 25.3 (1996): 313–16.

Shattuck, Roger. *The Innocent Eye*. New York: Farrar, Straus & Giroux, 1984.

Shih, Shu-Mei. *The Lure of the Modern: Writing Modernism in Semicolonial China, 1917–1937*. Berkeley: University of California Press, 2001.

James Siegel, *Fetish, Recognition, Revolution*. Princeton, NJ: Princeton University Press, 1997.

Sinha, Mrinalini. *Colonial Masculinity: The "Manly" Englishman and the "Effeminate Bengali" in the Late Nineteenth Century*. Manchester: Manchester University Press, 1995.

Spivak, Gayatri Chakravorty. "Can the Subaltern Speak?" In *Marxism and the Interpretation of Culture*. Ed. Cary Nelson and Lawrence Grossberg. Urbana and Chicago: University of Illinois Press, 1988. 271–313.

———. *A Critique of Postcolonial Reason: Toward a History of the Vanishing Present*. Cambridge, MA: Harvard University Press, 1999.

Stead, Christina. "The Writers Take Sides." *Left Review* 1.11 (1935): 453–62.

Stoler, Ann. "Making of Empire Respectable: The Politics of Race and Sexual Morality in 20th-Century Colonial Cultures." *American Ethnologist* 1.4 (1989): 634–60.

Tam Ích. "Nhân đọc: *Tôi kéo xe* của Tam Lang" [Tam Lang's *I pull a rickshaw*]. *Nhân Văn* [Humanities] 5 (1972): 37–43.

Tam Lang. "I Pulled a Rickshaw." In *The Light of the Capital: Three Modern Vietnamese Classics*. Trans. Greg Lockhart and Monique Lockhart. Kuala Lampur: Oxford University Press, 1996. 51–120.

———. *Tôi kéo xe* [I pull a rickshaw]. 1932. Repr., Los Alamitos, CA: NXB Xuân thu, 1988.

Tanabe, Akio, and Yumiko Tokita-Tanabe. "Introduction: Gender and Modernity in Asia and the Pacific." In *Gender and Modernity: Perspectives from Asia and the Pacific*. Ed. Yoko Hayami, Akio Tanabe, and Yumiko Tokita. Kyoto: Trans Pacific Press, 2003. 1–16.

Taylor, Keith. "Authority and Legitimacy in 11th-Century Vietnam." In *Southeast Asia in the 9th to 14th Centuries*. Ed. David Marr and Anthony Crothers Millner. Singapore: Institute of Southeast Asian Studies, 1986. 139–76.

Thạch Lam. "Hà Nội ban đêm" [Hanoi at night]. *Phong hóa* [Customs], March 10, 1933, 2.

———. "Hà Nội ban đêm." *Phong hóa*, April 28, 1933, 2.

———. "Hà Nội ban đêm." *Phong hóa*, May 5, 1933, 2.

———. "Hà Nội ban đêm." *Phong hóa*, June 16, 1933, 2.

———. "Hà Nội ban đêm." *Phong hóa*, July 7, 1933, 2.

———. "Hà Nội ban đêm." *Phong hóa*, July 28, 1933, 4.

Thanh Lãng. *Bảng lược đồ văn học Việt Nam* [A concise history of Vietnamese literature]. 2 vols. Saigon: NXB Trình bầy, 1967.

———. *Phê bình văn học thế hệ 1932* [A literary critique of the 1932 generation]. 2 vols. Saigon: Phong trào văn hóa, 1972.

———, ed. *13 năm tranh luận văn học* [Thirteen years of literary debates]. 3 vols. Repr., Ho Chi Minh City: Nhà xuất bản văn học, 1995.

Thế Lữ. "Những sợi dây trói buộc tôi" [The ropes that bound me]. *Văn nghệ* [Literature and the arts] 41 (1953): 14–20.

Thiếu Sơn. "Hai quan niệm về văn học" [Two literary perspectives]. In *13 năm tranh luận văn học* [13 years of literary debates]. Ed. Thanh Lãng. 1935. 3 vols. Ho Chi Minh City: Hội nghiên cứu và giảng dạy văn học, 1995. 1:105–9.

———. "Nghệ thuật với đời người" [Art and human life]. In *13 năm tranh luận văn học* [13 years of literary debates]. Ed. Thanh Lãng. 1935. 3 vols. Repr., Ho Chi Minh City: Hội nghiên cứu và giảng dạy văn học, 1995. 1:109–14.

———. "Văn học bình dân" [Popular literature]. In *13 năm tranh luận văn học* [13 years of literary debates]. Ed. Thanh Lãng. 1935. 3 vols. Repr., Ho Chi Minh City: Hội nghiên cứu và giảng dạy văn học, 1995. 1:114–18.

Thiong'o, Ngũgĩ Wa. *Decolonising the Mind: The Politics of Language in African Literature*. Portsmouth, NH: Heinemann, 1986.

Thomas, Megan. *Orientalists, Propagandists, and Ilustrados: Filipino Scholarship and the End of Spanish Colonialism*. Minneapolis: University of Minnesota Press, 2012.

Thượng Sỹ. "Thân thể và sự nghiệp Tam Lang" [The life and work of Tam Lang]. In *Cuộc đời viết văn, làm báo: Tam Lang, "Tôi kéo xe"* [A life of literature and journalism: Tam Lang, "I pull a rickshaw"]. Ed. Thế Phong. 1996. Repr., Hanoi: NXB Tổng hợp Đồng Nai, 2004. 5–11.

Tracol-Huynh, Isabelle. "Between Stigmatisation and Regulation: Prostitution in Colonial Northern Vietnam." *Culture, Health & Sexuality* 12 (2010): S73–S87.

———. "The Shadow Theater of Prostitution in French Colonial Tonkin: Faceless Prostitutes under the Colonial Gaze." *Journal of Vietnamese Studies* 7.1 (2012): 10–51.

Tran, Nhung Tuyet. "Woman as nation: Tradition and modernity narratives in Vietnamese histories." *Gender & History* 24.2 (2012): 411–430.

Trần Hữu Tá. *Vũ Trọng Phụng, hôm qua và hôm nay* [Vũ Trọng Phụng, yesterday and today]. Ho Chi Minh: Nhà xuất bản Thành phố Hồ Chí Minh, 1992.

Trần Thị Phương Hoa. "From Liberally Organized to Centralized Schools: Education in Tonkin, 1885–1927." *Journal of Vietnamese Studies* 8.3 (2013): 27–70.

Trinh Van Thao. *Vietnam du confucianisme au communisme: Un essai d'itinéraire intellectual* . Paris: L'Harmattan, 2007.

Trương Chính. Dưới mắt tôi [Beneath my eyes]. Hanoi: n.p., 1939.

———. "Nhất Linh." In Tự Lực văn đoàn: trong tiến trình văn học dân tộc [Self-Strengthening Literary Group and the development of national literature]. Ed. Mai Hương. Hanoi: Nhà xuất bản văn hóa—thông tin, 2000. 233–40.

Trường Chinh. Chủ nghĩa Mác và văn hóa Việt Nam [Marxism and Vietnamese culture]. Hanoi: NXB Sự thật, 1974.

Trương Tửu. "Cái buồn lãng mạn và các thi sĩ Thế Lữ, Lưu Trọng Lư, Phạm Huy Thông, Nguyễn Vỹ" [Romanticism's sorrow and the poets Thế Lữ, Lưu Trọng Lư, Phạm Huy Thông, Nguyễn Vỹ]. *Quốc Gia* [Nation], September 9, 1938, 1.2, 1.4.

———. "Địa vị Vũ Trọng Phụng trong văn học Việt Nam cận đại" [Vũ Trọng Phụng's place in modern Vietnamese literature]. In *Tao Đàn 1939* [Literary Coterie 1939]. Ed. Nguyễn Ngọc Thiện and Lữ Huy Nguyên. Hanoi: Văn học, 1999.

———. "Khi ông Nhất Linh muốn làm nhà xã hội học" [When Nhất Linh wanted to be a sociologist]. In *Tiểu thuyết Thứ Năm: Tác giả và tác phẩm* [Authors and works of *Thursday Novel*]. Ed. Anh Chi. 2 vols. 1938. Repr., Hanoi: NXB Văn học, 2002. 2:685–97.

———. "Tóm tắt và so sánh *Tố Tâm, Nửa chừng xuân, Đoạn tuyệt*" [Summarizing and comparing *Pure heart, In the midst of spring, Breaking away*]. In *Tuyển tập nghiên cứu, phê bình* [Selected research and criticism]. Ed. Nguyễn Hữu Sơn and Trịnh Bá Đĩnh. Hà Nội: NXB Lao động, 2007.

———. "Văn-chương lãng mạn ở xứ ta" [Our romanticist literature]. *Quốc Gia* [Nation], September 9, 1938, 1.2.

———. "Văn học Việt Nam hiện đại" [Modern Vietnamese literature]. In *Tuyển tập nghiên cứu, phê bình* [Selected research and criticism]. Ed. Nguyễn Hữu Sơn and Trịnh Bá Đĩnh. Hanoi: NXB Lao động, 2007. 84–164.

Tứ Ly. "Bên đường dừng bước" [On the side of the road]. *Phong hóa* [Customs], March 2, 1934.

Vũ Gia. *Nhất Linh trong tiến trình hiện đại hóa văn học* [Nhất Linh and the modernization of literature]. Hanoi: NXB Văn hóa, 1995.

Vũ Ngọc Phan. *Nhà văn hiện đại* [Modern authors]. 3 vols. 1941. Repr., Saigon: NXB Thanh Long, 1960.

———. "Quan niệm về lịch sử" [An approach to history]. *Sông Hương* [Perfume River] 1 (August 1, 1936).

———. "Về sử học, muốn gần sự thật, cần phải theo phương pháp" [On history, to get at the truth is to have method]. *Sông Hương* 2 (August 8, 1936).

Vũ Tam Giang. "Bàn thêm về đổi mới nhận thức lịch sử" [Further renovating the historical truth]. *Tạp chí Văn học* [Journal of literature] 3 (1991): 1–5.

Vũ Trọng Phụng. "Cơm thầy cơm cô" [Household Servants]. In *Phóng sự Việt Nam 1932-1945* [Vietnamese reportage, 1932–1945]. Ed. Phan Trọng Thưởng, Nguyễn Cừ, and Nguyễn Hữu Sơn. 3 vols. Ho Chi Minh City: NXB Văn học, 2000. 3:731–69.

———. "Để đáp lời báo *Ngày nay*: Dâm hay là không dâm" [To answer the journal *Ngày nay*: Obscene or not obscene]. In *Vũ Trọng Phụng, tài năng và sự thật* [Vũ Trọng Phụng, talent and truth]. Ed. Lại Nguyên Ân. Hanoi: NXB Văn học, 1997. 211–20.

———. *Dumb Luck*. Trans. Peter Zinoman and Nguyễn Nguyệt Câm. Ann Arbor: University of Michigan Press, 2002.

———. *Household Servants*. In *The Light of the Capital: Three Modern Vietnamese Classics*. Trans. Greg Lockhart and Monique Lockhart. Kuala Lumpur: Oxford University Press, 1996. 121–56.

———. *Làm đĩ*. In *Vũ Trọng Phụng: Toàn tập* [Vũ Trọng Phụng: Complete works]. 1936. Repr., Hanoi: NXB Hội Nhà văn, 1999. Trans. Shaun Malarney as *Lục xì*. Honolulu: University Hawai'i Press, 2011.

———. "Lời giao hẹn với độc giả trước khi đọc truyện" [A preface to the reader]. *Sông Hương* [Perfume River] 2 (August 8, 1936).

Wagner, Rudolph. *Inside a Service Trade: Studies in Contemporary Chinese Prose*. Cambridge, MA: Harvard University Press, 1992.

Wang, David Der-wei. *Fictional Realism*. New York: Columbia University Press, 1992.

Wilcox, Wynn. "French Imperialism and the Vietnamese Civil Service Examinations." *Journal of American–East Asian Relations* 21.4 (2014): 373–93.

———. "Women, Westernization and the Origins of Modern Vietnamese Theatre." *Journal of Southeast Asian Studies* 37.2 (2006): 205–24.

Wittgenstein, Ludwig. *Philosophical Investigations*. Trans. G. E. M. Anscombe. Oxford: Blackwell, 2001.

Wollaeger, Mark, with Matt Eatough, eds. *The Oxford Handbook of Global Modernisms*. New York: Oxford University Press, 2012.

Woodside, Alexander. *Community and Revolution in Modern Vietnam*. Boston: Houghton Mifflin, 1976.

———. *Lost Modernities: China, Vietnam, Korea, and the Hazards of World History*. Cambridge, MA: Harvard University Press, 2006.

———. *Vietnam and the Chinese Model: A Comparative Study of Nguyễn and Ch'ing Civil Government in the First Half of the Nineteenth Century*. Cambridge, MA: Harvard University Press, 1971.

Xuân Diệu. "Dứt khoát" [Without question]. In *Văn nghệ* [Literature and the arts] 41 (1953): 21–27.

"Xuân thủ đàm ân." *Phong hóa* [Customs], January 31, 1936.

Zinoman, Peter. *Vietnamese Colonial Republican: The Political Vision of Vu Trong Phung*. Berkeley: University of California Press, 2013.

INDEX

Adorno, Theodor W.: *Dialectic of Enlightenment* (with Horkheimer), 74, 137n34
aesthetic modernity in Vietnam: accelerated change and, 124; as contingent on the everyday, 11–12, 13, 48, 122–23, 158n5; cultural manifestations, 4–5; depicted through women's sexuality, 24; differences with Europe, 5; gender dynamics and, 4, 5–6, 8, 10–11, 19, 22, 116–18; impressionism and, 22; modernism distinguished from, 13, 106, 122–23; post-mandarin description, 4; Rancière's view of, 13–14, 48–51, 61, 62, 138–39n56, 144n2; realism's importance in, 50; reportage's centrality in, 21, 22; Self-Strengthening group and, 69–70, 135n25. *See also* modernism
Aira, César, 14
Andaya, Barbara Watson: *The Flaming Womb*, 8
Anderson, Benedict: on anticolonialism and culture, 13; on autoethnography, 142n18; "imagined community" concept, 14, 45; on importance of print capitalism for nation creation, 49–50, 121–22, 133–34n21; on nation-ness as "cultural artefacts," 139n57; on "spectre of comparisons," 120
An Nam tạp chí (journal), 117
anticolonialism: literary modernism and, 12–13, 17–18, 124; post-mandarin intellectuals' views, 3–4, 7, 23, 27, 66–67, 73–75, 119, 141n14, 142n18; reportage and, 13, 67, 141n14; supression of, 133n18
Appadurai, Arjun, 31
Aragon, Louis, 155n11
art for art's sake vs. art for life's sake debate, 107, 110–13, 154n5, 155–56n18; Nguyễn's *Kép Tư Bền* and, 112–18

August Revolution of 1945, 18, 113
autobiography as genre, 89–90, 91–92
autoethnography, 24–26, 31, 39, 52, 121, 142n18

Balzac, Honoré de, 12, 48–49, 50; *Le curé de village*, 61
Benveniste, Émile, 91–92, 93
Bergson, Henri, 140n2
Berman, Jessica: *Modernist Commitments*, 12–13
Bloch, Ernst, 154n5, 155n18
Bolaño, Roberto, 13
Bourdieu, Pierre, 94
Brecht, Bertolt, 155n11
Brennan, Timothy, 154n6
Bukharin, Nikolai, 113
Buzard, James, 25, 30

Cabral, Amilcar, 13
Campany, Robert, 149n17
Chakrabarty, Dipesh, 74
Cheah, Pheng, 7, 74, 120, 121, 154–55n8
China, Confucianism in, 130n3
Choisy, Maryse, 30; *Un mois chez les filles*, 36–37
Chow, Rey, 13
Cochinchina, 69, 135n26
Colet, Louise, 157n37
colonial modernity in Vietnam: change from vertical to horizontal social orientations, 89; compressed temporality of, 49–50, 105–6, 124; cosmopolitan women as initiators of, 10–11, 40–41, 55–56, 61–65, 120; cultural transformations, 4, 24–25, 43; depicted through women's sexuality, 8, 10–11; gender relations, 25, 53, 55–56, 119–20, 121, 122; intellectuals' uncertain position, 30, 32, 34; juxtapositions and inequalities, 13–14, 15–16, 19, 87, 100,